Cannon County Tennessee

Chancery Court Minutes

- 1840-1880 -

By:
Thomas E. Partlow

Southern Historical Press, Inc.
Greenville, South Carolina

Please Direct All Correspondence and Book Orders to:

Souther Historical Press, Inc.
PO Box 1267
375 West Broad Street
Greenville, S.C. 29602

ISBN # 0-89308-760-2

Printed in the United States of America

This Book

Is

Respectfully Dedicated

To

BUDDY and LINDA GRANSTAFF

Who Had Ancestors In Cannon County

PREFACE

Chancery Court records are of great value because they contain estate settlements of people who have died intestate. Oftentimes, such information cannot be found elsewhere. In addition to estate settlements, these records also include divorces, and after 1865, some Civil War information.

Thomas E. Partlow
December, 2000

Be it remembered that on the 3rd day of August, that being the 1st Monday in said month 1840, Chancery Court met in the town of Woodbury in Cannon County. Broomfield L. Ridley, presiding. Henry (Trott) was appointed Clerk & Master by the Chancellor. (Pp. 1-2)

Court stands adjourned until the next term of court. 3 Aug 1840. (P. 2)

(Page 3 is blank)

Be it remembered that on the first Monday in Feb 1841, Chancery Court met in the town of Woodbury. Broomfield L. Ridley, presiding. Henry (Trott), Jr. was appointed as Clerk & Master. (Pp. 4-6)

BENJAMIN PENDLETON, Executor of John Brown, versus NANCY BROWN, JAMES BROWN, ANNA BROWN, POLLY BROWN, HENDERSON YOAKUM, H. TROTT, J. J. TROTT, JACOB WRIGHT, and all other creditors. The widow of John Brown is given her dower. 2 Feb 1841. (Pp. 6-8)

JAMES BURGE versus WILLIAM STONE CLAIBORNE. There is no equity in complainant's bill. The bill is dismissed. 2 Feb 1841. (P. 8)

SARAH P. BROWN by next friend versus JAMES M. BROWN and others. The injunction is dissolved. 2 Feb 1841. (P. 9)

Chancery Court met in the town of Woodbury on the 2nd day of Aug 1841, it being the first Monday of said month. Chancellor Broomfield L. Ridley of the Fourth Chancery Division, presiding. (P. 9)

JANE McLAUGHLIN versus DAWSON McLAUGHTON. The death of the defendant is suggested. This suit is hereby abated. 2 Aug 1841. (P. 10)

DAVID McGILL versus JAMES McGILL. James Pogue, William Pogue, and   Pogue are infants under the age of 21 years. Henry Trott, Jr. is appointed as guardian. 2 Aug 1841. (P. 10)

JACOB and SAMUEL E. BURGER versus JAMES WOODS, Executor. The injunction is dissolved. 2 Aug 1841. (P. 10)

JAMES W. McADOW versus BIRD W. SMITH and others. This cause is dismissed. 2 Aug 1841. (P. 11)

CHARLES PORTERFIELD'S Administrator and heirs. The petitioners is the widow of Charles Porterfield who died in the year 1839 leaving the persons mentioned in the petition as his children. He died intestate. Defendants David and Alexander McKnight have been appointed his administrators. At the time of his death, the said Charles Porterfield was seized and possessed of a tract of land containing 115 acres. The petitioner has not had her dower assigned to her. 2 Aug 1841. (P. 11)

BENJAMIN PENDLETON, Executor, versus THE CREDITORS OF JOHN BROWN. The Clerk has sold the negro girl, Lucy, and her child,

1

Dick, to Robert H. Stephens for $500. The sale is confirmed. The dower has not yet been assigned to Nancy Brown. Commissioners are appointed to lay off the dower. 2 Aug 1841. (P. 12)

WILLIAM C. ODUM Et Al, Administrator of Samuel Corn versus JOSEPH RAMSEY and the other creditors. 2 Aug 1841. (P. 13)

JAMES W. BURGER versus SAMUEL GUNTER Et Al. The bill is dismissed. 2 Aug 1841. (P. 13)

Chancery Court of the Fourth Division in the State of Tennessee met in the town of Woodbury on the 7th day of Feb 1842, it being the first Monday in Feb 1842. Broomfield L. Ridley, presiding. (P. 14)

JAMES HARPER and JOHN CARPENTER versus DAVIS KING and ANDERSON KING, Administrators of Thomas King. The death of Anderson King is suggested. 7 Feb 1842. (P. 14)

SAMUEL CORN'S Administrators versus THE CREDITORS. 8 Feb 1842. (Pp. 14-15)

HENRY HART versus E. WRIGHT and others. Pleasant A. Thomason who had been previously appointed a receiver refused and neglected to act. 8 Feb 1852. (P. 15)

MARIAH E. PORTERFIELD versus CHARLES PORTERFIELD'S Heirs and Administrator. The said Mariah E. Porterfield is assigned her dower. 8 Feb 1842. (Pp. 16-17)

BENJAMIN PENDLETON, Executor of John Brown, versus THE CREDITORS, WIDOW, and HEIRS. Commissioners are appointed to lay off the dower to the widow. 8 Feb 1842. (Pp. 17-21)

DAVID McGILL versus JAMES McGILL and others. Final Decree. James McGill departed this life in 1838. Complainant and David Patton were appointed as administrators. There are six children, to wit, John McGill and Elizabeth Laughlin being two. Their shares have been purchased by David McGill who is likewise an heir. James McGill and Robert McGill are also the minor heirs of James E. Pogue who intermarried with Nancy (now also dead), one of the children of said James McGill. David McGill has been appointed by the court as guardian of the minors. 8 Feb 1842. (Pp. 21-23)

Chancery Court met in the town of Woodbury on Monday, 1 Aug 1842. Broomfield L. Ridley, presiding. (P. 23)

RICHARD BERRY versus CHARLES B. WALKER. This cause is continued. 1 Aug 1842. (P. 24)

JACOB BURGER and SAMUEL E. BURGER versus JAMES WOOD, Executor of John Wood. The bill is dismissed. 1 Aug 1842. (P. 24)

JOHN MULLINS VERSUS JOHN CHILDRESS. Complainant executed a deed to the defendant. The Clerk is to take an account and report to the court the state of indebtedness of the said Childress to the said complainant. 2 Aug 1842. (Pp. 24-25)

JOHN H. WOOD versus JOHN C. MARTIN. This cause is continued. 2 Aug 1842. (P. 25)

MATHEW EDWARDS versus ISAAC MARKS. Complainant to pay the costs. 2 Aug 1842. (P. 26)

CHARLES F. LOWE versus MATHEW EDWARDS, G. W. THOMPSON, ISAAC MARKS, and POLLY W. EDWARDS. Motion to make (Paery) Edwards a defendant in this bill. 2 Aug 1842. (P. 26)

RICHARD BERRY versus C. B. WALKER and ALEXANDER. The demurrer is not well taken. 2 Aug 1842. (P. 27)

HARPER, CARPENTER, & COMPANY versus THOMAS KING'S Administrators. 2 Aug 1842. (Pp. 27-28)

JAMES W. McADOW versus JAMES M. ARMSTRONG Et Al. The injunction preventing the defendant from selling or moving the slave, Isaac, is made perpetual. 2 Aug 1842. (P. 28)

FRANCIS A. WILEY and (HENRY) WILEY, minors, by their next friend versus JAMES M. BROWN, SARAH P. BROWN, THOMAS C. WORD and others. Henry Trott, Jr. as Administrator of Henry Wiley, has never settled his accounts with James M. Brown as guardian of the complainants. 2 Aug 1842. (Pp. 29-30)

The Court met pursuant to adjournment on 6 Feb 1843. Clerk & Master gives his report. (Pp. 30-31)

JOHN H. WOOD versus JOHN C. MARTIN. John H. Wood makes a statement in which he releases John Hollis from all liability on said note. 6 Feb 1843. (Pp. 31-32)

ABRAHAM BURGER versus A. J. WOOD. Complainant dismisses the suit. 6 Feb 1843. (P. 32)

MARY ADAMS versus JOHN ADAMS and others. Leave is granted to complainant to take depositions. 6 Feb 1843. (P. 32)

HENRY HART versus EBENEZAR WRIGHT and others. The death of Henry Hart was suggested. The cause is revived in the name of Manson M. Brien, Administrator of the said Henry Hart. 6 Feb 1843. (Pp. 32-33)

A number of causes are continued. (Pp. 33-35)

On the first Monday in Aug 1843, the same being the 7th day of the month, Chancery Court met in the town of Woodbury in Cannon County. Thomas L. Williams, presiding. (P. 36)

John C. Ransom has been appointed as Clerk & Master of the Chancery Court in Woodbury. 7 Aug 1843. (Pp. 36-37)

JOHN MULLINS versus JOHN CHILDRESS. The report of the Clerk is set aside. 7 Aug 1843. (P. 37)

A number of causes are continued. (P. 38)

J. JONES and BARBARY LEFEVRE, Administrator of John Lefevre, versus JAMES D. PATTIE and others. Defendant Pattie, while acting as Constable of Coffee County, received a note for collection. The claim was placed in the hands of John Lefevre, another constable of Coffee County, for collection. John Lefevre, having died, complainant was named as administratrix. 7 Aug 1843. (Pp. 39-40)

3

JACOB (MOORE) and others versus ALEXANDER McWHIRTER, Administrator of Thompson Newby. This cause is continued. 7 Aug 1843. (P. 40)

PHEBE NICHOLS and ABAGAIL NICHOLS versus EPHRAIM ANDREWS and THOMAS N. YOURIE, Administrators of Joshua Nichols, JOSEPH W. NICHOLS, MARY E. NICHOLS, and LOUISA E. NICHOLS, heirs of Joshua Nichols. The Court is of the opinion that the land in the will descended to the complainants. Defendants to pay the costs. 7 Aug 1843. (Pp. 40-41)

JOHN MARTIN, Administrator of Richard Butcher, versus JOSEPH RAMSEY and the PRESIDENT AND DIRECTORS OF THE BANK OF TENNESSEE at Shelbyville. The demurrer is overruled. 7 Aug 1843. (P. 41)

FANNIE A. WILEY and HENRY WILEY, Infant heirs of Henry Wiley who sue by their next friend versus HENRY TROTT, JR., Administrator of Henry Wiley, and others. An account of the estate. 7 Aug 1843. (Pp. 42-49)

JAMES BURGER versus WILLIAM J. ELLEDGE. This cause is continued. 7 Aug 1843. (P. 49)

Chancery Court met in the town of Woodbury in Cannon County on the first Monday in Feb 1844, it being the date assigned by law. 5 Feb 1844. (P. 50)

HARPER, CARPENTER, & COMPANY versus DAVIS, KING, and others. The Clerk makes his report. 6 Feb 1844. (Pp. 50-53)

JOHN MULLINS versus JOHN CHILDRESS. The death of the defendant is suggested. 6 Feb 1844. (P. 53)

JAMES BURGER versus WILLIAM F. ELLEDGE. Final Decree. Defendant became trustee of the trust set forth in this bill for the benefit of William Gunter. It appears that the beneficiary was satisfied. 6 Feb 1844. (Pp. 53-54)

MANSON M. BRIEN, Administrator of Henry Hart, versus EBENEZAR WRIGHT and others. 6 Feb 1844. (Pp. 54-55)

FRANCES A. WILEY and HENRY WILEY by their next friend versus JAMES M. BROWN and others. The Clerk makes his report. 6 Feb 1844. (Pp. 56-58)

PRESIDENT AND DIRECTORS OF THE BANK OF TENNESSEE versus JOHN HOLLIS and others. Final Decree. The equities in this bill have been fully met. 6 Feb 1844. (P. 58)

JOSHUA JONES and BARBARA LEFEVRE, Administrator of John Lefevre, versus JOHN D. PATTIE. The Clerk makes his report. 6 Feb 1844. (Pp. 51-52)

WILLIAM RING versus ELIZABETH TENNISON Et Al. The bill is taken for confessed. The order against Hiram Tennison, late husband of the said Elizabeth, is set aside. She is given leave to file as guardian of the heirs of the said Hiram. 6 Feb 1844. (P. 59)

4

ELIZABETH BEATY and ALLEN BEATY versus ISAAC W. ELLEDGE. This cause is continued. 6 Feb 1844. (P. 59)

JOSEPH RAMSEY versus THOMAS H. HOPKINS. HIRAM TENNISON'S Heirs, and WILLIAM RING. Elizabeth Tennison is appointed as guardian of the heirs of Hiram Tennison. She has failed to answer. 6 Feb 1844. (P. 60)

JOSEPH RAMSEY and ROBERT H. STEPHENS VERSUS JOHN MARTIN, JR. On 25 Aug 1840, said John Martin, Jr. was indebted to the complainant. Land was ordered to be sold in order to settle the debt. 6 Feb 1844. (Pp. 61-62)

JOHN MARTIN, Administrator of Richard Butcher, versus JOSEPH RAMSEY and others. It appears to the Court that the title of complainant's intestate to the slave, Daniel, is in dispute. 6 Feb 1844. (Pp. 62-63)

Chancery Court met in the town of Woodbury on 5 Aug 1844, it being the day assigned by law. Broomfield L. Ridley, presiding. (P. 64)

CHARLES F. LOWE versus MATHEW EDWARDS, POLLY EDWARDS, GEORGE W. THOMPSON, ISAAC (MEEKES), and PATIA EDWARDS. Isaac Meekes sold to Mathew Edwards a tract of land in Coffee County on the head waters of Elk River containing 104 acres. A balance of the purchase money is due. It appears that afterwards, Mathew Edwards and Polly W. Edwards sold said land to complainant. He paid them the purchase money for which Patia Edwards to whom the note was payable took judgment against complainant. The said Mathew Edwards, Polly Edwards, and Patia Edwards are perpetually enjoined from collecting all or any part of the judgment. 5 Aug 1844. (Pp. 65-66)

WILLIAM YOUNG versus WILLIAM SHANKS. There is no equity in complainant's bill. 5 Aug 1844. (P. 67)

HARPER & CARPENTER versus DAVIS, KING, and others. 5 Aug 1844. (Pp. 67-68)

RICHARD BERRY versus CHARLES B. WALKER and A. M. ALEXANDER. This cause is remanded to the Rules. 5 Aug 1844. (P. 68)

JOHN W. HALE versus MILAS F. TRAVES, WILLIAM A. TRAVES, and WILLIAM NICHOLS. Complainant on 6 Feb 1843 recovered a judgment against defendants for $101. A tract of land is to be sold to satisfy the judgment. 5 Aug 1844. (Pp. 69-70)

CATHARINE KEELE, a femme covert, and FRANCES E. KEELE, an infant, by their next friend versus JOHNATHAN or JOHN KEELE. Final Decree. In 1842, the parties Catharine and John Keele intermarried in Coffee County where they have heretofore resided. They had issue, Frances E. Keele, an infant child, seventeen months old. Some time after their marriage and before the commencement of this suit, the said Catherine conducted herself as a prudent and chaste wife. The defendant offered to her such indignities that she was compelled to withdraw from him. The bonds of matrimony are dissolved. 5 Aug 1844. (Pp. 70-71)

JOHN MARTIN, JR. and JOHN MARTIN, SR. versus JOSEPH RAMSEY and THE BANK OF TENNESSEE at Shelbyville. 5 Aug 1844. (Pp. 71-72)

JOHN MULLINS versus JOHN CHILDRESS. The death of the defendant has been suggested. No steps have been taken to revive the suit. 5 Aug 1844. (P. 72)

WILLIAM RING versus HIRAM TENNISON'S Heirs and SAMUEL RICHARDSON and wife. It appears from the proof that Hiram Tennison did not absconb as charged. Complainant to pay the costs. 5 Aug 1844. (Pp. 72-73)

Chancery Court of the 4th Chancery Division in the State of Tennessee met in the Courthouse in Woodbury on the 3rd day of Feb 1845. Broomfield L. Ridley, presiding. (P. 74)

WILLIAM P. HARRIS, Administrator of Ezekiel Robertson; MARY ROBERTSON, widow of said decedant; and Lewis M., Laura, Martha, Sibthe E., Maney F., John W., and Mary E. Robertson, heirs of said decedent. Petition to sell lot. 3 Feb 1845. (P. 75)

A number of causes are continued. (Pp. 75-77)

JOSEPH RAMSEY versus WILLIAM RING, THOMAS H. HOPKINS, WILLIAM TENNISON, ISAAC A. TENNISON, MARY J. TENNISON, MARTHA A. TENNISON, JOHN F. TENNISON, HIRAM TENNISON, and ELIZABETH TENNISON. Final Decree. About 1 Feb 1842, Samuel Richardson and wife executed to Defendant Thomas H. Hopkins a deed for a tract of land containing about 115 acres. The deed was cancelled and destroyed. A deed was executed by them to Hiram Tennison. Tennison and Ring entered into an obligation conditioned that said Tennison should convey said lands to said Ring if he (Tennison) could proven title to the land. On 9 Jul 1842, said land was levied on as the property of said Hopkins. Said land was sold as the property of said Hopkins and purchased by Complainant Ramsey. 3 Feb 1845. (Pp. 78-79)

WILLIAM WILLARD, LARKIN KEETON and wife MARY, WILLIAM R. JAMES and wife ISABELAH, BEVERLY WILLARD, MARTHA E. WILLARD, ISAAC A. WILLARD, DAVID B. WILLARD, FINIS H. WILLARD, and FANNIE M. WILLARD versus SAMUEL C. ODUM, WILLIAM C. ODUM, and others. Final Decree. The demurrer is sustained and the bill is dismissed. 3 Feb 1845. (Pp. 79-80)

FRANCIS PARKES versus GEORGE W. THOMPSON and others. The negro girl, Esther, mentioned in the pleadings is the property of complainant. Defendants are perpetually enjoined from selling said girl. 3 Feb 1845. (P. 80)

Chancery Court met in the town of Woodbury on 4 Aug 1845. Broomfield L. Ridley, presiding. (P. 81)

A number of causes are continued. (P. 81)

HARPER & CARPENTER versus DAVIS, KING, and others. 4 Aug 1845. (Pp. 82-83)

ELIZABETH BEATY and ALAN BEATY versus ISAAC W. ELLEDGE.

The Court finds that Allen Beaty is indebted to Isaac W. Elledge. 4 Aug 1845. (Pp. 83-84)

JAMES W. McADOW versus LEWIS PATTERSON and others. Motion to dissolve the injunction. 4 Aug 1845. (P. 85)

A number of causes are continued. (Pp. 85-86)

Be it remembered that since the last term of court, John C. Ransom, Clerk & Master, has submitted his resignation. The Chancellor proceeded to appoint Caleb B. Davis as Clerk & Master until the present time. The Chancellor now appoints the said Davis to a full term of office. 27 Apr 1846. (Pp. 87-90)

DANIEL HARDAWAY versus HUGH DAVIDSON. Final Decree. The equity in complainant's bill is fully met. 27 Apr 1846. (P. 90)

JOSEPH RAMSEY versus JOHN MARTIN. Final Decree. The cause is dismissed. 27 Apr 1846. (Pp. 90-91)

ELIZABETH PHILLIPS versus BENJAMIN L. PHILLIPS. The parties have compromised. 27 Apr 1846. (P. 91)

HANNAH A. TROTT versus HENRY TROTT. Final Decree. The parties have compromised. 27 Apr 1846. (P. 92)

THOMAS G. WOOD versus BENJAMIN PENDLETON, Executor of John Brown, and the creditors. 27 Apr 1846. (Pp. 92-93)

A. BURGER versus BENJAMIN CAMP). Benjamin (Cam) and Benjamin G. Cam) are non residents of this state. The bill is taken for confessed. 27 Apr 1846. (P. 93)

ROBERT WILSON and ELIZABETH WITHERSPOON versus ELIHU WITHERSPOON and TRAVIS. Final Decree. Ebenezar Witherspoon died intestate. Elihu Witherspoon was appointed as administrator. Said intestate left no children or widow or father. His brother and sister are next of kin. Eliza Witherspoon, being his sister, is entitled to a distributive share. She has received her share. She has waived her rights to Robert William. Said Elihu Witherspoon has refused to turn over to the said Robert Wilson his share of the estate. The Clerk is ordered to give an account. 27 Apr 1846. (Pp. 94-96)

WILLIAM P. HARRIS, Administrator of E. M. Robertson, versus THE BANK OF TENNESSEE and other creditors. 27 Apr 1846. (P. 96)

ESTHER BRIDGES and SAMUEL HANCOCK versus ALLEN BRIDGES and others. Complainants have to amend their bill. 27 Apr 1846. (P. 96)

ZACHARIAH BUSH and AARON BYFORD versus BLAKE SAGELY and B. B. DICKENS. The injunction heretofore granted has been dismissed so far as to permit said Sagely to prosecute his action of ejectment. 27 Apr 1846. (P. 97)

RICHARD BERRY versus CHARLES B. WALKER. 27 Apr 1846. (Pp. 97-99)

Chancery Court met in the town of Woodbury for its October term. (P. 100)

ESTER BRIDGES versus ALLEN BRIDGES and others. This cause is transferred to the Chancery Court at Manchester. (P. 100)

ROBERT WILSON and ELIZA WITHERSPOON versus ELIHU WITHERSPOON. Final Decree. It appears to the Court that there is in the hands of Defendant Elihu Witherspoon, Administrator of Ebenezar Witherspoon to which Complainant Robert Wilson is entitled in right of Eliza Witherspoon for her distributive share of the Estate of the said decedant the sum of $63.50. Oct 1846. (Pp. 100-101)

MELINDA CAUPENHAUR versus DAVID CAUPENHOUR. This cause is continued. Oct 1846. (P. 101)

JOHN W. STONE and wife SARAH versus NANCY BROWN. This cause is continued. Oct 1846. (P. 101)

RICHARD BERRY versus C. B. WALKER and A. M. ALEXANDER. Final Decree. Complainant's bill is dismissed. Oct 1846. (P. 102)

BUSH & BYFORD versus TAYLOR & SAGELY. Final Decree. Oct 1846. (P. 103)

JOHN MARTIN, SR. and JOHN MARTIN, JR. versus JOSEPH RAMSEY and the BANK OF TENNESSEE. 27 Oct 1846. (Pp. 103-104)

JOSEPH RAMSEY versus PETER FLEMING, ALBERT FLEMING, SAMUEL FLEMING, and LEVI ·BOLING. The demurrer of the defendants is not well taken. 27 Oct 1846. (P. 104)

GEORGE BOGLE, SR., Executor of John Higgin; JAMES MILLIKEN and wife ELIZABETH, WILLIAM HIGGIN, ALEXANDER HIGGIN, ELIJAH HIGGIN, JOHN D. ELKINS, HIRAM Y. TITTLE and wife MARY, WESLEY HIGGIN, JAMES HIGGIN, JOSEPH MORAH and wife SARAH, ELIZABETH? ARMSTRONG and wife MARGARET, JOHN HIGGIN, SAMUEL TITTLE, CARROL ANDERSON and wife MARGARET, JOHN TITTLE, MARY TITTLE, SUSANNAH TITTLE, ERMELIA TITTLE, WILLIE JANE TITTLE, and MISSOURI M. TITTLE, the six last named are minors. Ex Parte. John Higgin, late of Cannon County, died several years since seized and possessed of 125 acres in the 11th District. He left a last will and testament in which he devised the tract of land to his widow, Mary Higgin, during her natural life and at her death to be sold and the proceeded equally divided among his heirs. George Bogle, one of the petitioners, was appointed as Executor with John McMinn who has since died. Mary Higgin is now dead. The petitioners are the heirs. They are petitioning to sell the land. 27 Oct 1846. (Pp. 105-106)

HENRY TROTT, SR. versus A. G. CAMPBELL. Final Decree. Complainant has secured a judgment against Albert G. Campbell. Defendant has no property for which a lien can be made. Parties were join owners of a tract of land on the south side of Stone's River. The Clerk is to sell the defendant's share. 27 Oct 1846. (Pp. 106-107)

D. F. ( ) versus JOHN C. MARTIN. Final Decree. Defendant to pay the costs. 27 Oct 1846. (P. 107)

A number of causes are continued. (Pp. 107-108)

Chancery Court met at the Courthouse in the town of Woodbury for the April Term 1847. Broomfield L. Ridley, presiding. (P. 109)

LUCY BROGAN versus JOHN A. BROGAN. The bill is taken for confessed. A hearing is set. 26 Apr 1847. (P. 109)

(LUCY) EWELL versus (DABNEY) EWELL. Complainant dismisses her bill. 26 Apr 1847. (P. 109)

Be it remembered that since the last term of court, Caleb B. Davis tendered to the Chancellor his resignation as Clerk & Master. The Chancellor was pleased to appoint Zeno   C. Ross as Clerk & Master. (Pp. 110-112)

A number of causes are continued. (P. 112)

JAMES R. TAYLOR, HENRY CANNON and his wife AGNES. Ex Parte. On 12 Aug 1840, Edmond Taylor settled on Agnes P. Cannon, his daughter, a deed of gift of a woman slave named Lavina and her three children, Martha, William, and John to her sole and separate use. The slaves were transferred to James R. Taylor in trust for her. The said James R. Taylor was named as trustee without his knowledge or consent. The Clerk is to report to the next term of court a suitable person for the job. 27 Apr 1847. (Pp. 112-113)

LUCY BROGAN versus JOHN A. BROGAN. Complainant and defendant were married as charged and lived together as charged in Cannon County for more than two years previous to the filing of this bill. Defendant has been guilty of the indignity and cruel treatment towards the complainant as charged. The bonds of matrimony are dissolved. Parties have agreed as to alimony. 27 Apr 1847. (Pp. 113-114)

JACOB ADCOCK versus ADAM ELROD. The injunction is dissolved. 27 Apr 1847. (P. 114)

DAVID EDWARDS and wife versus NATHAN FINLEY Et Al. Final Decree. The defendant's demurrer is well taken. 27 Apr 1847. (P. 115)

MALINDA CAUPENHAUR versus DAVID CAUPENHAUR. Complainant and defendant were lawfully married and have lived together as husband and wife. Complainant has always conducted herself as a prudent, discreet wife and has been faithful to the marriage vow. Defendant has treated her with great personal indignities and has improperly inflicted personal violence on her in disregard of his obligations as a husband. The bonds of matrimony are dissolved. Complainant is given custody of her infant daughter. 27 Apr 1847. (Pp. 115-117)

JOHN W. BOWEN and wife SARAH JANE and others. Ex Parte. Petitioners John W. Bowen and wife Sarah Jane, together with Henry C. Barkley, Nancy Ann Barkley, Mary Isabella Barkley, William A. Barkley, and Robert A. Barkley who are minors and petition by their mother Elizabeth Barkley, petition to sell a negro girl named Agnes. 27 Apr 1847. (Pp. 117-119)

ROBERT CARSON versus JAMES PRICE. Complainant sold to

defendant a tract of land. Complainant recovered a judgment in Circuit Court against the defendant who has no personal estate. The Court decrees that the land should be sold to satisfy the debt. 27 Apr 1847. (Pp. 119-120)

GEORGE BOGLE, Executor of John Higgin, and others. Ex Parte. 27 Apr 1847. (P. 121)

ESTHER BRIDGES by her next friend versus ALLEN H. BRIDGES and JOHN HOWARD, Administrator of William Howard, and WILLIAM HOWARD. Complainant and defendants all reside in Coffee County. This cause is transferred to Chancery Court at Manchester. 27 Apr 1847. (P. 122)

Chancery Court met in the town of Woodbury on the 25th day of Oct 1847. It appears to the Clerk & Master by instruction of the Chancellor that he would not be in attendance to hold the court at the present term. The Court was adjourned until the 5th Monday in Nov next. (P. 123)

Chancery Court met in the town of Woodbury on the 29th day of Nov 1847. The Chancellor not appearing, the court was adjourned. (P. 123)

JAMES T. C. McKNIGHT, Executor and legatee of David McKnight; JAMES L. KELTON and wife ELIZA EUGENIA; JOHN M. ANDERSON and wife SARAH J.; SAMUEL H. A. McKNIGHT: and GEORGE D. A. McKNIGHT, the two last of whom are minors. Ex Parte. The Clerk is to take proof as to whether it is to the advantage of the parties that a sale be had. 2 Dec 1847. (Pp. 123-124)

DAVID M. JARRATT, Administrator of George St. John; WILLIAM ST. JOHN, THOMAS ST. JOHN, BESSY ST. JOHN, ARTHUR ST. JOHN, MARTIN ST. JOHN, GOODALL and wife NANCY, and BERRY ST. JOHN, children of Abner St. John who was a son of the intestate. Ex Parte. The Clerk is to take proof as to whether it is to the advantage of the parties that a sale be held. 2 Dec 1847. (P. 124)

JOSEPH RAMSEY versus JOHN MARTIN, SR. and JOHN MARTIN, JR. 2 Dec 1847. (Pp. 124-125)

WILLIAM BARTON. Ex Parte. The report is given as to the Estate of David McKnight. 2 Dec 1847. (Pp. 125-128)

DAVID M. JARRATT, Administrator of George St. John; JOHN ST. JOHN, WILLIAM ST. JOHN, THOMAS ST. JOHN, BESSY ST. JOHN, ARTHUR ST. JOHN, MARTIN ST. JOHN, sons of George St. John; GOODALL and wife NANCY and HENRY ST. JOHN, children of Abner St. John who was a son of the intestate and who also is now deceased of Alexander, Warren; GARLAIN THORNTON and wife SARAH JANE, HENRY THORNTON and wife ELIZABETH CATHARINE, GEORGE W. WARREN, MARTHA WARREN, ARTHUR WARREN, and WILLIAM WARREN, the four last are minors without guardian and appear by their father Arthur Warren and they together with the said Alexander, Sarah Jane, and Elizabeth, being the children of Martha or Patsy Warren who was a daughter of the intestate and died before him. Martha intermarried with   , Nancy Ann intermarried with. Catharine Miles and Mahaley Miles are children of Catharine.

Said Catherine was a daughter of the intestate. 2 Dec 1847. (Pp. 128-129)

MALAKIAH CUMMINGS and wife LUCINDA versus JOHN A. GEORGE, Administrator of Charles P. Alexander, CALVIN SULLIVAN, and others. Final Decree. Charles P. Alexander was the regular appointed guardian of the complainant, Lucinda who is one of the children and heirs of William Sullivan, late of Warren County, Tennessee. At the death of Charles P. Alexander who died intestate, John A. George was appointed as his administrator. The said Lucinda has intermarried with the complainant, Malakiah Cummings. Complainants are seeking their share of the estate. 2 Dec 1847. (Pp. 129-130)

JOHN BARRY versus MARIA BARRY. Bill for divorce. Complainant seeks to dismiss his suit. 2 Dec 1847. (P. 130)

WILLIAM GARMANY versus DAVID JONES and others. The suit has been compromised. 2 Dec 1847. (P. 130)

MARY MEDFORD versus HENRY MEDFORD. The suit is compromised. 2 Dec 1847. (P. 131)

GEORGE BOGLE, Executor of John Higgins, and others. 2 Dec 1847. (P. 131)

JAMES W. McADOW versus SHADRACH SMITH and others. The bill is dismissed. 2 Dec 1847. (Pp. 131-132)

Chancery Court was held at the Courthouse in Woodbury, Cannon County on 7 Sep 1848. Broomfield L. Ridley, presiding. (P. 133)

DAVID JARRATT, Administrator of George St. John and others. Ex Parte. 7 Sep 1848. (Pp. 133-134)

LUCY HOPKINS versus JOHN P. HOPKINS. This cause is continued. 7 Sep 1848. (P. 134)

LYDIA MEARS versus WILLIAM MEARS. The suit is dismissed. 7 Sep 1848. (P. 135)

ABRAHAM BURGER VERSUS ZENO C. ROSS and the TRUSTEES OF (LAWSON) ACADEMY. Defendant Ross is indebted to Abraham Burger in the sum of ninety dollars. Said Ross has abandoned and left the country. 7 Sep 1848. (Pp. 135-136)

HENRY HOWERSTON versus MARGARET HOWERSTON. The suit is dismissed. 7 Sep 1848. (P. 136)

HIRAM MORRIS and others versus CICERO B. DUNCAN, Surviving partner of the firm of T. W. DUNCAN & LAW. 7 Sep 1848. (Pp. 136-138)

DAVID HOLLIS by his guardian Joseph Hollis and (SAMSON) HOLLIS versus JAMES R. TAYLOR. This cause is referred to Rules. 7 Sep 1848. (P. 138)

LUCY BATES VERSUS HARMON ST. JOHN and wife. This cause is dismissed. 7 Sep 1848. (P. 138)

JOSEPH RAMSEY versus PETER FLEMING and others. 7 Sep 1848.

(Pp. 139-140)

C. C. HANCOCK versus ARCHIBALD STONE and JOHN W. STONE. The equity in the bill is fully met. The injunction is dissolved. 7 Sep 1848. (Pp. 140-141)

EPHRAIM C. GROSS versus RICHARD HANCOCK and JOSIAH SPURLOCK. The demurrer is not well taken. 7 Sep 1848. (P. 141)

THOMAS C. WORD versus ALBERT G. CAMPBELL. Defendant is indebted to the complainant. He has no personal property. Land is ordered to be sold. 7 Sep 1848. (Pp. 141-142)

JAMES T. C. McKNIGHT, Executor of David McKnight, and others. Ex Parte. 7 Sep 1848. (Pp. 142-149)

Chancery Court met in the town of Woodbury on 8 Mar 1849. The Chancellor not appearing, the Court was adjourned. (P. 149)

ALBERT M. McKNIGHT AND ANDREW M. McKNIGHT, Surviving Executors of John M. McKnight and WILLIAM R. AKINS and wife MARY E. and other heirs of John M. McKnight. Ex Parte. 9 Mar 1849. (Pp. 149-150)

MARTHA J. ST. JOHN versus HARMON ST. JOHN. The bill is taken for confessed. A hearing is set. 9 Mar 1849. (Pp. 150-151)

LUCY HOPKINS versus JOHN P. HOPKINS. Bill for divorce. The cause is continued. 9 Mar 1849. (P. 151)

HENRY SCOTT versus NANCY SCOTT. Complainant is a minor. He has no right to prosecute a suit. The suit is dismissed. 9 Mar 1849. (P. 151)

JAMES T. C. McKNIGHT, Executor of David McKnight, and others. Ex Parte. 9 Mar 1849. (Pp. 151-152)

GEORGE W. HANAGAR versus WILLIAM T. C   ) and others. 9 Mar 1849. (Pp. 152-153)

MALINDA COUGHAMOUS versus DAVID COUGHAMOUS. The Clerk is ordered to take an account with the said Malinda and charge her with all such valuable articles and property as defendant delivered to her in their separation except the land. 9 Mar 1849. (P. 153)

JOHN A. BAIRD and wife and HENRY WILEY by his guardian versus HENRY TROTT, JAMES J. TROTT, and others. 9 Mar 1849. (P. 154)

A. G. MILLIKEN versus (INDE) MILLIKEN. The bill is taken for confessed. 9 Mar 1849. (Pp. 154-155)

Chancery Court met at the Courthouse in the town of Woodbury on 6 Sep 1849. Thomas G. Wood, Clerk & Master, adjourned court until the next day. (P. 156)

James A. Spurlock was admitted to the Bar as a practicing attorney. 7 Sep 1849. (P. 156)

JOHN A. BAIRD and wife, FRANCES ANN and HENRY WILEY versus HENRY TROTT, Administrator of Henry Wiley, and others. The order

12

taking this bill for confessed is set aside. 7 Sep 1849. (P. 156)

On motion, it appears that the Clerk & Master has omitted to spread his receipts for state and county revenues for the year 1848. (P. 157)

ELIZA PENDLETON by her husband and next friend Benjamin Pendleton versus S. B. SPURLOCK and others. 7 Sep 1849. (P. 158)

ALBERT G. MILLIKEN versus JESSE MILLEKEN. The bill is taken for confessed. A hearing is set. Ex Parte. 7 Sep 1849. (P. 158)

JOHN W. PARKER versus EDWARD BRAGG and others. The Clerk is ordered to take proof. Complainant John W. Parker is a pauper and is entitled to present his suit without giving security. 7 Sep 1849. (P. 158)

EPHRAIM C. GROSS versus JOSIAH SPURLOCK and RICHARD HANCOCK. 7 Sep 1849. (Pp. 158-159)

Sheriff Robert A. Smith is fined five dollars for neglect to give attendance in court while in discharge of public business. 8 Sep 1849. (P. 159)

ALBERT G. MILLIKEN versus JESSE MILLEKEN. Complainant and defendant have been partners in trade with the power to purchase and sell property. It is the opinion of the Court that the complainant is part of the partnership debts. 7 Sep 1849. (Pp. 159-160)

CHRISTOPHER C. HANCOCK versus ARCHEBALD STONE and JOHN W. STONE. Final Decree. The equity of complainant's bill is met and denied. 8 Sep 1849. (P. 161)

DAVID HOLLIS by his guardians Joseph Hollis and Simeon Hollis and SIMEON HOLLIS and JOSEPH HOLLIS versus JAMES R. TAYLOR. All the equity in the bill is fully met. 8 Sep 1849. (P. 161)

JACOB ADCOCK versus ADAM ELROD and ZACHARIAH HAGEWOOD. Final Decree. The equity in the bill is fully met. 8 Sep 1849. (Pp. 161-162)

JOHN W. PARKER versus EDWARD BRAGG and others. Complainant is a pauper and is not entitled to prosecute his suit without giving security. 8 Sep 1849. (P. 162)

ISAAC A. KEETON versus ISAAC ADAMS. Injunction. 8 Sep 1849. (P. 162)

ALBERT M. McKNIGHT and ANDREW McKNIGHT, Surviving executors of John M. McKnight, and others. Ex Parte. 8 Sep 1849. (P. 163)

THOMAS C. WORD versus ALBERT G. CAMPBELL and others. The Clerk has sold the land and mills in the pleading. 8 Sep 1849. (P. 164)

JOSEPH P. LASSITER versus LUKE LASSITER and others. This

cause is remanded to the Rules. 8 Sep 1849. (P. 164)

LUCY HOPKINS versus JOHN P. HOPKINS. Complainant and defendant were married and lived together as man and wife as set forth in the bill of complainant. The defendant has wilfully and maliciously deserted the complainant. He has absconded with one Hannah J. Johnson and has been and still is living with her in adultery. The bonds of matrimony are dissolved. 8 Sep 1849. (Pp. 164-165)

ELIZA PENDLETON by her husband and next friend Benjamin Pendleton versus S. B. SPURLOCK and others. 8 Sep 1849. Eliza Pendleton (formerly Eliza McAdoo) intermarried with Benjamin Pendleton about the 26th day of Jan 1848. On 18 Aug 1848, William McAdoo conveyed by deed of gift to his daughter, Eliza Pendleton, three slaves, to wit, Mary, Violet, and Martha and their increase. Since the execution of said conveyance, the slave, Mary, has been delivered of a child named Tennessee. The said S. B. Spurlock, assignee of Cli Bailey, recovered a judgment against Benjamin Pendleton. The said Eliza filed suit for an injunction to enjoin the said Spurlock and his securities from selling the slave and her increase. 8 Sep 1849. (Pp. 165-167)

MARTHA J. ST. JOHN versus HARMON ST. JOHN. Final Decree. Complainant intermarried with defendant as stated in the bill. It further appears to the Court that Complainant is one of the heirs and distributees of William Bates. All the property she receives as one of the legatees is settled upon her free and apart from her husband. 8 Sep 1849. (P. 167)

MALINDA CAUGHINSUR versus DAVID CAUGHENSUR. This cause is referred to the Master to take an account. 8 Sep 1849. (P. 168)

CICERO B. DUNCAN, Surviving partner, versus JOSIAH FUSTON and others. The demurrer is not well taken. 8 Sep 1849. (P. 168)

JAMES R. TAYLOR, JOHN L. TAYLOR, and other heirs of Edmond Taylor. The Clerk is to take an account to determine the amount of advancements made by Edmond Taylor to each of his children in his lifetime whether in property, money, or in paying debts for them. 8 Sep 1849. (P. 169)

ALEXANDER INGLISH versus JOHN RODGERS, WILLIAM RODGERS, JAMES RODGERS, JANE RODGERS, ALEXANDER MORGAN and wife CATHARINE, HENRY RODGERS, WILLIAM RODGERS, and ELIZABETH RODGERS. On 2 Jan 1843, the complainant executed to John Rodgers, the ancestor of defendants a deed of trust to secure a debt. A tract of land is to be sold to satisfy the debt. 8 Sep 1849. The said John Rodgers left his widow, Elizabeth, and his children who are the defendants in this cause. 8 Sep 1849. (Pp. 170-174)

Chancery Court met in the town of Woodbury at the Courthouse on 7 Mar 1850. Broomfield L. Ridley, presiding. (P. 175)

14

JOSEPH P. LASSITER versus LUKE LASSITER and others. Final Decree. This cause is dismissed. 7 Mar 1850. (P. 175)

DAVID M. JARRATT, Administrator of George St. John, and others. Ex Parte. 7 Mar 1850. (Pp. 176-177)

AGNES HENDERSON and others. Ex Parte. The Clerk is to take proof to determine if it is in the interest of the minors, Baldy and Robert C. Henderson, two of the petitioners, that the land be sold. 7 Mar 1850. (P. 177)

SUSAN NOKES and WILLIAM NOKES, Administrators of Thomas Nokes, and others versus MEDFORD CAFFEY. 7 Mar 1850. (P. 177)

ROBERT WOODRUFF versus MOSES H. GLASSCOCK and others. 7 Mar 1850. (Pp. 177-178)

ALBERT M. McKNIGHT and ANDREW McKNIGHT, Executors of John M. McKnight and others. 7 Mar 1850. (Pp. 178-183)

JOHN W. PARKER versus EDWARD BRAGG Et Al. 7 Mar 1850. (P. 183)

ALEX MORGAN and others versus ELIZABETH RODGERS and others. The Clerk is to hear proof and report back the value of the slaves. 7 Mar 1850. (Pp. 183-184)

THOMAS C. WORD versus A. G. CAMPBELL Et Al. The lands mentioned in the pleadings have been sold. 7 Mar 1850. (Pp. 184-186)

ALBERT G. MILLIKEN versus JESSE MILLIKEN. 7 Mar 1850. (Pp. 186-187)

MALINDA CAUGHINSUR versus DAVID CAUGHINSUR. One third of defendant's estate is decreed to complainant for the support of herself and her infant daughter. 7 Mar 1850. (Pp. 188-189)

JOSHUA (VAPER) versus STEPHEN A. MITCHELL. 7 Mar 1850. (P. 190)

JAMES W. McADOO versus JOHN ORRAN and others. There is no equity in the bill. 7 Mar 1850. (P. 191)

NELSON COOPER versus JOHN McIVER. The equity in the bill was in favor of complainant. 7 Mar 1850. (P. 192)

WILLIAM GIBSON versus WILLIAM CATHEY. It appears to the Court that the complainant was mustered into the service of the United States as a volunteer soldier in the late war with Mexico for the term of twelve months before the expiration of which time he was discharged. He became by the Act of Congress of 11 Feb 1847 to a certificate of warrant from the War Department for 160 acres or treasury script. William Gibson, a brother of the complainant also enlisted in said service for the same time during which time he died of sickness contracted in said service. The said William Gibson left no wife, child, father, or mother, no sister or brothers other than the complainant. The said Richard Gibson was appointed administrator of the estate. It appears that the defendant fraudulent obtained the certificate of discharge of the complainant and his brother. 7 Mar 1850.

(Pp. 193-195)

BENJAMIN PENDLETON and wife ANN ELIZA and JOSEPH SPURLOCK. Ex Parte. The petitioner, Ann Eliza Pendleton, is the owner of a tract of land in Cannon County containing between 65 and 80 acres. The said Benjamin Pendleton and the said Ann Eliza are lawfully intermarried and that with a view of removing to the State of Texas, they contracted to sell the land to the said Joseph Spurlock at the price of ten dollars per acre which is a fair price for it. They intend to reinvest the money in lands in Texas to be settled to the sole and separate use of the said Ann Eliza. Doubts have arisen as to the power of the said Benjamin and Ann Eliza to sell and convey the said land. The Court rules that they have the right to sell and convey said land. 7 Mar 1850. (Pp. 195-196)

JAMES R. TAYLOR, Administrator of Edmond Taylor, versus JOHN L. TAYLOR, JOSIAH F. MORFORD and wife JANE, HENRY CANNON and wife AGNES, WILLIAM FERRELL, ELIZA ANN FERRELL, MARTHA F. FERRELL, JUDATH FERRELL, and MARGARET FERRELL. The Clerk made his report as to the advancements received by the legatees during the lifetime of the said Edmond Taylor. The legatees are James R. Taylor, Josiah F. Morford and wife Jane B., Edmond H. Taylor, Henry Cannon and wife Agnes, John L. Taylor, Nathaniel M. Taylor, Leyhton Ferrell and wife Elizabeth (now deceased). 7 Mar 1850. (Pp. 197-201)

JOHN A. BAIRD and wife and HENRY WILEY versus HENRY TROTT and others. 7 Mar 1850. (Pp. 201-202)

ALEXANDER INGLIS versus WILLIAM RODGERS, JOHN RODGERS, ALEXANDER MORGAN and wife CATHARINE, JAMES RODGERS, JANE RODGERS, HENRY RODGERS, WILLIAM RODGERS, and ELIZABETH RODGERS. The original indebtedness of complainant to John Rodgers, the ancestor of defendants was one hundred dollars. 7 Mar 1850. (Pp. 202-203)

EPHRAIM C. GROSS versus RICHARD HANCOCK and JOSIAH SPURLOCK. 7 Mar 1850. (Pp. 203-206)

JAMES T. McKNIGHT, Executor, and legatees of David McKnight. Ex Parte. 7 Mar 1850. (Pp. 206-213)

Chancery Court met in the town of Woodbury on the 5th day of Sep 1850. Broomfield L. Ridley, presiding. (P. 214)

EMILY JANE ROBINSON, MARTHA AN ROBERTSON, LOUCINDA ROBERTSON, WILLIAM J. ROBERTSON, and MARY P. ROBINSON by their guardian William McGill; NANCY E. ROBINSON, SILAS A. ROBINSON, Administrator of Jesse Robinson, and (JAMES) McGill. Ex Parte. The petitioners are the children of the said Jesse B. Robinson. Nancy E. Robinson is the widow. The said Jesse B. Robinson was the original owner of 121 acres which he sold on 14 Dec 1847 to James McGill for $1200. All the purchase money has been paid except for $265 for which the Administrator still holds the note. All the parties desire rescinding said note (which is alleged to be in accordance with the request of the said Jesse B. on his death bed. 5 Sep 1850. (Pp. 214-215)

HUGH ROBINSON'S Administrator and heirs versus BERRY WILLIAMS and others. William McGill has been appointed the regular guardian for Emily, Martha, Louisa, William J., and Mary P. Robinson, minor heirs of Jesse B. Robinson. 5 Sep 1850. (P. 216)

ISAAC A. KEETON versus ISAAC ADAMS and R. A. SMITH. This cause is continued. 5 Sep 1850. (P. 216)

FRANCES HANCOCK by her next friend Charles J. Hancock versus (LOUIS) HANCOCK. The Clerk is to take proof and report back to the Court. 5 Sep 1850. (P. 217)

WILLIAM J. DAWSON versus W. J. RAGLAND. The parties have compromised. 5 Sep 1850. (P. 217)

EMILY JANE ROBINSON and the other heirs of Jesse B. Robinson. Ex Parte. 5 Sep 1850. (Pp. 217-219)

STEPHEN A. MITCHELL versus JOSHUA VASSER Et Al. The defendant is to give bond and security. 5 Sep 1850. (Pp. 220-221)

JOHN L. TAYLOR versus RAYMON H. (MASON) and JOHN R. SULLIVAN. The suit has been compromised. 5 Sep 1850. (P. 221)

JAMES M. COMER versus JOHN TILFORD Et Al. The complainant is entitled to the relief sought. 5 Sep 1850. (P. 221)

BENJAMIN GASAWAY versus WILLIAM GLENN. The demurrer of the defendant was not sustained by the proof. 5 Sep 1850. (P. 222)

MARY ANN FLOYD versus GEORGE W. FLOYD. Complainant and defendant were lawfully married. The treatment of defendant toward complainant has been so cruel that it is unsafe and improper for her to live and cohabit with him. The bonds of matrimony are dissolved. 5 Sep 1850. (P. 223)

BENJAMIN WEBBER versus B. B. DICKENS and DAVID PATTON. On motion of complainant, John A. Webber is released as security for complainant in prosecuting this cause. 5 Sep 1850. (Pp. 223-224)

JOHN W. PARKER versus J. C. MARTIN Et Al. It appears to the Court that defendant Edward Bragg entered into a contract with Sarah Parker, widow of Levi Parker and mother of complainant to purchase the tract of land in the proceedings. 5 Sep 1850. (Pp. 224-226)

JAMES R. TAYLOR, Administrator of Edmond Taylor, versus JOHN L. TAYLOR and others. 5 Sep 1850. (Pp. 227-230)

EPHRAIM C. GROSS versus RICHARD HANCOCK and JOSIAH SPURLOCK. Final Decree. 5 Sep 1850. (Pp. 230-232)

HARMON ST. JOHN and wife MARTHA JANE versus MARTIN WALE and SAMUEL R. JAMES. The death of Martin Wale is suggested. This cause is revived in the name of Lucy James. 5 Sep 1850. (P. 233)

JAMES RODGERS and others versus ELIZABETH RODGERS, SR. and

others. 5 Sep 1850. (Pp. 233-234)

FRANKLIN COLEMAN versus F. D. WRATHER and D. M. JARRATT. Defendant to pay the costs. 5 Sep 1850. (P. 234)

JAMES T. C. McKNIGHT and the legatees of David McKnight. Ex Parte. 5 Sep 1850. (Pp. 234-235)

FRANCES HANCOCK by her next friend versus LEWIS CARSWELL. Seventy-five dollars would be a reasonable allowance to the complainant for her support until the next term of this court. 5 Sep 1850. (Pp. 236-237)

MARIA WEEDON by her next friend versus DANIEL J. WEEDON. The complainant is allowed seventy-five dollars for her support until the next term of court. 5 Sep 1850. (P. 237)

FRANCES HANCOCK versus LEWIS HANCOCK. 7 Sep 1850. (Pp. 237-238)

MEDFORD COFFEE versus SUSAN NOKES, Administratrix, and WILLIAM NOKES, Administrator of Thomas Nokes; and MARTHA NOKES, MARY NOKES, SARAH NOKES, and WILLIAM NOKES. William Nokes has not been appointed guardian for the minor defendants. He is hereby appointed. 7 Sep 1850. (Pp. 238-239)

Chancery Court met in the town of Woodbury on 6 Mar 1851. Broomfield L. Ridley, presiding. (P. 240)

Chancery Court met in the town of Woodbury on 4 Sep 1851. Broomfield L. Ridley, presiding. (P. 241)

Clerk & Master Thomas G. Wood presented his receipts from 1849-1850. (Pp. 241-242)

JOHN S. BROWN, Trustee, versus ELI and JOHN P. BAILEY. The bill is taken for confessed. 4 Sep 1851. (P. 242)

ALBERT G. MILLIKEN versus JESSE MILLIKEN. The Clerk is to take an account and report back. 4 Sep 1851. (Pp. 242-243)

WILLIAM NOKES, D. M. JARRATT, SUSAN NOKES, and others versus MEDFORD COFFEE. 5 Sep 1851. (Pp. 243-244)

WILLIAM H. McCABE versus EPHRAIM NESBITT and WILLIAM STACY. All the equity in complainant's bill is fully met. 5 Sep 1851. (P. 244)

SARAH E. WEEDON by her next friend versus AUGUSTUS M. WEEDON and others. The parties have compromised. 5 Sep 1851. (P. 245)

JOHN M. COOPER and wife LUCKEY P. versus FRANCIS BRYSON, CHRISTOPHER OWEN and wife PERMELIA, WILLIAM BRYSON, and JOHN W. SUMMERS. The bill is taken for confessed. Samuel Bryson died intestate many years since, leaving the defendant, Francis, as his widow and the complainant Lockey P., wife of John M. Cooper and the defendant Permelia, wife of Christopher Owen, and William Bryson as his only children and heirs. There are two slaves, Christina and her child Andy to be distributed among the heirs. They are to be sold at auction. 5 Sep 1851. (Pp. 245-246)

DAVID M. JARRATT, Administrator of George St. John, and others. Ex Parte. 5 Sep 1851. (Pp. 247-248)

ISAAC A. KEETON versus ZACHARIAH THOMASON. The defendant is to have leave to file his demurrer. 5 Sep 1851. (Pp. 248-249)

BENJAMIN F. WOOD versus JOHN H. WOOD Et Al. The cause is continued. 5 Sep 1851. (P. 249)

FRANCES HANCOCK by her next friend versus LEWIS HANCOCK. The complainant dismisses her suit. 5 Sep 1851. (P. 249)

WILLIAM FERRELL versus AGNES W. HENDERSON and JAMES T. HENDERSON. Final Decree. All the equity in the bill is met. 5 Sep 1851. (Pp. 249-250)

JESSE PIERCE versus LEGRON C. WHERRY. The defendant is a non resident of Tennessee. The bill is taken for confessed. A hearing is set. 5 Sep 1851. (P. 250)

JOSIAH FUSTON versus CICERO B. DUNCAN and others. 5 Sep 1851. (Pp. 250-252)

ISAAC A. KEETON versus ISAAC ADAMS and ROBERT A. SMITH. Final Decree. 5 Sep 1851. (Pp. 252-253)

JAMES T. C. McKNIGHT, Executor and legatee of James L. Kelton and wife ELIZA EUGENIA: JOHN M. ANDREWS and wife SARAH, JR.: SAMUEL H. A. McKNIGHT, AND GEORGE D. McKNIGHT, Legatees of David McKnight. Ex Parte. 5 Sep 1851. (Pp. 253-254)

JOHN A. BAIRD and wife and HENRY WILEY versus HENRY TROTT and others. 5 Sep 1851. (Pp. 254-255)

DANIEL LEMAN versus J. T. D. WALE and DAVID M. JARRALL. 5 Sep 1851. (Pp. 255-256)

LARKIN KEATON versus ZACHARIAH THOMASON and R. H. SMITH. The injunction is dissolved. 5 Sep 1851. (Pp. 256-257)

MARIA L. WEEDON by her next friend versus DANIEL F. WEEDON. The suit is dismissed. 5 Sep 1851. (P. 257)

NANCY C. McADOW versus WILLIAM McADOW Et Al. Parthenia Ann McAdoo, Thomas B. McAdoo, Margaret J. McAdoo, Azaline McAdoo are all minors and have no regular guardian. William C. Luck is appointed as guardian. 5 Sep 1851. (P. 257)

MARK L. YOUNG versus WILLIAM L. McADOW. The defendant is a non resident. The bill is taken for confessed. A hearing is set. 5 Sep 1851. (P. 258)

STEPHEN A. MITCHELL versus JOSHUA VASSAR and others. This cause is continued. 5 Sep 1851. (Pp. 258-260)

Chancery Court met in the town of Woodbury on 4 Mar 1852. Broomfield L. Ridley, presiding. (P. 261)

JOHN ST. JOHN'S Heirs. Petition to sell land. Special commissioners are appointed to make a report to the court at the next term. 4 Mar 1852. (Pp. 261-262).

POLLY SUTTON, Widow and Executrix of Edmond Sutton; WILLIAM W. McKNIGHT and wife ELIZABETH, and the other heirs and legatees of Edmond Sutton deceased versus WILLIAM H. MOSES and wife ALEY and ARMSTED G. SUTTON. The bill is taken for confessed. 4 Mar 1852. (P. 262)

JOHN M. COOPER and wife LOCKEY P. versus FRANCIS BRYSON and others. The Clerk on 1 Oct 1851 at public auction did sell the slave Christina and child to John M. Cooper, he being the highest bidder. 5 Mar 1852. (P. 263)

ZEBULON L. BREVARD versus J. L. FARR, JOSEPH PINKERTON and wife NANCY, MARTHA BREWER, SUSAN BREWER, ROBERT BREWER, WILLIAM BREWER, JOHN BREWER, ALFRED D. FUGETT, CHARLES T. NEW, CALEB ESLEY and wife ELIZA, THOMAS W. BREWER, and ERASMUS G. BREWER. On 24 Jun 1850, complainant recovered a judgment against Jonathan L. Farr before T. B. Brevard, a Justice of the Peace. On 5 Jan 1849, the said Farr purchased from Erasmus Kees a lot in Woodbury known as Lot No. 43. He executed a note for a part of the purchase money which was endorsed by said Kees to Jesse Brewer and Benjamin Brewer deceased. Defendants Alfred D. Fugett and Charles T. New are administrators. The other defendants, except Farr, are their heirs. 5 Mar 1852. (Pp. 264-265)

LEWIS JETTON, Trustee, and AUGUSTUS M. WEEDON and wife SARAH E. Ex Parte. It appears to the Court that Augustus M. Weedon heretofore purchased land in Cannon County for which he executed a note to Arthur Warren. The land is to be sold to settle the debt. 5 Mar 1852. (Pp. 266-267)

ALBERT G. MILLIKEN versus JESSE MILLIKEN. Ex Parte. Land is being sold to settle a debt. 5 Mar 1852. (Pp. 267-268)

JOSHUA VASSAR versus STEPHEN A. MITCHELL. 5 Mar 1852. (Pp. 269-270)

REZIN FOWLER and others versus ELI BAILEY and others. Defendant recovered a judgment against complainant. 5 Mar 1852. (Pp. 270-271)

JAMES W. McADOW versus WILLIAM C. LEECH and others. The demurrer is not well taken. 5 Mar 1852. (P. 271)

JASPER RUYLE versus JOSIAH SPURLOCK and others. The equity in the complainant's bill is not well take. 5 Mar 1852. (P. 271)

BENJAMIN WEBBER versus (BAXTER) B. DICKENS and DAVID PATTON. 5 Mar 1852. (Pp. 272-274)

ISAAC N. JOHNSTON versus WILLIAM M. HOOKER, R. F. MARSHALL, THOMAS COX and wife ELIZA J., D. C. MARSHALL, H. L. MARSHALL, JOHN J. MARSHALL, and F. L. MARSHALL: WILLIAM SMITH and wife MARTHA C. The cause is dismissed. 5 Mar 1852. (P. 275)

SUSAN NOKES and others versus MEDFORD COFFEE. Final Decree. Title to a tract of land is vested in David M. McKnight. 5 Mar 1852. (Pp. 275-280)

HARMON ST. JOHN and wife MARTHA JANE versus DAVID M. JARRATT, Administrator of William Bates; FRANCES M. (SEWEL) and wife (ABYEL), ELIZABETH BATES, SUSAN BATES, ULIUS BATES, WILLIAM L. BATES, LUCY BATES, AZARIAN BATES, and (LUCY) BATES, widow of William Bates, and R. FOWLER. William Bates died, intestate, in Dec 1847. All of the above named parties except David M. Jarratt and R. Fowler are heirs and distributees of the said William Bates. David M. Jarratt has been appointed as administrator of the estate. The Clerk is ordered to take an account with the said Jarratt. 5 Mar 1852. (Pp. 280-282)

JOHN L. TAYLOR versus R. H. MASON. The death of John L. Taylor is suggested. 5 Mar 1852. (P. 282)

JOHN A. BAIRD and others versus HENRY TROTT, JR. and others. 5 Mar 1852. (P. 283)

CHARLEY B. SPURLOCK versus JOHN W. STROUD and others. The demurrer is not well take. 5 Mar 1852. (P. 284)

REZIN FOWLER versus ELIJAH MEARS. 5 Mar 1852. (Pp. 285-286)

WILLIAM H. McCABE versus EPHRAIM NESBITT and WILLIAM STACY. The parties have agreed to submit the matter to arbitration. 5 Mar 1852. (Pp. 286-287)

Chancery Court met in the town of Woodbury on the 30th of Sep 1852. Broomfield L. Ridley, presiding. (P. 288)

Thomas G. Wood, Clerk & Master submits his report. 30 Sep 1852. (Pp. 288-289)

JOHN H. BYFORD versus SUSANNAH BYFORD. Final Decree. The complainant asks that the cause be dismissed. 30 Sep 1852. (P. 289)

ALFRED ST. JOHN versus ELIZABETH ST. JOHN. This cause is dismissed. 30 Sep 1852. (P. 290)

JESSE PERRER versus LEGRAN C. WHERRY and others. Defendant Wherry has left the State of Tennessee and has gone to parts unknown. 30 Sep 1852. (Pp. 290-291)

ARCHEBALD WEATHERFORD versus G. W. SILVERTOOTH and others. The Clerk is to report to court at next term. 30 Sep 1852. (P. 291)

ELIZABETH ADAMS versus WILLIAM ADAMS and JOSEPH SIMPSON. Complainant is the wife of defendant William Adams. In Jul 1849, the defendant abandoned the complainant (they then being citizens of Cannon County) and from thence to the State of Arkansas where he has since remained leaving his wife in Cannon County unprovided for and in a very destitute condition, she being very old. Defendant Joseph Simpson has in his possession a note or bill on a man by the name of Allan Lea who lived in the State of Alabama which belonged to defendant William Adams. The sum of money owed in the note is to be paid to the said Elizabeth Adams. Defendant William Adams is enjoined from collecting it. 30 Sep 1852. (Pp. 291-292)

ELIJAH MEARS versus HENRY D. McBROOM and BENJAMIN T. Mc-BROOM. Final Decree. 30 Sep 1852. (Pp. 292-294)

FRANCES HANCOCK by her next friend William L. Adams versus LEWIS ADAMS. Complainant and defendant intermarried and they were and had been citizens of Tennessee for two whole years before the filing of this bill. Defendant Lewis Hancock has been guilty of cruel and inhuman treatment of the said Frances and have afforded her such indignities to her person so as to render her condition intolerable. The bonds of matrimony are dissolved. 30 Sep 1852. (Pp. 294-296)

POLLY SUTTON, Widow and Executrix of Edmond Sutton; John H. Wood and wife Roxana, John Tegue and wife Sarah E., and others, heirs and legatees of Edmond Sutton versus WILLIAM H. MOSES and wife ALCY and A. G. SUTTON. Edmond Sutton departed this life in 1824, leaving complainant Polly, his widow, who has never since married and as his only children Roxana P. who has since married with John H. Wood; Mary intermarried with Alexander Tassey; Elizabeth intermarried with William W. Mc-Knight; Sarah E. intermarried with John Teague; Margaret intermarried with Daniel Fite; and the defendants Alcy who married William H. Moses; and Armstead G. Sutton. 30 Sep 1852. (Pp. 296-297)

STEPHEN A. MITCHELL versus JOSHUA VASSAR and WILLIAM H. PEYTON. The contract for the sale of the tract of land referred to in the pleadings has been rescinded and set aside by a decree of the Supreme Court of Tennessee. 30 Sep 1852. (P. 298)

JAMES W. McADOW versus WILLIAM C. LEECH and others. Defendant received a judgment against the complainant for $502. A tract of land is to be sold to satisfy the judgment. 30 Sep 1852. (Pp. 299-301)

NANCY C. McADOW versus WILLIAM McADOW and others. This cause is continued. 30 Sep 1852. (P. 301)

ASA TODD, Administrator of Hugh Robertson; Pleasant Cathron and wife Jane, Robert Gordon and wife Luma, Hannah McCaslin, Silas Robertson, James K. P. Robertson, a minor, who sues by his guardian Silas Robinson, all heirs of Hugh Robinson versus BERRY WILLIAMS: and Emily, Martha Ann, Louisa Jasper, heirs of Jesse B. Robinson. Hugh Robinson died, intestate, in Cannon County in the year 1848. Asa Todd is his administrator. The Clerk is ordered to sell a tract of land belonging to the deceased. 30 Sep 1852. (Pp. 301-303)

WOOD & STONE versus JOSEPH BAILEY, JOHN N. BAILEY, and JOHN YOUNG. The bill is taken for confessed. 30 Sep 1852. (Pp. 304-306)

JOHN R. TAYLOR, Administrator of Edmond Taylor, versus JOHN L. TAYLOR and others. 30 Sep 1852. (Pp. 306-309)

POLLY SUTTON and others versus WILLIAM H. MOSES and others. 30 Sep 1852. (Pp. 309-310)

ARCHEBALD WEATHERFORD versus GEORGE W. SILVERTOOTH. Com-

22

plainant obtained the fiat of this court restraining defendant from receiving from the Administrator of his father his portion of said estate. The injunction in this cause is dissolved. 30 Sep 1852. (P. 310)

B. F. WOOD versus JAMES WOOD and others. This cause is continued. 1 Oct 1852. (P. 311)

THOMAS G. WOOD versus DABNEY SANDRIDGE and CAROLINE SANDRIDGE. Complainant is the legal owner of three fifth's parts. Defendants are the owners of two fifths parts of the tract of land in the petition or bill containing about 1200 acres. The Court is of the opinion that complainant is entitled to a partition or division of the land. 1 Oct 1852. (P. 311)

HARMON ST. JOHN and wife MARTHA JANE versus DAVID M. JARRATT, Administrator of William Bates, and others. 1 Oct 1852. (Pp. 312-313)

JOHN M. COOPER and wife LEATHY P. versus FRANCES BRYSON and others. 1 Oct 1852. (P. 313)

ZACHARIAH L. BREVARD versus J. L. FARR and others. 1 Oct 1852. (P. 314)

JOHN WEBB and T. B. SMITH versus ISAAC RAINS and others. The injunction is overruled. 1 Oct 1852. (Pp. 314-315)

SAMUEL VANCE and others versus A. D. FUGET and C. L. NEW, Administrators of B. Brewer. Complainants are not entitled to the relief prayed for. The demurrer is well taken. Complainants' bill is dismissed. 1 Oct 1852. (P. 315)

FRANCES HANCOCK by her next friend versus LEWIS HANCOCK. Defendant is to pay A. M. Savage for services rendered. 1 Oct 1852. (Pp. 315-316)

S. B. SPURLOCK versus JOHN W. STROUD, WALTER STROUD, ?. J. GOOD, MARY A. STROUD and others. The death of Defendant Walter Stroud is suggested. 1 Oct 1852. (P. 316)

ELIJAH MEARS versus HENRY D. McBROOM and BENJAMIN T. McBROOM. (P. 316)

A. D. FUGET and T. C. NEW, Admintrators of Jesse Brewer and of Benjamin Brewer; ROBERT H. BREWER, WILLIAM M. BREWER, JOHN L. BREWER, and ELIZABETH BREWER, children and minor heirs of Jesse Brewer who sue by Benjamin Fugett, their regular guardian, versus WILLIAM C. (MILLS) and wife MARTHA, JOSEPH PINKSTON and wife NANCY, MARTHA BREWER, THOMAS W. BREWER, ERASMUS BREWER, JOHN COLLIER and wife SUSAN, EASLEY and wife ELIZA. 1 Oct 1852. (Pp. 317-320)

ADAM ELROD versus GOVERNOR WILLIAM B. CAMPBELL and others. This cause is dismissed. 1 Oct 1852. (P. 320)

JAMES R. TAYLOR. Ex Parte. 1 Oct 1852. (P. 320)

LARKIN KEATON versus ZACHARIAH THOMASON. This cause is continued. 1 Oct 1852. (P. 321)

A. D. FUGETT and C. T. NEW, Administrators of Jesse Brewer
and Benjamin Brewer; ROBERT BREWER, WILLIAM M. BREWER, JOHN
L. BREWER, and ELIZABETH L. BREWER, minors under the age of 21
years and heirs of Jesse Brewer by their regular guardian Benjamin Fugett versus WILLIAM C. MILLER and wife MARTHA, JOSEPH
PARKER and wife NANCY, and other heirs of Jesse Brewer and
Benjamin Brewer deceased. 1 Oct 1852. (Pp. 322-323)

WILLIAM M. HOOKER, ROBERT F. MARSHALL, THOMAS COX and wife
ELIZA J., DAVID C. MARSHALL, HUGH L. MARSHALL, JOHN J. MARSHALL,
F. L. MARSHALL, WILLIAM SMITH and MARTHA SMITH. 1 Oct 1852.
(Pp. 323-324)

The Chancellor is pleased to order that all the causes be
enrolled. And then the Chancellor is pleased to adjourn the
Court until the next regular term. BROOMFIELD L. RIDLEY.

CHANCERY MINUTES MAR 1853-APR 1861

Chancery Court was held in the town of Woodbury in Cannon County on Thursday after the fourth Monday, it being the 31st day of Mar 1853. Broomfield L. Ridley/ presiding. (P. 1)

POLLY SUTTON, Executrix of Edmund Sutton and others versus WILLIAM H. MOSES and others. 31 Mar 1853. (Pp. 1-3)

PRUDENCE R. HUBBARD and ELIZABETH RUCKS versus JAMES T. HENDERSON. The Clerk is ordered to appoint a receiver. 31 Mar 1853. (P. 3)

BENJAMIN F. WOOD versus JAMES WOOD and JOHN H. WOOD. This cause is dismissed. 31 Mar 1853. (Pp. 3-4)

ASA TODD, Administrator of Hugh Robinson, and others versus BERRY WILLIAMS and others. 31 Mar 1853. (Pp. 4-5)

ARCHEBALD WEATHERFORD versus GEORGE W. SILVERTOOTH. Final Decree. The bill is dismissed. 31 Mar 1853. (P. 5)

JAMES R. TAYLOR, Trustee for A. F. CANNON. Ex Parte. Henry Cannon, the husband of Agnes F. Cannon, is a suitable person to be appointed her trustee. 31 Mar 1853. (P. 6)

FRANCES HANCOCK versus LEWIS HANCOCK. Special commissioners are appointed to go on the premises of the defendant and to make division of the property mentioned. The slaves to be divided were Rhitta, about 30 years and infant child; Boy Frank, age about 8 years; Girl Adline, age 6 years; Frances, a cripple child of the woman considered and estimated to be of no value; Manual, age about 68 or 70 years and valued at $200. 31 Mar 1853. (Pp. 7-8)

THOMAS G. WOOD versus DABNEY SANDRIDGE and CAROLINE SANDRIDGE. Commissioners appointed to partition the land mentioned in the proceedings. 31 Mar 1853. (Pp. 9-11)

ARCHEBALD STONE and JOHN H. WOOD versus JOHN N. BAILEY, JOSEPH BAILEY, and JOHN YOUNG. Final Decree. 31 Mar 1853. (P. 12)

S. B. SPURLOCK versus JOHN H. STROUD. The death of Walter Stroud and Sarah Jane Good was suggested at the last term of court. It not being known who are the heirs at law of the said Sarah Jane Good and Walter Stroud. It is ordered that Thomas G. Wood, Clerk & Master, be appointed as receiver. 31 Mar 1853. (P. 13)

NELSON COOPER versus JOHN McIVER. The parties in the proceedings erected the mills mentioned in the pleadings. The Clerk is to take an account in this cause. 31 Mar 1853. (Pp. 13-14)

LUCY BOMAN versus WILLIAM J. BOMAN. The bill is taken for confessed. Parties were lawfully married in Cannon County. The conducted of the defendant towards complainant has been such as to render it unsafe and improper for her to cohabit with him and be under his dominion. Complainant at the time of the marriage had a life estate in the land whereon she lived. The bonds of matrimony are dissolved. 31 Mar 1853. (P. 14)

JESSE BREWER'S and BENJAMIN BREWER'S Administrators and others versus WILLIAM C. MILLER and others. Bill of account and distribution. 31 Mar 1853. (Pp. 14-16)

MARK L. YOUNG versus WILLIAM S. McADOW. Time is granted to the complainant to file. 31 Mar 1853. (Pp. 16-17)

JOHN W. (SUMMAR), Guardian of Sarah Cooper versus B. B. COOPER and others. The bill is taken for confessed against Nathaniel Hayes. 31 Mar 1853. (P. 17)

BENJAMIN WEBBER versus BAXTER B. DICKENS and DAVID PATTON. Final Decree. Complainant recovers of defendants. 31 Mar 1853. (Pp. 17-18)

Chancery Court met in the town of Woodbury on Thursday after the 4th Monday in Sep, it being the 29th day of Sep 1853. Broomfield L. Ridley, presiding. (P. 19)

ASA TODD, Administrator of Hugh Robinson and others versus BERRY WILLIAMS Et Al. James M. Avant, the attorney in this cause, is to be paid. 29 Sep 1853. (P. 19)

NELSON COOPER versus JOHN McIVER. The death of the defendant is suggested. 29 Sep 1853. (P. 19)

HARMON ST. JOHN and wife MARTHA J. versus SAMUEL R. JAMES. The complainant dismisses the suit. 29 Sep 1853. (P. 20)

A number of causes are continued. (P. 20)

WILLIAM J. SMITH and wife MARTHA C. versus THOMAS COX and wife ELIZA J., DAVID C. MARSHALL, HUGH E. MARSHALL, JOHN J. MARSHALL, and FINIS L. MARSHALL. The bill is taken for confessed. Complainant Martha C. Smith and defendants are all the children and heirs of John C. Marshall deceased. Defendant Eliza J. is his widow, but since intermarried with the defendant Thomas Cox. The tract of land in the pleadings descended from John C. Marshall who died intestate to his heirs who are jointly entitled to the same. It appears to the Court that the land can be beneficially partitioned. 29 Sep 1853. (Pp. 21-22)

HENRY D. McBROOM and BENJAMIN T. McBROOM versus ELIJAH MEARS. The defendant has failed to pay the note due. The town lot is to be sold to pay the debt due. 29 Sep 1853. (Pp. 22-23)

HARMON ST. JOHN and wife MARTHA JANE versus DAVID M. JARRATT, Administrator of William Bates, FRANCIS M. SEAWELL and wife ABIGAIL, ELIZABETH BATES, SUSAN BATES, ULYSSES BATES, WILLIAM L. BATES, LUCY ANN BATES, and LUCY JAMES. Order for distribution. The money is to be distributed equally amongst the co-defendants, the widow and children of William Bates deceased. The widow, Lucy Bates, has married Samuel R. James. 29 Sep 1853. (Pp. 23-24)

WILLIAM H. GRIMMETT versus JOHN W. SUMMER, THOMAS SUMMER, ARMSTEAD FRANCIS, ARMSTEAD G. ODUM, NICHOLAS SMITH. Final Decree. The allegations are not sustained. 29 Sep 1853. (P. 24)

ELIZABETH RUCKS and JAMES R. HIBBITT, Administrators of Prudence R. Hubbard, versus JAMES T. HENDERSON and WILLIAM MILLER. Final Decree. James Taylor bequeathed to Elizabeth Rucks during her lifetime a negro named James and at her death to Prudence R. Hubbard, the intestate of James R. Hubbard. The negro came into the hands of James T. Henderson, Executor of said James Taylor. He refuses to deliver him to the said Elizabeth Rucks who is entitled to him. The Clerk is to take possession of the said slave and deliver him to the rigtful owner. 29 Sep 1853. (Pp. 24-26)

JOHN WEBB and T. B. SMITH versus ISAAC RAINS and ELI BAILEY. The defendant Rains was not entitled to collect the amount of the original judgment which was rendered void. 29 Sep 1853. (Pp. 26-27)

WILLIAM F. GEORGE versus GEORGE W. COOPER, JOHN COOPER, Administrators of Thomas Cooper; BERRY COOPER, PHILLIP COOPER, MARY COOPER, MARTHA COOPER, LOUISA COOPER, and JANE COOPER. George W. Cooper is appointed as guardian for the said Phillip, Mary, Martha, Louisa, and Jane Cooper, minor heirs of the said Thomas Cooper deceased. 29 Sep 1853. (P. 27)

POLLY SUTTON, Executrix of Edmond Sutton, and others versus WILLIAM H. MOSES and wife Et Al. 29 Sep 1853. (Pp. 27-29)

JOHN M. ODENHEIMER and others versus JESSE PIERCE. Complainants, together with their late co-partner A. B. Smith, now deceased, sold to the defendant Lot No. 12 in the town of Woodbury. The lot was bounded east by the Public Square. The lot was purchased by credit which is now due. The lot is to be sold to satisfy the debt. 29 Sep 1853. (Pp. 29-30)

WILLIAM J. SMITH and wife MARTHA C. versus THOMAS COX and wife ELIZA J. and others. The Clerk is to make a study to determine if the land can be beneficially divided. The land contains the dower of Eliza J. Cox who is the late widow of John C. Marshall. 29 Sep 1853. (Pp. 31-32)

SARAH McBROOM by her husband and next friend Henry D. McBroom, JOHN D. McBROOM, WILLIAM T. McBROOM, BENJAMIN T. McBROOM, ABEL McBROOM, JR., WILLIAM BARTON and wife SARAH. Ex Parte. Petition to sell land. Abel McBroom, Sr. conveyed by deed of gift, bearing date of 2 Aug 1842, to William Barton and Benjamin T. McBroom, in trust for Sarah McBroom, wife of Henry D. McBroom, during her natural life and at her death to be divided equally between the petitioners, all the children of said Sarah and Henry D. McBroom the property, lands, etc. in the pleadings. Said Sarah is quite ok and does not require all of said property for her support. The Court is of the opinion that the land should be sold. 29 Sep 1853. (Pp. 32-33)

MARK L. YOUNG versus WILLIAM S. McADOW and others. Nancy McAdoo; Berthina Ann, Margaret J., Azaline, and Thomas B. McAdoo were all before the court by virtue of a summons. All, except William S. and Nancy were minors. P. J. Leech is appointed guardian for the minors. They are minor heirs of the said William S. Title to a tract of land is divested out of the heirs of the said William S. McAdoo and vested in the complainant Mark L. Young. 29 Sep 1853. (Pp. 33-35)

JOHN M. COOPER and wife LOCKEY P. versus FRANCIS BRYSON and others. Final Decree. 29 Sep 1853. (Pp. 35-36)

S. B. SPURLOCK & COMPANY versus JOHN W. STROUD and others. The heirs of Walter Stroud are minors without guardian. The heirs of Sarah J. Good are without guardian. George W. Cooper is appointed as guardian. 29 Sep 1853. (Pp. 36-37)

Chancery Court met in the town of Woodbury on the Thursday after the fourth Monday, it being the 30th day of Mar 1854. Broomfield L. Ridley, presiding. (P. 38)

SARAH McBROOM by her next friend Henry McBroom and others. Ex Parte. 30 Mar 1854. (Pp. 38-40)

WILLIAM J. SMITH and wife MARTHA C. versus THOMAS COX and others. 30 Mar 1854. (Pp. 40-42)

DANIEL S. FORD versus JAMES GOODNER. Final Decree. The complainant's bill was not sustained by the proof. 30 Mar 1854. (P. 42)

CLERK & MASTER versus LUVINA BURTON, Administratrix. This cause is remanded to the Rules. 30 Mar 1854. (P. 42)

JOHN F. PRESTON versus NANCY C. McADOO, HENRY YOUNG'S Heirs, and others. The bill is taken for confessed against all the defendants except Nancy C. McAdoo who has leave to answer. 30 Mar 1854. (Pp. 42-43)

JOHN M. ODENHEIMER, JAMES TENNANT, SAMUEL B. DERICKSON, JOHN W. GILLY, JOHN PEARSON, SAMUEL W. BARLOR, and FRANCIS CAMPBELL, JAMES MARTIN, and ROBERT G. SMITH versus JESSE PIERCE. The town lot ordered to be sold was sold to the said Robert G. Smith for $736. 30 Mar 1854. (Pp. 43-44)

POLLY SUTTON, Executor of Edmond Sutton, and others versus WILLIAM H. MOSES and others. Petition to sell lands. 30 Mar 1854. (Pp. 44-45)

ELIZABETH WRATHER by her next friend George W. Cooper versus JAMES M. ROBERTS, JONATHAN L. FARR, DAVID M. JARRATT, and others. Complainant's next friend has given security. The Court is of the opinion that the next friend has no right to file as a pauper. 30 Mar 1854. (Pp. 45-46)

WILLIAM F. GEORGE for himself and others versus GEORGE W. COOPER and others. The said William F. George recovers from the creditors of Thomas Cooper deceased. 30 Mar 1854. (P. 46)

LARKIN KEATON versus Z. THOMASON and R. A. SMITH. Injunction. 30 Mar 1854. (Pp. 46-47)

JOHN R. SUMMAR versus SARAH COOPER. There is to be a jury trial in order to determine whether the defendant was a person of unsound mind. The jury cannot agree. 30 Mar 1854. (Pp. 47-48)

N. L. ORRAND versus JONATHAN HENDRICKSON and others. The complainant recovers. 30 Mar 1854. (Pp. 48-49)

POLLY SUTTON and others versus WILLIAM H. MOSES and others. 30 Mar 1854. (Pp. 49-52)

SARAH McBROOM and husband and others. Petition to sell land and town lots. 30 Mar 1854. (Pp. 52-53)

T. B. SMITH versus JESSE PIERCE and others. Final Decree. 30 Mar 1854. (P. 54)

S. B. SPURLOCK & COMPANY versus JOHN W. STROUD and wife MARY ANN, SARAH J. GOOD, WALTER STROUD, and others. Complainant recovered a judgment against defendant John W. Stroud. The said John W. Stroud purchased of the defendants Margaret Hall, A. Taylor, and Walter Stroud several tracts of land lying mostly in the 5th District. He has paid all of the purchase money, but he has only title bonds and not deeds. John W. Stroud fraudulently and without consideration transferred said lands to defendant Sarah J. Good who in like manner conveyed the same to Mary Ann Stroud, wife of John W. Stroud. The transfer is null and void. 30 Mar 1854. (Pp. 55-56)

NELSON COOPER versus JANE R. McADOO. Final Decree. Report of the Clerk. 30 Mar 1854. (Pp. 56-58)

DAVID M. JARRATT, Administrator of George St. John; WILLIAM ST. JOHN, THOMAS ST. JOHN, BERRY ST. JOHN, ARTHUR ST. JOHN, MARTIN ST. JOHN, the sons of George St. John, and others. Ex Parte. 30 Mar 1854. (Pp. 59-60)

Resolution by the Bar noting the fact that Chancellor Broomfield L. Ridley has consented to become a candidate for selection to the Supreme Court. 30 Mar 1854. (Pp. 60-61)

Chancery Court held in the town of Woodbury on the Thursday after the fourth Monday, it being the 28th day of Sep 1854. Samuel D. Frierson, presiding. (P. 62)

Chancery Court met in the town of Woodbury on 2 Oct 1854. Broomfield L. Ridley, not appearing, the Clerk adjourned court. (P. 63)

Chancery Court met in the town of Woodbury on the first Monday, it being the second day of Apr 1855. Broomfield L. Ridley, presiding. (P. 64)

The Clerk & Master, Thomas G. Wood, presents his receipts. 2 Apr 1855. (P. 64)

JOHN F. PRESTON versus WILLIAM McADOW and others. Process has been served on the infant defendants. Delphia Young has since the commencement of this suit intermarried with Joseph Borum. William Young is appointed guardian for Fielding and Granville Young. 2 Apr 1855. (P. 65)

ANN D. SULLIVAN versus JOHN R. SULLIVAN and Z. L. BREVARD. The suit is dismissed. John R. Sullivan is to pay all of the costs. 2 Apr 1855. (P. 66)

BERRY WILLIAMS versus JOHN McCLAIN. The demurrer is not well taken. 2 Apr 1855. (P. 66)

Be it remembered that the term of office for Thomas G. Wood as Clerk & Master has expired. The Chancellor is pleased to re-appoint the said Thomas G. Wood as Clerk & Master. 2 Apr 1855. (Pp. 66-68)

SARAH McBROOM by her husband and next friend Henry D. Mc-Broom, WILLIAM BARTON and wife SARAH, JOHN D. McBROOM, WILLIAM T. McBROOM and others. Decree. 2 Apr 1855. (Pp. 68-69)

JOHN S. BRIEN, Trustee, versus ELI BAILEY and JOHN P. BAILEY. 2 Apr 1855. (Pp. 69-70)

NELSON COOPER versus JANE R. McIVER, Executrix of John McIver. Sale of a tract of land. 2 Apr 1855. (Pp. 70-71)

ISAAC M. ASHTON versus ABEL McBROOM, JR. and others. 2 Apr 1855. (Pp. 71-72)

S. B. SPURLOCK versus JOHN W. STROUD and others. Final Decree. Sale of a tract of land. 2 Apr 1855. (P. 2)

WILLIAM GIVAN and wife, LEVI REED, and others versus DAVID TRAVIS and others. The bill is amended to make William C. Barrett, the Administrator of William Travis, a defendant. 2 Apr 1855. (P. 73)

CLERK & MASTER versus DANIEL F. WEEDON and LEVINA BURTON. H. M. Burton is the attorney of Maria Weedon and by agreement with her and said Daniel F. Weedon is entitled to $150. Said H. M. Burton is dead. Lavina Burton is his administratrix. Said administratrix is entitled to the money. 2 Apr 1855. (Pp. 73-74)

JOHN S. BREWER and A. D. FUGETT and C. T. NEW, Administrators of Benjamin Brewer, Surviving partner. The bill is not sustained by the proof. 2 Apr 1855. (P. 74)

STEPHEN A. MITCHELL versus DANIEL W. MITCHELL and others. Complainant's bill is dismissed. 2 Apr 1855. (Pp. 74-75)

WILLIAM J. SMITH and wife MARTHA C. versus THOMAS COX and wife ELIZA J., DAVID C. MARSHALL, HUGH R. MARSHALL, JOHN J. MARSHALL, and FINIS L. MARSHALL. Petition to sell land. 2 Apr 1855. (Pp. 75-76)

JOHN R. SUMMER versus SARAH COOPER. Writ of lunacy. The findings of the jury was not warranted. The Chancellor is pleased to set it aside. A new trial is ordered. 2 Apr 1855. (Pp. 77-78)

JOHN E. MASON versus ISAAC N. FULLER. James N. Fuller has left the county. Process cannot be served. It appears that William West has sold the land in the pleadings to Fuller. Said land is on the west side of the Public Square. Fuller has paid all the purchase money except six dollars. Complainant recovers of the defendant. The house and lot are to be sold to satisfy a debt. 2 Apr 1855. (Pp. 78-79)

JOHN B. PARRIS versus JANE COOPER and others. Final Decree.
The bill is taken for confessed. It appears to the Court that
the conveyance of the three shares in the proceeds of the sale
of the real estate of Thomas Cooper was made to delay and hinder creditors and is void. 1 Apr 1855. (P. 79)

ZACHARIAH THOMPSON versus LARKIN KEATON. Final Decree.
Complainant recovers of the defendant. 1 Apr 1855. (Pp. 80-
82)

RICHARD HANCOCK versus E. C. GROSS and others. 1 Apr 1855.
(Pp. 83-84)

REZIN FOWLER versus ELIJAH NEELY. 1 Apr 1855. (P. 84)

JOHN E. MASON versus ISAAC N. FULLER. Report. 1 Oct 1855.
(P. 85)

AMANDA M. BUSH versus WILLIS W. BUSH. Final Decree. The
bill is taken for confessed. Amanda M. Bush is the wife of
Willis W. Bush. They have the following named slaves, to wit,
Nancy, about 47; Rose, about 22; Jessy, about 9; Maria, about
14; Letha, about 12; Collins, about 8; Caroline, about 29;
Frances, about 11; Emeline, about 9; Henderson; Green, 7.
The said Willis W. Bush is a man of very limited means besides
the property above named. The slaves shall be divested out of
the defendant and vested in complainant. 1 Oct 1855. (Pp. 86-
87)

MARTIN ARMSTRONG versus OWEN ALEXANDER and ELAM ALEXANDER.
In 1849, Owen Alexander, as the agent of Elam Alexander, purchased of W. W. McKnight the tract of land described in the
pleadings for $824. 1 Oct 1855. (P. 88)

JOSEPH M. BASHAM versus MARABLE BASHAM. Complainant and
defendant were married in Warren County about three years since.
They had one child. The defendant has an ungovernable temper.
It is unsafe for the complainant and child to live with him.
The bonds of matrimony are dissolved. 1 Oct 1855. (P. 89)

LUCY ANN BYNUM versus GEORGE W. BYNUM. The bill is taken
for confessed. Complainant and defendant were married in
Rutherford County in Aug 1854. Defendant drove the complainant off from his house and offered such indignities to her
person that it would be improper and unsafe for her to live
and cohabit with him. The bonds of matrimony are dissolved.
1 Oct 1855. (P. 89)

ELIZABETH M. HICKS versus ABRAHAM HICKS. Final Decree.
The bill is taken for confessed. Defendant has abandoned the
complainant for more than two whole years before the filing of
this bill without any just cause. The bonds of matrimony are
dissolved. The defendant is forever enjoined from taking or
meddling with the children. 1 Oct 1855. (P. 90)

JOHN B. SUMMER versus SARAH COOPER. Final Decree. The
defendant recovers of the complainant. 1 Oct 1855. (Pp. 91-
92)

WILEY'S Heirs versus HENRY TROTT Et Al. 1 Oct 1855. (P.

92)

NANCY C. McADOW versus WILLIAM McADOW, ROBERT A. SMITH, PARTHENIA ANN McADOW, AND OTHERS versus JOHN F. PRESTON. The land mentioned in the pleadings belonged to the heirs of Henry Young and was sold by a decree of the Court. John F. Preston became the purchaser. 2 Oct 1855. (Pp. 92-94)

JOHN W. SEXTON and others versus ABLE McBROOM and others. Complainant's bill is dismissed. 2 Oct 1855. (P. 94)

WILLIAM GIVEN and wife, Levi Read, and others versus DAVID TRAVIS, WILLIAM SMART, and others. Complainants dismiss their bill as to Margaret Earthman, she having no representatives and died out of the limits of the State. The parties are given time to take proof. 2 Oct 1855. (Pp. 94-95)

BERRY WILLIAMS versus JOHN McCLAIN. Complainant purchased of one Hugh Robinson a tract of land in the 4th District of Cannon County. Complainant took from the said Hugh Robinson his bond for title and executed to him his note. After the death of the said Robinson, his heirs gained a judgment against complainant. A writ of possession is issued to complainant. 2 Oct 1855. (P. 96)

JOHN W. SUMMER versus SARAH COOPER. Complainant is not entitled to the relief sought in his bill. 2 Oct 1855. (Pp. 96-97)

Chancery Court met in the town of Woodbury at the Courthouse on the fifth Monday and 31st day of Mar 1856. Broomfield L. Ridley, presiding. (P. 98)

JOSEPH CLARK, Administrator, and others versus ELIZABETH SUBLETT, Executor of George A. Sublett and others. The demurrer is sustained. The cause is continued. 1 Apr 1856. (P. 99)

JOSEPH CLARK, Administrator, and others versus LEWIS JELTON, Executor of John L. Jelton, and others. The demurrer is sustained. The cause is continued. 1 Apr 1856. (P. 99)

JOSEPH CLARK, Administrator, and others versus A. R. HAMMER, Administrator of Henry Trott deceased. The cause is continued. 1 Apr 1856. (P. 99)

ELIZABETH BARLOW versus JOHN H. BARLOW. Final Decree. The bill is taken for confessed. Complainant and defendant were married in the State of Virginia several years since. The defendant's conduct towards complainant was so cruel and inhuman that it was unsafe for complainant to be under the dominion and control of defendant. More than one year before the filing of this bill, defendant abandoned the complainant. The bonds of matrimony are dissolved. 1 Apr 1856. (Pp. 100-101)

E. H. CAMPBELL and others versus JAMES ST. JOHN and others. James St. John, Emily St. John, and Lydia St. John are minors without guardian. W. M. Burger is appointed as guardian. 1 Apr 1856. (P. 101)

E. H. CAMPBELL, Administrator of Thomas St. John, and others versus JAMES ST. JOHN and others. The Administrator has exhausted all of the personal estate of said decedent. Land is to be sold to pay the debts. 1 Apr 1856. (Pp. 101-102)

JAMES R. ESPEY and others versus JOHN ESPEY and others. Petition to sell land. The Clerk is to take proof as to the value of the land. 1 Apr 1856. (Pp. 103-104)

R. H. PHILLIPS versus B. H. F. PHILLIPS. The verdict of the jury is ordered to be spread upon the Minutes of the Court. Robert H. Phillips is appointed as guardian of the said Benjamin H. F. Phillips. 1 Apr 1856. (P. 105)

B. B. COOPER, Executor, versus F. COOPER and others. This cause is referred to the Master. 1 Apr 1856. (P. 106)

LUNFIELD SMITH versus EDWARD G. STEEL. The bill is taken for confessed. The defendant purchased of the complainant on 29 Apr 1853 a tract of land in the 5th District containing about 412 acres. The defendant has failed to pay anything toward the land. Complainant is entitled to the relief sought. 1 Apr 1856. (Pp. 107-108)

PERRY WILLIAMS versus JOHN McCLAIN. Report of the Clerk. 1 Apr 1856. (Pp. 108-109)

M. FRANCIS, Guardian of James Francis and Sarah A. Francis, Margaret D. Francis, Elizabeth Francis, children and minor heirs. The Clerk is to report if it is to the advantage of the minors to sell the slave Juda. 1 Apr 1856. (Pp. 109-110)

B. H. F. PHILLIPS versus PETER H. PHILLIPS. It appears to the court that complainant has become of unsound mind and has been so declared by a jury of Cannon County which has been approved by a decree of this court. Robert H. Phillips is appointed as regular guardian. This suit is revived in the name of the said Robert H. Phillips. 1 Apr 1856. (Pp. 110-111)

SAMUEL VANCE versus DANIEL TENPENNY. The injunction is granted. 2 Apr 1856. (P. 111)

WILLIAM GIVENS and wife versus DAVID TRAVIS and others. This cause is revised in the names of William Earthman, Isaac Earthman, Mary Travis and husband David, John Todd and wife Margaret, (Steven) McLain and wife Sarah. The cause is continued. 2 Apr 1856. (P. 111)

FOUNTAIN OWEN and wife ALAMINTA versus A. L. HANCOCK, C. C. HANCOCK, and P. G. LEECH, Administrator of Robert Hancock. The demurrer is well taken. 2 Apr 1856. (Pp. 111-112)

SARAH ALFORD versus WILLIAM ALFORD. This cause is continued. 2 Apr 1856. (P. 113)

RICHARD HANCOCK'S Heirs versus E. C. GROSS and others. Motion of P. G. Leech, Administrator of Richard Hancock. The Court is to consider dissolving the injunction. 2 Apr 1856. (P. 114)

ROBERT H. PHILLIPS versus BENJAMIN H. F. PHILLIPS. It appears to the Court that it is necessary to sell the property set forth in the amended bill. 2 Apr 1856. (P. 114)

THOMAS J. PRESTON, Administrator of W. S. McAdoo. The plaintiff is to pay to defendant Nancy C. McAdow $650 out of the funds arising from the sale of the land which he had enjoined. 2 Apr 1856. (P. 115)

BREWER'S Administrators versus JOSEPH PINKERTON and others. 2 Apr 1856. (Pp. 115-116)

JOSEPH CLARK, Administrator, and others versus HENRY TROTT'S Administrator. Depositions ordered to be taken. 2 Apr 1856. (P. 117)

Chancery Court met in the town of Woodbury on the fifth Monday, it being the 29th day of Sep 1856. Broomfield L. Ridley, presiding. (P. 118)

MARY D. WOODALL versus WILLIAM C. WOODALL. It appears to the Court from the production of the record from the Criminal Court of Rutherford County, that the defendant William C. Woodall on 16 May 1853 was sentenced to the penitentiary of the State of Tennessee for the term of six years commencing with that day and he was rendered infamous. Publication has been made in this cause. The bonds of matrimony are dissolved. 29 Sep 1856. (P. 118)

M. FRANCIS, Guardian of James J. Francis, Sarah A. Francis, Margaret D. Francis, and Elizabeth Francis. Ex Parte. Sale of the slave Juda to Melchisadic Francis. 29 Sep 1856. (Pp. 118-119)

JOHN D. CAMPBELL and wife versus RICHARD MARTIN. 29 Sep 1856. (Pp. 120-121)

SANFIELD SMITH versus E. G. STEEL. Title to a tract of land is divested out of the said E. G. Steel and is vested in the said Sanfield Smith. 29 Sep 1856. (P. 121)

DAVID M. JARRATT, Administrator of George St. John, and others. Ex Parte. 29 Sep 1856. (Pp. 121-123)

BARBERY M. SMITH versus JOHN R. SMITH. Complainant and defendant were married in Cannon County and lived together as man and wife. Complainant conducted herself properly during the time they lived together. Defendant has continued his abandonment for more than two years before the filing of this bill. He is gone to parts unknown. The bonds of matrimony are dissolved. 29 Sep 1856. (P. 123)

A. D. FUGETT and T. C. NEW, Administrators of Brewer brothers. Bill for final settlement. 29 Sep 1856. (Pp. 123-125)

L. G. LEECH, Administrator of Richard Hancock, versus E. C. GROSS and others. There is no equity in complainant's bill. The bill is dismissed. 29 Sep 1856. (P. 126)

E. H. CAMPBELL, Administrator of Thomas St. John, and others versus EMALINE ST. JOHN and others. 29 Sep 1856. (Pp.

126-128)

JAMES R. ESPEY and others versus JOHN ESPEY and others. Petition to sell land of John Espey deceased. Title to 142 acres is divested out of the heirs of John Espey and vested in James Jameson subject to a lien on the purchase money. 30 Sep 1856. (Pp. 128-130)

JOHN H. WOOD versus ARCHEBALD STONE. Complainant and defendants were partners as merchants in the town of Woodbury. They had dissolved their partnership. It appears to the Court that they were co-equal partners. 30 Sep 1856. (Pp. 130-131)

JOSEPH CLARK, Administrator of John A. Beard, FRANCES ANN BEARD, and HENRY WILEY versus A. R. HAMMER, Administrator of Henry Trott; ELIZABETH SUBLETT, Executrix of George A. Sublett; LEWIS JELTON, Executor of John L. Jelton; JOHN WEBB and wife Sarah P. Webb. Henry Wiley died intestate in Warren (now Cannon) County in 1838, leaving two children, to wit, Frances Ann, now the widow of John A. Beard, and Henry Wiley, both of whom were minors and who had not arrived at the age of 21 years at the filing of this bill in 1848. It appears that Henry Trott, at the Jul term 1839 of the County Court of Warren County, was appointed the administrator of the said Henry Wiley. He gave bond in the sum of $15,000 with Sarah P. Wiley, George A. Sublett, and John L. Jelton. Henry Wiley left a large estate which came into the hands of the administrator, Henry Trott. Henry Trott has since died and this suit has been revived against his administrator. The said George A. Sublett and John L. Jelton have died and this suit has been revived against their executors. James M. Brown, guardian of the complainants is seeking to have certain property attached for the benefit of the complainants, he having absconded and left the county. 30 Sep 1856. (Pp. 132-135)

MARY YOUNG versus ISAAC B. YOUNG, Executor of Isaac Young; BURTON L. McFERRIN and wife MARTHA and others, legatees and distributees of Isaac Young deceased. Isaac Young, the ancestor, died in the year 1853 testate. Isaac B. Young is his executor, B. L. McFerrin having renounced. Isaac Young by deed of gift on 1 Jun 1844 to complainant Mary Young, his wife, a negro girl named Mary, about 5 years of age, and some personal property. The will leaves property to his wife, children, and grandchildren. 30 Sep 1856. (Pp. 135-136)

ASA TODD, Administrator of William Icisom, and SARAH ICISOM, Widow of said deceased, versus ALBERT, EVELINE, CALVIN, SARAH C., and WILLIAM ICISOM, minor heirs of said deceased. Petition to lay off dower and to sell land. 30 Sep 1856. (P. 137)

BENJAMIN H. F. PHILLIPS and wife versus ROBERT H. PHILLIPS. 30 Sep 1856. (Pp. 138-140)

JAMES R. TAYLOR & COMPANY versus SOLOMON SPICER and others. The suit has been compromised. 30 Sep 1856. (P. 140)

SARAH ALFORD versus WILLIAM ALFORD, EDWARD ALFORD, and BENJAMIN CARSON. The suit is dismissed. 30 Sep 1856. (P. 140)

MARY A. HALEY versus ISAAC T. HALEY. Complainant and defendant married some twenty-five years since. They have five children, the issue of their marriage. Two of them are married and three living with them. Defendant is a dissipated man and likely to waste his property. Complainant is a prodent business woman and well calculated to manage the property. Defendant agrees for his property to settle on the complainant. The complainant will have full power and authority to control the use of the property as if she was a femme sole for the benefit and support of herself and family and defendant if he will remain at home with his family and enjoy the same. 30 Sep 1856. (Pp. 140-142)

SARAH E. WEEDON versus LEWIS JELTON, Trustee. Final Decree. On 10 Nov 1850, A. M. Weedon conveyed a deed of trust to the defendant Lewis Jelton as trustee three slaves, Eliza, Daniel, and Nick. Daniel has died since the making of the trust deed. The property conveyed by said trust deed was and is for the use and benefit of complainant and the children she then had or might have by the said A. M. Weedon who was the husband of the said Sarah E. 30 Sep 1856. (Pp. 142-144)

FOUNTAIN OWEN and wife versus A. L. and C. C. HANCOCK and others. Depositions are ordered to be taken off the file. 30 Sep 1856. (Pp. 144-145)

A. M. WEEDON versus SARAH E. WEEDON. Cross bill. This bill is dismissed. 30 Sep 1856. (P. 145)

C. B. ODOM, Administrator of William C. Odom, versus FOUNTAIN OWEN, C. C. ODOM, and others, heirs and distributees of William C. Odom. William C. Odom died in Cannon County in 1855 intestate. Complainant was appointed his administrator. The decedent several years since had bought two tracts of land of Defendant Owen. Said decedent lived on one of the tracts at the time of his death. It is where his widow now lives. The estate is insolvent. The Clerk is ordered to sell the balance of the land. 30 Sep 1856. (Pp. 146-147)

B. B. COOPER, Executor of Christopher Cooper, versus F. COOPER, Co-executor; ABRAHAM COOPER and others, heirs and distributees of Christopher Cooper. Final Decree. 30 Sep 1856. (Pp. 148-152)

R. H. F. PHILLIPS versus PETER H. PHILLIPS. 30 Sep 1856. (P. 152)

R. H. Mason, Deputy Clerk & Master, asked to be discharged from further duties which was done. The Clerk then appointed James H. Wood as Deputy Clerk & Master. 30 Sep 1856. (P. 153)

Chancery Court met in the town of Woodbury on the fifth Monday, it being the 30th day of Mar 1857. Broomfield L. Ridley, presiding. (P. 154)

JOHN L. BRIEN, Trustee, versus ELI BAILEY and JOHN P. BAILEY. The suit is dismissed. 30 Mar 1857. (P. 154)

B. H. F. PHILLIPS and wife versus R. H. PHILLIPS. Final

36

Decree. The report of the Clerk is in all things confirmed. 30 Mar 1857. (Pp. 155-158)

JOHN H. WOOD versus ARCHEBALD STONE. A receiver is appointed. 30 Mar 1857. (P. 158)

ASA TODD, Administrator of William Scissim and others versus ALBERT SCISSIM and others. All the rights and title of the children and heirs of William Scissim are divested out of them and vested in the widow and relic of the said William Scissim. 30 Mar 1857. (Pp. 158-161)

B. H. PHILLIPS by his guardian versus PETER H. PHILLIPS. 30 Mar 1857. (Pp. 161-162)

REBECCA WEBBER versus BENJAMIN WEBBER. This cause has been compromised. 30 Mar 1857. (P. 163)

EXENA E. BOGLE, Administrator, versus MATHEW L. BOGLE and others. Defendants Elizabeth H., George A., Thomas N., and Josephine E. Bogle are all minors without guardian. James B. Thomas is appointed as guardian. 30 Mar 1857. (P. 163)

REZIN FOWLER versus ELIJAH NEELY. Report of the Clerk. 30 Mar 1857. (Pp. 163-165)

MARY SUSAN DEWITT versus DANIEL G DEWITT. The bill is taken for confessed. A hearing is set. 30 Mar 1857. (Pp. 165-166)

C. B. ODOM, Administrator of William C. Odom, and others versus FOUNTAIN OWEN and others. Report of the Clerk. 30 Mar 1857. (Pp. 166-167)

JOHN D. CAMPBELL and wife and others versus RICHARD MARTIN and others. The demurrer is overruled. 30 Mar 1857. (P. 167)

JOSEPH CLARK, Administrator of John A. Baird and others versus A. R. HAMMER, Administrator of Henry Trott and others. The Clerk is to make his report at next term. 30 Mar 1857. (Pp. 167-168)

MARY YOUNG versus ISAAC B. YOUNG, Executor. Isaac B. Young and Martha McFerrin were charged each in testator's book with sixty dollars more than they received. There is due to the complainant from the estate of the testator the sum of $1625. 30 Mar 1857. (P. 169)

MARY SUSAN DEWITT versus DANIEL G. DEWITT. The bill is taken for confessed. Defendant and complainant have been married. From this marriage, complainant had one infant female child. Complainant is a woman of good character. The conduct of the defendant toward the complainant has been so cruel and inhuman that it was unsafe for her to cohabit with and to be under his dominion and control. The bonds of matrimony are dissolved. 30 Mar 1857. (Pp. 169-170)

OWEN and wife versus C. C. HANCOCK and others. Robert Hancock died, intestate, on 15 Jul 1855, leaving his wife and children, complainant Alaminta and defendants Alfred L. and Christopher C. Hancock surviving him. Defendant Leech qualified

as administrator of intestate's estate. Intestate's widow has
relinquished and conveyed all her interest in said estate in
consideration of certain property, leaving complainant and defendants A. L. and C. C. alone interested in said intestate's
estate. Jacob Adams by his last will and testament in the State
of Virginia in the year 1807 bequeathed to his daughter, Mary
Cooper, who was afterwards married to said intestate and is the
mother of complainant Alaminta and defendants A. L. and C. C. a
negro girl, Celia, during her lifetime. If she died without
any heirs, said Celia and her increase were to return to intestate's estate and be divided among his other children. The intestate gave to his daughter, Alaminta, on her marriage to Complainant Fountain two slaves, Gincy, and child, Minda-- said
Celia's child and grandchild. Their worth was about $600. They
have been held ever since by complainants as their property.
Said intestate held and claimed said girl Celia and all her increase, except such as he gave to his children, down to the
death of said inteste's first wife, said Mary Cooper. Said
complainant was under the belief that the slaves did not belong
to the intestate, but were entailed property. The intestate had
in his possession at the time of his death old Celia and her
following named descendants, to wit, Newton, Mary, Sarah, Alford,
Ann, Dill, Silva, John, Elizabeth, Dice and her child Darthula,
Jim, Ann, and one whose name is not given, being fifteen in all.
Said fifteen slaves went into the possession of the said C. C.
after the death of the intestate. Said intestate's first wife,
Mary Cooper, took absolute title to said slave Celia and her
increase under the will of said Jacob Adams. Said Richard Hancock by his intermarriage with said Mary Cooper took possession
of old Celia and her increase. He did not part with his title
during his lifetime. The court is of the opinion that the complainants are entitled to the relief that they seek. 31 Mar
1857. (Pp. 170-174)

EXEMA E. BOGLE, Administrator, versus MATTHEW L. BOGLE and
others. Joseph H. Bogle died intestate on 4 Sep 1856, leaving
his widow and defendants as his heirs. Complainant has qualified as executrix. Said intestate died seized and possessed of
the tract of land described in complainant's bill in which complainant is entitled to dower. Some of the defendants have
asked for a sale of the balance of the land. The Clerk is to
determine if it is in the best interest of the heirs to have a
sale. 31 Mar 1857. (Pp. 174-175)

Chancery Court met in the town of Woodbury on the first
Monday, it being the 5th day of Oct 1857. Broomfield L. Ridley,
presiding. (P. 176)

ASA TODD, Administrator of William Scissom, versus ALBERT
SCISSOM Et Al. Report. 5 Oct 1857. (Pp. 176-177)

E. H. CAMPBELL, Administrator of Thomas St. John, and
others versus JAMES ST. JOHN and others. Final Decree. 5 Oct
1857. (P. 178)

WILLIAM WHARTON versus WILEY W. BELL Et Al. It is agreed
that the matter is controversy will be settled by arbitration.

5 Oct 1857. (Pp. 178-179)

WILLIAM GUNTER versus WILLIAM CAMPBELL and wife Et Al. The bill is dismissed. 5 Oct 1857. (P. 179)

JOHN W. WOOD versus ARCHEBALD STONE. Final Decree. 5 Oct 1857. (Pp. 180-183)

LUCINDA GREEN versus POLLY ANN GREEN. Petition in case of lunacy. The said Polly Ann Rodgers is an idiot and utterly incapable of managing her own affairs with safety to herself and others. She has an undivided interest in 200 acres and other property as well. Ellis Williams and Lydia Ann (Nunley) are her children. The Court decrees that Lucinda Green be appointed guardian of the said Polly Ann Rodgers. 5 Oct 1857. (Pp. 184-185)

JAMES TODD, SR. versus ROBERT W. ESPEY and others. It appears to the Court that Robert Laswell has qualified as administrator of Robert W. Espey. All of the equities in the bill are denied. The bill is dismissed. 5 Oct 1857. (P. 185)

DENNIS SMITH versus S. E. GILBERT and others. The injunction is dissolved. 5 Oct 1857. (P. 186)

A number of causes are continued. (Pp. 186-187)

C. B. ODOM, Administrator of William C. Odom, versus FOUNTAIN OWEN and others. 5 Oct 1857. (Pp. 188-189)

EXEMA E. BOGLE, Administratrix, versus MATTHEW S. BOGLE and others. Commissioners appointed to lay out the dower have filed their report. (Pp. 189-194)

ADAM PARKER versus C. M. HOPPER. There is still an unpaid balance of the purchase money. The land is to be sold. 5 Oct 1857. (Pp. 194-195)

JAMES ESPEY and others versus JOHN ESPEY and others. (Mariah) Jamison, wife of James Jamison, and Narcissa Jamison, wife of Robert Jamison, are to have their share in the real estate. Robert Espey is one of the distributees. 5 Oct 1857. (Pp. 196-197)

Chancery Court met in the town of Woodbury on the fifth Monday in Mar, it being the 27th day of said month 1858. The Chancellor, being absent, court was adjourned. (P. 198)

Chancery Court met in the town of Woodbury on the first Monday after the fourth Monday in Sep, it being the 4th day of Oct 1858. Broomfield L. Ridley, presiding. (P. 199)

ADAM PARKER versus C. M. HOPPER. The Clerk is to sell the lands mentioned. 4 Oct 1858. (Pp. 199-200)

A number of causes are continued. (Pp. 200-201)

THOMAS G. WOOD versus P. G. LEECH, Administrator. The defendant to pay the costs. 4 Oct 1858. (Pp. 201-202)

ABRAHAM BURGES versus P. G. LEECH, Administrator. 4 Oct 1858. (P. 202)

A. R. HAMMER, Administrator, versus THOMAS J. JELTON Et Al. Mary Trott, Elizabeth Trott, and Franklin Trott were minors without guardian. Thomas G. Wood is appointed as guardian. 4 Oct 1858. (P. 203)

ELIZABETH R. THOMPSON versus GEORGE W. THOMPSON. Petition for divorce. Defendant is ordered to pay for the support and maintenace of complainant for the next six months. Defendant is to furnish the complainant the use of a servant to be selected by her out of any servants in his possession. 4 Oct 1858. (P. 203)

P. G. LEECH, Administrator de bonis non with the will of James B. Summer, and Administrator of Lehanna Summer; H. C. SUMMER, J. N. D. SUMMER, WILLIAM BOYLE and wife SARAH A., DANIEL TRAVIS and wife MARY; ELIZABĒTH SUMMER, Administratrix of (Robert) Summer; T. R. SUMMER, A. J. BRISON and wife SUSAN, WILLIAM M. ROBERTSON and wife IZY E., J. J. BRISON and wife CINDERILLA H., JAMES C. SUMMER, and MARY L. BOYLE by her next friend P. G. Leech versus DAVID D., WINEY A., WILLIAM H., M. P., JR., Z. T., JAMES M. SUMMER: MIRA L. ALEENA C., ans SARAH A. SUMMER; and Joel Bogle. Defendants are minors with the exception of Boyle and are without guardian. It appears to the Court that J. M. Summer would be a suitable person to act as guardian to protect the interest of said minors. 5 Oct 1858. (Pp. 204-205)

SERENA A. WILLIAMS versus BERRY WILLIAMS. The defendant came forward to file his answer. 5 Oct 1858. (P. 205)

P. G. LEECH, Administrator of Richard Hancock versus A. L. HANCOCK, C. C. HANCOCK, FOUNTAIN OWEN and wife (ALLIMINTA). Final Decree. A tract of land was sold to the said A. L. Hancock. 5 Oct 1858. (Pp. 206-207)

M. S. BOGLE and others. Petition for sale of land. The Clerk is to report if it is advantageous for the petitioners to sell the land. 5 Oct 1858. (P. 207)

CHARLES READY versus JOSEPH BRAGG and wife ELIZABETH. On 29 Jan 1853, complainant recovered a judgment against the defendant. Joseph Bragg was the legal owner of the tract of land mentioned in the pleading. It appears to the Court that said Joseph Bragg did fraudulently transfer title to the land to his wife Elizabeth Marilla Bragg. He did this to delay and hinder his creditors and especially the said Charles Ready. 5 Oct 1858. (Pp. 207-209)

WILLIAM GIVENS and wife MARGARET, LEVI REED and wife MARY, and others, heirs of William Travis, versus DAVID TRAVIS, MARGARET EARTHMAN, WILLIAM C. SMART, and others. The allegations in the bill are not sustained by the proof. The deed of conveyance was not a deed of trust, but an absolute conveyance in remainder after the death of William Travis of the land and slaves specified in said deed to Davis Travis. 5 Oct 1858. (Pp. 209-210)

JAMES R. ESPEY and others versus JOHN ESPEY and others.

The Clerk is directed to withhold the share of Robert Espey until the decision of the suit of Todd against said Robert Espey. He shall credit the amount of the share of Margaret Jamison, wife of James Jamison, on the notes of her husband. He is also to report the value of the fund the widow. 5 Oct 1858. (Pp. 210-212)

ALFRED JONES versus MARY E. JONES. Complainant and defendant married about seven years ago and lived together about three or four months as husband and wife. Defendant left the complainant without just cause and has continued his wilful and malicious desertion for more than two years. The bonds of matrimony are dissolved. 5 Oct 1858. (P. 212)

JAMES S. ODOM, Guardian. Petition to sell slave. Armstead G. Odom died leaving a will which has been proven. He left four minor children, to wit, John S., Mathew M., R. L., and James H. Odom, all of tender years. Petitioner was appointed as guardian. A negro girl named Louisa was bequeathed to the minors. Said girl was disobedient and could not be controlled without whipping. Guardian is seeking to sell the slave. 5 Oct 1858. (P. 213)

ASA TODD Et Al versus ALBERT SCISSIM and others. 5 Oct 1858. (P. 214)

M. S. BOGLE Et Al. Petition for the sale of land. James W. McAdoo states that he knows well the land that was allotted to the widow of James H. Bogle as her dower and containing 171 acres. He lives near said land. He states that the land cannot be advantageously divied into six equal shares among the petitioners. He states that there are only two or three building sites on the land. The lots would be too small for a settlement. The land is ordered to be sold. 5 Oct 1858. (Pp. 215-217)

SARAH BOWERAMAN and others versus JESSE MILLIKEN and others. George Kelton is appointed Administrator of Michael Boweraman. 5 Oct 1858. (P. 217)

BENJAMIN JOHNSON, Executor of John Smith, versus JOHN S. DAVIS and R. S. SMITH. John S. Davis is a non resident of the State of Tennessee. 5 Oct 1858. (P. 218)

HENRY WILEY Et Al versus HENRY J. TROTT Et Al. The bill is taken for confessed as to James J. Trott, James M. Brown, Sr., James M. Brown, Jr., Joseph D. Morgan, Edmund Pendleton, Thomas Pendleton, Andrew Pendleton, Benjamin Pendleton, Stay A. Pendleton, Catherine Pendleton, Mary Pendleton, and Dillard Pendleton. The defendants are non residents of the State of Tennessee. The bill is taken for confessed. 5 Oct 1858. (Pp. 219-220)

P. G. LEECH, Administrator, versus MATTHEW S. BOGLE and others. Enxina C. Bogle was Administratrix of Joseph H. Bogle. On 1 Nov 1857, she intermarried with James S. Wamack. She died intestate on 23 Aug last. P. G. Leech has qualified as the administrator. The suit is revived in the names of P. G. Leech and James S. Wamack. 5 Oct 1858. (Pp. 220-224)

A number of causes are continued. (Pp. 225-226)

Thomas G. Wood, Clerk & Master, presented to be spread upon the minutes of the court the Comptroller's statement of revenue. 29 Oct 1857. (Pp. 226-227)

POLLY KEATON by her next friend William Keaton versus JOHN WILLARD and others. The defendants bill is well taken. Complainant is to pay the cost. 6 Oct 1858. (P. 227)

C. B. ODOM, Administrator of William C. Odom, versus FOUNTAIN OWEN and others. The Clerk is to make a distribution among the creditors. 6 Oct 1858. (Pp. 228-238)

MARY JANE HAYES versus JOHN HAYES Et Al. The demurrer is well taken. The bill is dismissed. 6 Oct 1858. (P. 238)

R. L. OWEN versus P. G. LEECH, Administrator. The administrator is ordered to deliver the negro boy to the complainant. 6 Oct 1858. (Pp. 238-239)

P. G. LEECH, Administrator, Et Al versus DAVID L. SUMMER Et Al. John Bogle is a non resident. The bill is taken for confessed. James B. Summer departed this life some time in 1855 in Cannon County, having previously making a will. He was seized and possessed of a tract of land granted to him by the State of Tennessee by Grant No. 23126. It is bounded on the south by John and Carrol Davenport. The Clerk is to report as to whether it would be advantageous to divide the land or to sell it. 6 Oct 1858. (Pp. 240-242)

ISAAC GUNTER versus JAMES B. ELLEDGE. The injunction is dissolved. 6 Oct 1858. (Pp. 243-244)

WILLIAM L. ALEXANDER Et Al versus JOHN A. GEORGE Et Al. Nancy A. George, William Crane, Mary Crane, Margaret C. Alexander, A. K. Alexander, and Hampton Sullivan have been served. Nancy A. George is a non resident of the State of Tennessee. The bill is taken for confessed. 6 Oct 1858. (P. 244)

FOUNTAIN OWEN and wife versus C. C. HANCOCK, A. L. HANCOCK, and P. G. LEECH, Administrator. All of the exceptions in the report are disallowed. The fifteen slaves may be hired out before they are sold. 6 Oct 1858. (Pp. 245-246)

JAMES C. QUARLES and others versus A. C. THOMAS and others. The bill is taken for confessed. 6 Oct 1858. (P. 247)

Chancery Court met at the Courthouse in the town of Woodbury on the first Monday and 4th day of Apr 1859. Broomfield L. Ridley, presiding. (P. 248)

JAMES T. QUARLES and JAMES H. JOHNSON versus WILLIAM C. LEECH and others. The bill is taken for confessed. 4 Apr 1859. (P. 249)

E. H. CAMPBELL, Administrator, versus JAMES ST. JOHN and others. John Pendleton purchased one of the tracts of land. 4 Apr 1859. (P. 250)

ASA TODD, Administrator, and SARAH SISSON versus ALBERT SISSON and others. 4 Apr 1859. (P. 251)

LUCINDA MELTON and others versus WILLIAM GRIZZLE and others. William Melton departed this life intestate, leaving a widow and heirs. They are the complainants and defendants. He left considerable real estate. The widow has not been endowed out of the said land. It is in the interest of the heirs that the land be sold. 4 Apr 1859. (P. 251)

JAMES R. ESPEY and others versus JOHN ESPEY and others. Report of the Clerk. 4 Apr 1859. (Pp. 252-254)

A. R. HAMMER, Administrator of Henry Trott, versus THOMAS J. JELTON and others. The personal assets of the decedent is between eighteen and nineteen hundred dollars. The indebtedness amounts to four thousand dollars. A sale of a tract of land will be necessary. 4 Apr 1859. (Pp. 255-256)

A. R. HAMMER, Administrator of Henry Trott, versus NELSON COOPER. 4 Apr 1859. (Pp. 256-257)

M. S. BOGLE and others. Petition for sale of land. 4 Apr 1859. (Pp. 258-259)

BENJAMIN JOHNSON, Executor of John Smith, versus JOHN Z. DAVIS and ROBERT G. SMITH. Defendant Robert G. Smith on 1 Sep 1854 sold to defendant Davis a house and lot in the town of Woodbury. Two notes were held by John Smith who departed this life testate. The notes are due. Land will be sold to satisfy the debt. 4 Apr 1859. (Pp. 259-261)

J. T. WOODRUFF versus JOHN W. A. KNOX and ALEXANDER McKNIGHT, Executor. This cause is continued. 4 Apr 1859. (P. 261)

Statement of the revenue collected by the Clerk & Master. 4 Apr 1859. (Pp. 261-262)

JOHN F. WEEDON, Administrator of William C. Miller, versus MARTHA E. MILLER and others. William C. Miller died in Cannon County in 1857 intestate. Complainant was appointed as the administrator. It does not appear to the court that all the children or minor heirs of the said William C. Miller are before the court. It is necessary to sell the tracts of land mentioned in the pleadings to satisfy the debts. It is suggested that a guardian be appointed for the minors. 4 Apr 1859. (P. 262)

The Chancellor is pleased to reappointed Thomas G. Wood as Clerk & Master for a term of six years. The said Wood takes his oath of office. 4 Apr 1859. (Pp. 263-264)

A. L. Seitz was admitted to the practice of law. 5 Apr 1859. (P. 265)

W. R. HILL versus DAVID ESPEY and H. S. CAWTHON. Final Decree. The bill is dismissed. 5 Apr 1859. (P. 266)

A. C. MILLIKEN, Administrator of John W. Milliken, versus JESSE MILLIKEN and JESSE N. MILLIKEN. The widow of John W. Milliken has intermarried. The personal estate of the decedent was insufficient to pay his debts. Jesse Milliken is guardian. Jesse A. Milliken is the only heir of John W. Milliken. The real estate is so situated that it cannot be divided and sold so as to pay the debts. (Pp. 267-268)

JOHN F. WEEDON, Administrator of William C. Miller, versus MARTHA E. MILLER, SARAH LORETTA MILLER, and others. It is necessary to sell the lands and town lot mentioned in the bill for the payment of debts of said estate. The Clerk is to determine whether all the children or all the heirs of William C. Miller are before the Court and have regular guardians or not. The Clerk reports that all of the children are before the Court. They are without guardian. William C. Miller died in Cannon County in 1857, leaving his widow, Martha E. Miller, and as his only children or heirs at law, the defendants Sarah Loretta Miller, Thomas T. Miller, Elizabeth J. Miller, William H. Miller, Elnora Miller, Terry W. Miller, and George D. C. Miller who are minors under the age of twenty-one years and have no regular guardian. 5 Apr 1859. (Pp. 269-272)

M. R. RUSHING versus G. W. THOMPSON and others. Process has been served. Defendants Elizabeth N. Sanford and William G. Thompson are both minors under the age of twenty-one years and are without guardian. Washington Britton is appointed as their guardian. 5 Apr 1859. (P. 272)

ELIZABETH J. BARTON by her next friend J. L. Farr versus WILLIAM BARTON and others. The demurrer is well taken. Defendants to pay the costs. 5 Apr 1859. (P. 273)

ZACHARIAH THOMASON versus LARKIN KEATON. Final Decree. The equity in the bill is fully met. The cause is dismissed. 5 Apr 1859. (Pp. 273-274)

A. BURGER versus F. REED and SUSAN REED, and others. The bill is sustained by the proof. 5 Apr 1859. (P. 274)

JOHN WILLIAMS versus DAVID EPLEY and NEEDHAM JERRIGAN. Final Decree. The equity in complainant's bill has been met. 5 Apr 1859. (P. 275)

LUCINDA MELTON Et Al versus WILLIAM GRIZZLE Et Al. It is in the interest of the heirs that the land be sold. It cannot be divided among them. 5 Apr 1859. (Pp. 276-277)

WILLIAM McFARLAN and wife versus W. S. MASSEY, Administrator, and others. Process has been served. The bill is taken for confessed. 5 Apr 1859. (P. 277)

SARAH J. RAINS, Administratrix of J. B. Rains, versus JAMES VANDERGRIFF and GABRIEL LANCE. It appears to the court that defendant Gabriel Lance sold to decedent J. B. Rains a tract of land and received a title bond. Said decedent has sold to the said Vandergriff the said land and executed a title bond. Complainant has received a judgment against said Vandergriff. The land will be sold to satisfy the debt. 5 Apr 1859. (P. 278)

James H. Wood is appointed as Deputy Clerk & Master. 5 Apr 1859. (P. 279)

ABEL and M. R. RUSHING, Executors of John Rushing, versus ANDERSON RUCKER and wife and others. Final Decree. Process has been served on Anderson Rucker and his wife Rem), David J. Wheeler and wife Elizabeth C., Jesse ( ) and wife Patience, John Landers, and Dorcas J. Petty. The bill is taken for confessed. John Rushing by a portion of his will bequeathed to his two granddaughters, Rebecca C. Davis and Dorcas J. Gilley, a sum of one thousand dollars each. It was to be expended by the executors for the purchase of small negro girls, one for each of the said grandchildren. The Court is of the opinion that after the death of Sarah Rushing, the widow of said John Rushing, then the estate is to be divided between Abel Rushing, M. R. Rushing, Permelia Rucker, and Elizabeth C. Wheeler, the two sons and two daughters of the said John Rushing who were living at the date of the will and the children of either of them that may be dead at the time of said division. 5 Apr 1859. (Pp. 279-281)

JAMES L. THOMAS and others versus WILLIAM C. LEECH and others. The Master's action is sustained. Process has been served on Amanda Leech. Publication has been made as to the defendants Ambrose M. Thomas, Iverson J. Thomas, Isaac Johnson and wife Sarah M. The bill is taken for confessed. A hearing is set. 5 Apr 1859. (Pp. 281-282)

ABEL RUSHING versus ARCHEBALD STONE and R. H. MASON. The injunction is dissolved. 5 Apr 1859. (P. 282)

JAMES S. ODOM, Guardian of John S. Odom, Martha M. Odom, R. L. Odom, and James H. Odom, minor heirs of A. Z. Odom. Ex Parte. 6 Apr 1859. (Pp. 283-284)

P. G. LEECH, Administrator, versus M. S. BOGLE and others. The Court states that the slave, America, did not belong to the intestate of complainant at his death, but that she belonged to one Jacob H. Thomas. 5 Apr 1859. (Pp. 284-287)

LUCINDA BUSH versus (MELCHISIDAC) BUSH. Divorce. 5 Apr 1859. (P. 287)

E. L. C. WITTY versus JOHN MURRAY. The bill is taken for confessed. Defendants John and Eli Muncy were indebted to complainant in about the sum of sixty dollars. A tract of land is ordered sold. 5 Apr 1859. (P. 288)

P. G. LEECH, Administrator, and others versus DAVID D. SUMMERS and others. 5 Apr 1859. (Pp. 289-291)

E. L. C. WITTY versus JOHN MURRAY and others. 5 Apr 1859. (Pp. 291-293)

ELIZABETH R. THOMPSON versus GEORGE W. THOMPSON. Bill for divorce. 5 Apr 1859. (Pp. 293-295)

ELIZABETH R. THOMPSON versus GEORGE W. THOMPSON. The suit has been compromised. The bill is dismissed. 5 Apr 1859. (P. 296)

Court adjourned until next regular term. (P. 296)

Chancery Court met in the town of Woodbury on the first Monday next after the fourth Monday in September, it being the third day of Oct 1859. (P. 297)

E. L. C. WITTY versus JOHN MUNCY and ELI MUNCY. Title to a tract of land is divested out of the defendants and vested in J. R. Neely. 3 Oct 1859. (P. 298)

LUCINDA MELTON, wife of William Melton deceased; JAMES MELTON and wife ELIZABETH, formerly Melton, JAMES BLAIR and wife CAROLINE, JOHN W. MELTON, ANSEL MELTON, WILLIAM J. MELTON, and GREEN MELTON versus WILLIAM GRIZZLE and wife MARY, JAMES GRIZZLE and wife MARTHA, MARY MELTON by her guardian James H. Wood, and JO D. MELTON, JR. by his guardian Jo D. Melton, Sr. Final Decree. Land is to be sold after the allotment of dower to complainant Lucinda Melton. 3 Oct 1859. (Pp. 298-301)

JOHN F. WEEDON, Administrator of William C. Miller, versus MARTHA E. MILLER, SARAH LORETTA MILLER, THOMAS T. MILLER, ELIZABETH J. MILLER, WILLIAM H. MILLER, ELENORA MILLER, (JENNY) W. MILLER, and GEORGE D. C. MILLER. Title to a tract of land is divested out of the heirs of William C. Miller and is vested in the purchaser. 3 Oct 1859. (Pp. 301-304)

A number of causes are continued. (Pp. 304-305)

SARAH J. RAINS, Administratrix of J. B. Rains versus GABRIEL LANCE and JAMES VANDERGRIFF. Final Decree. Sale of a tract of land. 3 Oct 1859. (Pp. 306-308)

A. R. HAMMER versus THOMAS J. JELTON, AMANDA BANKS, STEPHEN BANKS, MARY TROTT, ELIZABETH TROTT, and FRANKLIN TROTT. Defendant Jelton and Henry Trott deceased were joint owners of a tract of land which was sold. Title to the land was divested out of the complainants and defendants and vested in the purchaser. 3 Oct 1859. (Pp. 309-311)

A number of causes are continued. (Pp. 311-312)

WILLIAM CUMMINGS versus SARAH J. RAINS, Administratrix. It appears to the court that Isaac, Eliza Ann, and J. B. Rains are minors without guardian. A. Burger is appointed as guardian. (Pp. 312-313)

WILLIAM WHARTON versus WILEY W. BELL and others. Elizabeth S. and Mary W. Bell are minors without guardian. J. S. Brien is appointed as guardian. 3 Oct 1859. (P. 313)

M. FRANCIS, Guardian; JAMES J. FRANCIS, SARAH A. FRANCIS, D. J. FRANCIS, and ELIZABETH FRANCIS. Ex Parte. Petition to sell a slave. 3 Oct 1859. (Pp. 314-315)

ALBERT G. MILLIKEN, Administrator, versus JESSE MILLIKEN and JESSE A. MILLIKEN. Sale of a tract of land at twelve dollars an acre. 3 Oct 1859. (Pp. 315-316)

DAVID DODD and M. R. RUSHING versus JAMES SULLIVAN Et Al. Order to appoint a guardian for the minor heirs of William C. Miller. 3 Oct 1859. (P. 346)

RUTH MOORE versus SAMUEL MOORE. The defendant wilfully and maliciously abandoned the complainant. Complainant and defendant have two children, the issue of their said marriage. The bonds of matrimony are dissolved. Complainant is given control of the children. 4 Oct 1859. (Pp. 316-317)

WILLIAM McFARLAND and wife versus JAMES H. MITCHELL and others. The widow is entitled to a third of the real estate. The widow is now forty years of age. The widow is entitled to $1202. The Clerk is to state an account concerning the heirs at law of Adam Elrod. He shall charge each child with all advancements made. 4 Oct 1859. (Pp. 318-320)

C. B. ODOM, Administrator of William C. Odom, versus FOUNTAIN OWEN and the distributees and creditors. 4 Oct 1859. (Pp. 321-323)

BENNETT RUCKER by his next friend versus HENRY GOODLOE and wife Et Al. Guardian appointed for the minors, to wit, Joannah, Bennet, Henry, Jr., and James Goodloe. 4 Oct 1859. (P. 323)

E. L. C. WITTY versus JOHN CROSSLIN Et Al. Sale of land to satisfy a debt. 4 Oct 1859. (P. 324)

JOHN M. COOPER and wife versus WILLIAM BRYSON Et Al. William Bryson before his death had assigned his portion of the proceeds from the sale of Louisa and child to William Adamson. 4 Oct 1859. (P. 325)

A. R. HAMMER, Administrator of Henry Trott, versus NELSON COOPER and S. B. SPURLOCK. Sale of the mills and lands to satisfy a debt. 4 Oct 1859. (Pp. 325-327)

A. G. MILLIKEN, Administrator, versus JESSE MILLIKEN and JESSE A. MILLIKEN. Land is to be sold to satisfy a debt. 4 Oct 1859. (Pp. 327-328)

MARGARET BARRETT versus JAMES H. BARRETT. Complainant and defendant intermarried about Mar 1858 and lived together for three months. On account of cruel treatment from the defendant, complainant was forced to leave him. The bonds of matrimony are dissolved. 4 Oct 1859. (P. 329)

JAMES R. ESPEY, MARY ESPEY, and others versus A. B. CARNES and wife, and others. The bill is taken for confessed. John Espey departed this life intestate in Cannon County some years since, leaving complainants and defendants as his heirs except A. B. Carnes and wife, Richard Jones, and Samuel Jamison. The estate has been fully distributed. 4 Oct 1859. (P. 330)

A. Burger was this day appointed guardian of Benjamin H. T. Phillips, a person of unsound mind. 4 Oct 1859. (Pp. 330-331)

DAVID DODD versus JOHN F. WEEDON and others. The solicitor is willing to accept that the death of Malissa J. House is true. It appears to the court that the heirs of William Sullivan petitioned the Circuit Court for a decree to sell a certain tract of land. William C. Miller purchased the land be-

fore his death. The said Miller died before the note was due.
Malissa J. House is one of the heirs of William Sullivan deceased. She died before the decree was pronounced in said
cause, leaving children who were not made parties to the cause.
Therefore the sale is declared to be null and void. 4 Oct
1859. (Pp. 332-334)

M. R. RUSHING versus G. W. THOMPSON, Et Al. Final decree.
Elizabeth V. Sanford and William C. Thompson are minors and
are represented by their guardian. It appears to the court
that on the 14th day of Feb 1849, Elizabeth R. Taylor, then
being a single woman and owner of considerable real estate
and personal estate had agreed to marry Thomas B. Sanford.
Before the marriage, said Elizabeth R. and the said Thomas B.
entered into a written marriage contract in which she retained
her property free from the said Thomas B. Said parties were
married. Afterwards, the said Thomas B. died, leaving the said
Elizabeth his widow and the defendant, Elizabeth V., as the
only issue of their marriage. On 7 Mar 1854, the said Elizabeth
R. intermarried with defendant G. W. Thompson and on 13 Nov
1855, said Thompson and wife sold to complainant M. R. Rushing
344 acres of land, it being the same conveyed in said marriage
contract. The court decrees that the said Elizabeth R. retained
her absolute right to the land after the death of the said
Thomas B. George W. Thompson has marital rights in the land.
They have an absolute title to the land and are free to sell
it. 4 Oct 1859. (Pp. 334-336)

Chancery Court met in the town of Woodbury at the Courthouse
on the first Monday after the fourth Monday in March, it being
the second day of April 1860. Broomfield L. Ridley, presiding.
(P. 337)

P. G. LEECH and others versus DAVID D. SUMMER and others.
Some of the parties who are interested and heirs of James B.
Summer are left out of this proceeding. Their names are not
known. The Clerk is to ascertain the names of the ones left
out and report at the next term of court. 2 Apr 1860. (Pp.
337-338)

ENOCH BOWERS versus FRANCES BOWERS. It appears from the
proof that it was intolerable for the complainant to live with
the defendant as his wife and upon the ground of inhuman treatment. She was compelled to abandon him. The bonds of matrimony are dissolved. 2 Apr 1860. (P. 338)

A number of causes are continued. (Pp. 338-339)

LUCINDA BUSH versus ZACHARIAH BUSH. The complainant and
defendant were heretofore intermarried. The defendant since
said marriage has been guilty of cruel and inhuman treatment
towards the complainant. He has abused her person and threatened
her life. It is impossible for her to cohabit with him. The
bonds of matrimony are dissolved. The complainant is to select
all the interest in the estate of her father. 2 Apr 1860.
(Pp. 340-341)

A number of causes are continued. (Pp. 341-342)

WILLIAM WHARTON versus W. W. BELL and REBECCA BELL. The arbitrators determined that the house and lot did not belong to W. W. Bell, but did belong to Rebecca Bell. The Court determines that the house and lot is not liable to the satisfaction of Complainant Wharton's claims. 3 Apr 1860. (Pp. 342-343)

C. R. WATERS and wife ELIZABETH versus WILLIAM BARTON, Et Al. The testator of William Barton, Joshua Barton, died in Oct 1842 in Cannon County. He placed in the hands of his son David Barton the two slaves, Henry and Mack. He did not by a written or verbal gift give said slaves to his said son, but the said son received the slaves as "Bailor" and as such he carried them to the State of Texas where they remained as the possession of said David until the death of said David in 1844. After this, Joshua Barton legally appointed James R. Taylor to go to Texas and get said slaves and bring them to him in the State of Tennessee. They were brought back and placed in the possession of the said Joshua in 1845 and remained in his possession until his death in 1857. After the death of the said Joshua, complainant Elizabeth, who is the daughter of said David A. brought this suit. If the said David A. ever claimed the slaves as his own, the said Joshua had no knowledge of it. The Chancellor decrees that David A. Barton did not acquire any title to said slaves. 3 Apr 1860. (Pp. 343-346)

MARY ESPEY versus A. B. CARNES. The Clerk was to report what amount has been paid to each of the legatees and what would be a reasonable amount for the solicitors. 3 Apr 1860. (Pp. 346-347)

BENNETT RUCKER by next friend versus HENRY GOODLOE and others. The Clerk is to report to the court. 3 Apr 1860. (P. 349)

P. G. LEECH, Administrator, versus MATHEW L. BOGLE and others. 3 Apr 1860. (Pp. 349-358)

TURNER VAUGHN versus ASA SMITH and others. This cause is continued. 3 Apr 1860. (P. 359)

HENRY WILEY, WILLIAM L. COVINGTON, and wife versus JAMES J. TROTT Et Al. Henry Trott, Jr. departed this life since the commencement of this suit. He left the following heirs, to wit, Mary Trott, Elizabeth Trott, and Franklin Trott who are all minors and are non residents of the State of Tennessee. This cause is continued. 3 Apr 1860. (Pp. 360-361)

JOHN RUSHING'S EXECUTORS versus A. RUSHING and wife PARMELIA, D. J. WHEELER and wife. Said John Rushing left considerable money that will be going to his daughters, Parmelia Rucker and E. C. Wheeler at the death of their mother. It is agreeable to all parties that the money should be paid to their husbands. 3 Apr 1860. (Pp. 362-363)

WILLIAM CUMMINGS by next friend versus SARAH J. RAINS, Administratrix. Complainant sold the defendants the tracts of land mentioned in the pleadings. The notes have not been paid.

Land is to be sold to satisfy the debt. 4 Apr 1860. (Pp. 364-365)

WILLIAM BARTON versus THOMAS TOLBERT and others. Henry Trott deceased was in 1851 seized by title in fee simple of a house and lot in the town of Woodbury. The number of the lot was not known. Said Trott sold the lot to one of the defendants, J. J. Smith, for $100. Said Smith executed a note. The house and lot are to be sold to settle the debt. 4 Apr 1860. (Pp. 365-366)

A. N. FISHER versus GAINS, LEECH, and others. Said Fisher is to be permitted to file a cross bill. 4 Apr 1860. (Pp. 367-368)

A number of causes are continued. (Pp. 368-370)

THOMAS C. WOOD, Guardian of B. H. T. Phillips. Ex Parte. Commissioners are appointed to settle with the guardian. 4 Apr 1860. (Pp. 371-373)

ULYSSES BATES, WILLIAM L. BATES, and others, heirs and distributees of William Bates, versus ABRAHAM BURGER, REZEN FOWLER, and others. William Bates departed this life several years since possessed of considerable property. The administration was granted to D. M. Jarratt who has long since wound his administration up-- paid all the debts of the said estate and distributed the residue among the heirs. Said Bates was the owner of a large real estate living in Cannon, Warren, and Rhea Counties. In Aug 1850, a petition was filed in the County Court of Cannon County purporting to be filed by Rezen Fowler, guardian of Elizabeth, Susan, Ulysses, Lucy, William, and Azaline Bates, minor heirs of William Bates deceased and Frances M. Sewel and wife Abigal, Harmon St. John and wife Martha praying for a sale of a large quantity of real estate. Rezen Fowler was the Clerk of the County Court and was a petitioner to sell the land. Commissioners were appointed who stated that the land could not be advantageously partitioned. 4 Apr 1860. (Pp. 374-376)

JAMES JAMISON versus JOHN CUNNINGHAM. Complainant sold to defendant a tract of land in the 4th District of Cannon County. The notes on the land have not been paid. The Clerk is ordered to sell the land for the debt. 4 Apr 1860. (Pp. 376-377)

JAMES PETTY, Administrator of John Petty, and others. Ex Parte. Petition to sell slaves. John Petty, late of Cannon County, departed this life intestate. James Petty as been appointed his administrator. Said intestate died seized and possessed of four slaves, to wit, Mary, a woman and her three children, to wit, John, about 9, Lucy, and Hulda, about 5. There are several distributees, to wit, James Petty, John C. Petty, George W. Petty, Polly Goad, Ambrose Petty, David Petty, Nancy Runnells, Betsy Ann Williams, and Clementine Burke. Nancy Ann, Mary, and Isham Petty petition by their next friend and guardian Ambrose Petty as the children of their father, Isham Petty deceased, who was a son of the intestate and was entitled

to one share. Frances M. Williams and James Kellough are infant children of Margaret Allen deceased who was the daughter
of intestate and as such represent their deceased mother and
are entitled to one share. It appears to the Court that it
is impossible to divide the slaves without a sale. Said slave
and her children have been living in Murfreesboro eight or nine
years. Her husband resides there. Murfreesboro would be the
better market for said slaves. 4 Apr 1860. (Pp. 377-378)

F. OWEN and wife versus A. L. HANCOCK and C. C. HANCOCK,
and P. G. LEECH, Administrator of Richard Hancock. Final Decree. The Clerk gives his report. 4 Apr 1860. (Pp. 379-382)

ELIJAH LYON, Administrator of A. Whitfield, versus EMELINE
WHITFIELD and others. The bill is taken for confessed. S. H.
Woods received judgment against the complainant. A tract of
land is to be sold to settle the debt. 4 Apr 1860. (P. 383)

JOHN F. WEEDON, Administrator of William C. Miller, versus MARTHA E. MILLER and others. 4 Apr 1860. (Pp. 383-389)

JOHN S. BRIEN, Trustee, versus ELI and JOHN P. BAILEY.
The Clerk gives his report. 4 Apr 1860. (Pp. 389-395)

WILLIAM McFARLAND and wife ELIZABETH versus JAMES H. MIT-
CHELL and others. Final Decree. The Clerk shall charge each
child of Adam Elrod with all advancements. The Administrator
of John Elrod is one of the heirs of Adam Elrod deceased who
died after the death of his father Adam Elrod. Elizabeth Mcfarland is the widow of Adam Elrod. She has intermarried with
William McFarland. Said Elizabeth is entitled to a dower. The
following are the children of said Adam, to wit, William B. Ferrell and wife Eliza; John Ferrell and wife Margaret; James H.
Mitchell and wife Elizabeth; W. L. Roach and wife Sarah; W. E.
Justice and wife Josephine; Samuel Harmon; Nancy A. (Adams);
Benjamin F., Rachael, and David Elrod. The last named seven
distributees are minors without guardian. Josephine Justice is
a minor, but her husband is her guardian. 4 Apr 1860. (Pp.
396-406)

ELIJAH LYON, Administrator of A. Whitfield, versus EMELINE
WHITFIELD, Et Al. It appears to the court that (Milley) Whitfield, Andy M. Whitfield, Mary E. Whitfield, Christian M. Whitfield, and A. Whitfield are minors without guardian and are
heirs at law of A. Whitfield. Emeline Whitfield has been
served with process and has failed to answer. The bill is taken
for confessed against her. 4 Apr 1860. (P. 407)

EAKIN & COMPANY versus FURMAN & COMPANY. 4 Apr 1860. (P.
408)

Chancery Court met in the town of Woodbury on the first
Monday next after the fourth Monday in Sep, it being the first
of Oct 1860. Broomfield L. Ridley, presiding. (P. 409)

JAMES SULLIVAN and others versus ELIZA LEWIS and others.
Doug C. and Missouri Ann House are minors without guardian.
A guardian is appointed. 1 Oct 1860. (P. 409)

N. W. SUMMER and J. D. FRANCIS, Administrator, versus NANCY FRANCIS, MARTHA L. WILSON, and others. Mandy E. and Christopher C. Jones, Mary P. and Sarah Francis are minors without guardian. A. Burger is appointed as guardian. 1 Oct 1860. (Pp. 409-410)

JAMES JAMISON versus JOHN CUNNINGHAM. Final Decree. Report of sale of land. 1 Oct 1860. (Pp. 410-411)

SARAH J. RAINS, Administratrix, versus GABRIEL LANCE and JAMES VANDERGRIFF. 1 Oct 1860. (Pp. 412-413)

JOHN F. WEEDON, Administrator of William C. Miller, versus MARTHA E. MILLER Et Al. Report. 1 Oct 1860. (Pp. 413-415)

A. F. McFERRIN versus NANCY WILLIAMS Et Al. Williamson Williams, John R. Williams, Sallie Ann Williams, Joseph A. Williams, Zachariah Williams, Thomas A. Williams, Fannie E. Williams, and Nancy E. Williams are all minors without guardian. William Williams is appointed as guardian. 1 Oct 1860. (P. 416)

W. M. ROBERTSON versus A. J. BRYSON, Guardian of D. D. Summer. Taking care of, boarding, and clothing David D. Summer was worth at least ten dollars a month. The Clerk reports that the complainant's services is worth $100. 29 Aug 1860. (P. 417)

A number of causes are continued. (Pp. 417-418)

JAMES SULLIVAN and others versus ELIZA LEWIS Et Al. William House, the father of Davy C. and Missouri Ann House, was appointed their regular guardian. 2 Oct 1860. (P. 419)

Benjamin F. Phillips is a man of unsound mind and is a ward of the court. The Clerk is to make a report as to the proper amount to pay his guardian. 2 Oct 1860. (P. 420)

E. L. W. NAPIER versus ELIZA NAPIER. The defendant has failed to appear. The cause is taken for confessed. 2 Oct 1860. (P. 421)

E. L. NAPIER versus ELIZA NAPIER. The said Eliza Napier has wilfully abandoned her husband, the complainant. While living with the said husband, the said Eliza treated him extremely bad. She acted lewd and in an adulterous manner. The bonds of matrimony are dissolved. 2 Oct 1860. (P. 421)

A. R. HAMMER, Administrator of Henry Trott, versus THOMAS J. JELTON and others. 2 Oct 1860. (Pp. 422-423)

ROBERT ESTES versus NANCY J. ESTES. The bill is taken for confessed. The defendant was guilty of acts of adultery and violated her marital vows. The bonds of matrimony are dissolved. 2 Oct 1860. (Pp. 423-424)

(Page 425 is marked out)

JAMES SULLIVAN versus ELIZA LEWIS Et Al. The Clerk is to report if the land can be divided. 2 Oct 1860. (P. 426)

A. R. HAMMER, Administrator, versus NELSON COOPER Et Al. Judgment. 3 Oct 1860. (Pp. 427-430)

JAMES SULLIVAN Et Al versus ELIZA LEWIS Et Al. The Clerk reported that it is not advantageous to the parties that the land be partitioned. 3 Oct 1860. (Pp. 430-431)

WILLIAM E. JUSTICE and HENRY E. JUSTICE versus BYNUM & MITCHELL. (Pp. 431-432)

W. L. BATES and others versus WILLIAM CUMMINS and others. Process has been served on John D. Charlton, but he has failed to appear. It further appears that defendants David Brewer, Thomas Brewer and wife, Elizabeth Price, Sarah Price, Jackson Price, Elisha Price are all non residents of this State. Leave is granted to take depositions. 3 Oct 1860. (P. 433)

HENRY A. WILEY and others versus JAMES J. TROTT and others. 3 Oct 1860. (Pp. 434-437)

N. W. SUMMER and J. D. FRANCIS, Administrator, versus NANCY FRANCIS Et Al. John D. Francis is one of the administrators. A report is make to the court. 3 Oct 1860. (Pp. 437-440)

CLEM R. WATERS and wife ELIZABETH versus WILLIAM BARTON, Administrator of Joshua Barton; WILLIAM BARTON, JOSEPH RAMSEY and wife HANNAH, JAMES R. TAYLOR and wife ELIZABETH. 3 Oct 1860. (Pp. 440-442)

B. F. and PRESTON CARNAHAM versus THOMAS LILLARD, Administrator of William Summer Et Al. Final Decree. 4 Oct 1860. (Pp. 442-443)

JAMES R. ESPEY Et Al versus RICHARD JONES, Administrator. The Clerk is to make a report as to the advancements that have been made from the estate. 4 Oct 1860. (Pp. 443-446)

PARALEE DUNAWAY versus D. W. DUNAWAY. Complainant and defendant were intermarried in Rutherford County and lived together about two years. The defendant beat and abused complainant so that it became intolerable for her to live safely with him any longer on account of his cruel and inhuman treatment. The bonds of matrimony are dissolved. Complainant is to retain custody of her children. 4 Oct 1860. (P. 447)

HIRAM TODD Et Al versus JOHN BURKETT. The Clerk reported that it is necessary to sell the land. 4 Oct 1860. (Pp. 448-449)

A. F. TODD Et Al versus LEVINA GUNTER Et Al. The Clerk is to report at the next term of court. 4 Oct 1860. (Pp. 450-452)

JACKSON HUNTER and wife versus POLLY ROGERS and others. The bill is taken for confessed. 4 Oct 1860. (P. 452)

JACKSON HUNTER and wife TINSEY versus POLLY A. ROGERS and others. It appears to the court that Polly A. Rogers is a person of unsound mind and has been so declared by the court.

Her guardian is dead and she is without guardian. Lydia A. Nunley is a minor and has no guardian. Thomas A. Wilsher is appointed as guardian of Polly A. Rogers and Lydia A. Nunley. 4 Oct 1860. (P. 453)

JACKSON HUNTER and wife versus POLLY A. ROGERS and others. The Clerk is to determine the amount needed for the board, care, and attention needed for the said Polly A. Rogers and Lydia A. Nunley. 4 Oct 1860. (P. 454)

A number of causes are continued. (Pp. 454-455)

JACKSON HUNTER and wife versus POLLY A. ROGERS and others. 4 Oct 1860. (Pp. 455-456)

JOHN M. COOPER and wife LOCKEY versus FRANCIS BRYSON Et Al. William Bryson is entitled to one fourth of the fund arising from the sale of the slave mentioned in the pleading. 4 Oct 1860. (P. 457)

JOHN D. WEEDON, Administrator of William C. Miller versus MARTHA E. MILLER Et Al. 4 Oct 1860. (Pp. 458-459)

BENNETT RUCKER by his next friend versus HENRY GOODLOE and wife and others. 4 Oct 1860. (Pp. 459-460)

WILLIAM BARTON versus THOMAS TOLBERT and others. The Clerk gives his report. 4 Oct 1860. (Pp. 461-462)

SARAH BOWERMAN, GEORGE KELTON, Administrator of Mikiel Bowerman, versus N. G. MILLIKEN, JESSE MILLIKEN, WALKER TODD, and SAMUEL BOWERMAN. The bill is taken for confessed. Michael Bowerman died intestate. Complainant George Kelton is his administrator. Sarah Bowerman is his widow. The other complainants and defendants and Samuel Bowerman are his distributees. In his lifetime, the said Michael sold to Jesse Milliken 205 acres in the 4th District. This was paid by note. The Court rules that the complainants are entitled to recover the amount of the said notes. 4 Oct 1860. (Pp. 463-464)

WILLIAM L. BATES Et Al versus A. BURGER Et Al. 4 Oct 1860. (Pp. 465-469)

ELIJAH LYONS, Administrator of A. A. Whitfield, versus EMELINE WHITFIELD Et Al. The Clerk gives his report. 4 Oct 1860. (Pp. 469-470)

P. G. LEECH, Administrator of Joseph H. Bogle, and JAMES S. WAMACK, Administrator of Exema E. Wamack. The Clerk is to report to the court the amount paid out by him to the heirs of Joseph H. Bogle. 4 Oct 1860. (Pp. 470-472)

MATHEW S. BOGLE and others. Petition for sale of land. 4 Oct 1860. (Pp. 472-473)

EAKIN & COMPANY versus FURMAN & COMPANY. 4 Oct 1860. (Pp. 473-474)

Chancery Court met in the town of Woodbury on the first Monday next after the fourth Monday in Mar, it being the first day of Apr 1861. Broomfield L. Ridley, presiding. (P. 475)

HIRAM TODD and wife NANCY versus JOHN J. BURKETT Et Al.
Hiram Todd was the purchaser of the tract of land mentioned in
the pleadings. The said Hiram promised to pay the heirs of
Andrew Burkett. It appears to the court that Andrew Burkett
was indebted to Hiram Todd and to Nancy Todd as widow of the
said Andrew. (Pp. 476-477)

LUCINDA MELTON, Widow of William Melton, and others versus
WILLIAM GRIZZLE and others. 1 Apr 1861. (Pp. 478-480)

ANTHONY OWEN versus M. S. BOGLE and others. It appears to
the Court that defendant James S. Odum has died since the filing
of the answer of defendants. He was guardian of defendants
John S., Rufus, Mathew, and James S. Odom. Peter C. Talley has
been appointed as guardian of said minor defendants. 1 Apr
1861. (P. 481)

WILLIAM WOOD versus R. L. BOYD and others. Defendants
R. L. Boyd and Lucinda Boyd are non residents of Tennessee. The
bill is taken for confessed. 1 Apr 1861. (P. 482)

CLEM R. WATERS and wife ELIZABETH versus WILLIAM BARTON
Et Al. Report of the Clerk. 1 Apr 1861. (Pp. 482-484)

M. S. BOGLE Et Al. Petition to sell land. 1 Apr 1861.
(Pp. 485-486)

R. L. OWEN, Administrator, versus WILLIAM F. ODOM. Decree.
Defendant is indebted to James S. Odum. A tract of land is to
be sold to satisfy the debt. 1 Apr 1861. (Pp. 386-387)

JAMES SULLIVAN Et Al versus ELIZA LEWIS Et Al. Clerk's
report. 1 Apr 1861. (Pp. 487-489)

A number of causes are continued. (P. 490)

LUCINDA BUSH versus ZACHARIAH BUSH. This cause is continued. 1 Apr 1861. (P. 491)

A. F. McFerrin, Administrator of Thomas H. Williams versus WILLIAM WILLIAMSON Et Al. 1 Apr 1861. (Pp. 492-493)

THOMAS W. WOOD versus WILLIAM G. CARMICHAEL and others.
On 30 Nov 1860, William G. Carmichael and John St. John gave
his word as trustee to carry out the trust deed provisions. 1
Apr 1861. (Pp. 493-496)

J. M. ALEXANDER versus E. D. and J. H. ALEXANDER. Complainant's bill is overruled. 2 Apr 1861. (P. 497)

THOMAS CAMPBELL versus MERRITT and GIVENS. The demurrer
is well taken. Complainant recovers the costs of the demurrer. 2 Apr 1861. (P. 497)

STEPHEN COOK versus WILLIAM COSBEY. Judgment by motion.
2 Apr 1861. (Pp. 497-498)

MARTHA BARRETT by her next friend B. F. Barrett versus
G. C. BARRETT. It appears to the court that Z. C. Barrett was
in fact a mean man. He is perpetually enjoined from meddling
with the fund mentioned. 2 Apr 1861. (Pp. 498-499)

PARALEE DUNAWAY versus D. W. DUNAWAY. The Clerk is to take and state what would be a reasonable amount for the support of complainant and her two children each year according to the estate and condition in life of the defendant. 2 Apr 1861. (Pp. 500-501)

ROBERT BAILEY versus WILLIAM CUMMINGS. 2 Apr 1861. (Pp. 502-503)

MARY CARSON versus F. COLEMAN and MOSES THOMPSON. Said Coleman and Thompson have commenced proceedings to have Mary Carson declared a lunatic. The Court is of the opinion that The County Court has concurrent jurisdiction with Chancery Court in cases of idiotcy, lunacy, and other unsoundness of mind. David W. Smith is the agent for the said Mary Carson. 2 Apr 1861. (P. 503)

ROBERT BAILEY versus WILLIAM CUMMINGS. Inquisition of lunacy. William Cummings is a person of unsound mind and utterly incapable of managing his own affairs with safety to himself and others. The said William Cummings has a wife named Delphia and the following children, to wit, Elizabeth Ann Snow, Benjamin F. Cummings, Moses H. Cummings, Martha who has intermarried with , her husband's name not known, Panza Bailey, Julia Stone, Dallas Cummings, Polk Cummings, Adline Cummings, and also Jackson Cummings' heirs, to wit, F. A. Young, Malinda Melton, Malinda Gunter's heirs, to wit, Mary McCabe, P. D. Gunter, and some others whose names are not known. 2 Apr 1861. (Pp. 503-505)

ABEL RUSHING versus ARCHEBALD STONE and others. 2 Apr 1861. (Pp. 506-507)

GEORGE KELTON, Administrator of Michael Bowerman, SARAH BOWERMAN, and others versus A. G. MILLIKEN, JESSE M. MILLIKEN, and WALKER TODD. Jesse Milliken has not paid the amount due for the land. Land is to be sold to satisfy the debt. 2 Apr 1861. (Pp. 507-508)

WILLIAM CAWTHON versus H. L. BUSH. Report. 2 Apr 1861. (Pp. 509-510)

WILLIAM L. BATES and others. Ex Parte. Petition to sell land. 2 Apr 1861. (P. 511)

A. C. MILLIKEN, Administrator, versus JAMES MILLIKEN Et Al. The Clerk is to take an account with the administrator as to the amount that he paid out of his own funds. 2 Apr 1861. (Pp. 511-512)

J. W. EDWARDS versus M. J. EDWARDS. William Edwards and M. J. Edwards were intermarried several years since. The said M. J. Edwards was guilty of adultery with one Shockley. She wilfully abandoned the said J. W. about the year 1854, about six years since without reasonable cause and still persists in her abandonment. The bonds of matrimony are dissolved. 2 Apr 1861. (P. 512)

WILLIAM D. STROUD versus WILLIAM STROUD. The cause is dismissed. 2 Apr 1861. (P. 513)

SARAH J. RAINS, Administratrix, versus JOSEPH BOGLE. 2 Apr 1861. (Pp. 513-514)

REBECCA WEBBER versus BENJAMIN WEBBER and others. Divorce and alimony. Said Benjamin Webber is to pay into the office of the Clerk & Master for the support of said Rebecca until the next term of court. 2 Apr 1861. (P. 514)

WILLIAM McFARLAND and wife ELIZABETH versus ROACH, MITCHELL Et Al. The Clerk is to pay over the money arising from the sale of the land and slaves of Adam Elrod. 2 Apr 1861. (Pp. 514-516)

A. F. TODD, Administrator, and REBECCA GUNTER versus LAVINA GUNTER Et Al. E. J. Summer was the highest bidder for a tract of land. 2 Apr 1861. (Pp. 516-517)

JACKSON HUNTER and wife LINSEY versus POLLY ANN RODGERS Et Al. Report. 2 Aug 1861. (Pp. 517-519)

N. W. SUMMER and J. D. FRANCIS, Administrators of E. Francis, versus NANCY FRANCIS and others. 2 Aug 1861. (Pp. 520-522)

FURMAN & COMPANY and others versus H. K. FISHER and brother and others. Defendants on 4 Apr 1859 did convey a deed of trust to J. A. Barnes in trust for the benefit of the creditors of the firm of W. H. Fisher & Brother. 3 Apr 1861. (Pp. 522-524)

SARAH BOWERMAN and others versus JESSE MILLIKEN and others. 3 Apr 1861. (Pp. 525-526)

ANSEL MELTON Et Al versus WILLIAM GRIZZLE and wife Et Al. Mary Melton has intermarried with S. M. Gunter. It appears to the court that Isaac Gunter is a safe, prudent man. S. M. Gunter is not a prudent man. It appears to the court that Isaac Gunter is a suitable person to act as trustee for the said Mary Gunter. 3 Apr 1861. (P. 527)

Court is adjourned until the next regular term. (P. 528)

Chancery Court met at the Courthouse in the town of Woodbury on the first Monday next after the fourth Monday in Sep,
it being the second day of Oct 1865. John P. Steel of the Third
Chancery Division of the State of Tennessee presiding. (P. 1)

T. J. Jelton has been appointed as Clerk & Master of the
Chancery Court at Woodbury. 12 Jun 1865. (Pp. 1-2)

JAMES M. ROBERTS versus J. D. FRANCIS Et Al. Defendants
Thomas and Sarah Francis are minors without guardian. Thomas J.
Jelton is appointed as guardian. 2 Oct 1865. (P. 2)

C. B. ODOM, Administrator, versus WILLIAM R. BOGLE and others.
2 Oct 1865. (P. 3-4)

T. J. JELTON. Bond. 2 Oct 1865. (Pp. 4-6)

ROBERT BAILEY Et Al versus JANE BAILEY, JOHN W. SHERLEY and
wife, MARGARET C. BAILEY, JOSEPH BAILEY, JR., and RUTHA ANN
MELTON. A hearing is set. 2 Oct 1865. (P. 6)

HENRY A. WILEY and others versus JAMES J. TROTT and others.
2 Oct 1865. (P. 6)

ROBERT K. STEPHENS versus MARY JANE STEPHENS. Bill for
divorce. The bill is taken for confessed. A hearing is set. 2
Oct 1865. (P. 7)

ROBERT BAILEY versus WILLIAM CUMMINS. Petition of lunacy.
Warren Cummins was appointed as guardian for defendant William
Cummins who was a man of unsound mind. It is suggested and admitted that the said ward, William Cummins, is dead. The Clerk
is to take an account with the said Warren Cummins. 2 Oct 1865)

ANN MORRIS versus ELISHA MORRIS. The bill is taken for
confessed. Process has been served on the said Elisha Morris by
the Sheriff of Smith County. A hearing is set for the present
term of court. 2 Oct 1865. (P. 8)

Thomas C. Wood and Absolom Finley were sworn in as practicing
solicitors of this court. 2 Oct 1865. (P. 8)

COLE ANN MORRIS versus ELISHA MORRIS. Complainant and defendant were married in Cannon County in the year 1862. The defendant has wilfully and maliciously deserted the complainant for
more than two years. The bonds of matrimony are dissolved. 2
Oct 1865. (Pp. 8-9)

ROBERT K. STEPHENS versus MARY JANE STEPHENS. Final Decree.
It appears to the court that defendant Mary Jane Stephens has
since her marriage with complainant been guilty of acts of a-
dultery contrary to her marital vows. The defendant and complainant have three children, the issue of their marriage. The
bonds of matrimony are dissolved. The said Robert K. Stephens
is restored to all the rites and privileges of a young man single. The defendant is not a suitable person to have the charge
of the children. She has by her conduct forfeited all rite to
support or alimony. 2 Oct 1865. (P. 9)

JAMES SULLIVAN versus ELIZA LEWIS Et Al. James Sullivan,
one of the complainants in this cause is dead. It appears that

Jane Sullivan is the administratrix. The suit is revived in her name. The real estate of William Sullivan had been sold and converted into personal estate. 2 Oct 1865. (P. 9)

ROBERT BAILEY and others versus JANE BAILEY, JOHN W. SHERLEY and wife MARGARET E. Et Al. The Clerk is to give an account of the indebtedness of the estate of Joseph Bailey. The Clerk reports it will be necessary to sell about 120 acres of land. The said Joseph Bailey, Sr. departed this life in Cannon County in 1861, intestate, leaving a widow, Jane Bailey, and the following heir viz. Robert Bailey, the only living child of said deceased. The said deceased never had but one other child viz. John N. Bailey deceased. Jane Turner, Isabella M. Bailey, Margaret E. Sherley, Joseph Bailey, Jr. are the children of the said John N. Bailey. Rutha Ann Melton is the grandchild of the said John N. Bailey and the only child of her mother who is dead and was the daughter of the said John Bailey deceased. 2 Oct 1865. (Pp. 10-11)

R. L. OWEN, Administrator, and others versus MARY ODOM and others. The papers in this cause have been destroyed or mislaid. Notice is to be made to creditors by publication. 2 Oct 1865. (Pp. 11-12)

WILLIAM CUMMINS versus WILLIAM STONE. The suit is revived in the name of the heirs of William Cummins deceased, to wit, P. D. Cummins, Adaline Young, Malinda Melton, Mary McCabe, Pleasant D. Gunter, Nancy Gunter, William Gunter, Elizabeth Ann Susa, Benjamin F. Cummins, Moses H. Cummins, John F. King, Rhody King, Elizabeth King, William Ford, Elizabeth Ford, Parazada Bailey, Julian Stone, E. D. Cummins. 2 Oct 1865. (P. 12)

BETTY V. SANFORD versus JOHN F. WEEDON and others. The Rules docket of this court have been destroyed or mislaid. No process can be found on file. It appears to the Court that the bill was filed 22 Jan 1862 and the Rule Docket was the destroyed or mislaid. A considerable amount of real estate is mentioned in the bill. 2 Oct 1865. (Pp. 12-13)

ROBERT BAILEY Et Al versus JANE BAILEY Et Al. It appears to the court that all of the defendants are probably before the court. There were 1015 acres. The personal estate is exhausted. There are outstanding debts. It is necessary to sell a portion of the land. 2 Oct 1865. (Pp. 13-14)

HENRY DAUGHERTY, Administrator of T. M. Allison Et Al versus THOMAS ALLISON and others and creditors. Publication is to be made for the creditors. 2 Oct 1865. (Pp. 14-15)

S. J. ODOM versus WILLIAM C. LEECH and J. M. ODOM. The land in the bill is in the 11th District. The said William C. Leech is indebted to complainant. It is necessary to sell land in order to pay the debts. 2 Oct 1865. (P. 15)

W. L. BATES and others. Ex Parte. Petition to sell land. 2 Oct 1865. (Pp. 15-16)

B. L. and P. CARNAHAM versus WILLIAM B. LILLARD, Administrator of William Sunhill and others. 2 Oct 1865. (P. 15)

WILLIAM SAULS versus WILEY DAVENPORT and JOHN W. SUMMER. All the equity in complainant's bill has been met. The injunction is dissolved. 2 Oct 1865. (P. 16)

RICHARD TENPENNY versus D. M. JARRATT and others. Decree on demurrer. 2 Oct 1865. (Pp. 16-17)

Court adjourned until court in course. (P. 17)

Chancery Court met at the Courthouse in the town of Woodbury on the first Monday next after the fourth Monday in Mar, it being the second day of Apr 1866. (P. 18)

A. F. TODD, Administrator of P. A. Gunter, Et Al versus LAVINA GUNTER Et Al. Sale of a tract of land. 2 Apr 1866. (Pp. 18-19)

ASA TODD, Administrator of S. Lannom, versus S. GANNON Et Al. Defendants M. A., S. M., James N., J. K., and Sarah E. Gannon are minors without guardian. James S. Barton is appointed as guardian. 2 Apr 1866. (P. 19)

WILLIAM A. CLARK, Administrator of (?) Sisson, versus MARY A. SISSON Et Al. Defendants Mary Ann, C. W., I. G., and Sarah E. Sisson are all minors without guardian. James S. Barton is appointed as their guardian. 2 Apr 1866. (P. 19)

W. A. CLARK, Administrator, versus JAMES J. REED Et Al. Defendants James J., Amanda J., Mary E., Louisa C., Nancy C., Liddia E., and George W. Reed are minors without guardian. James S. Barton is appointed as guardian. 2 Apr 1866. (P. 20)

ISAAC McBROOM and wife Et Al versus ALFORD TENPENNY Et Al. Defendant is the executor of Daniel Tenpenny. The defendant as executor will pay the costs. 2 Apr 1866. (Pp. 20-21)

C. B. SUMMER, Administrator, versus ZACHARIAH SMITH Et Al. It appears to the court that Jefferson Summer of Cannon County and the children and heirs of Elijah Summer are unknown citizens of the State of Missouri. They are without guardian. 2 Apr 1866. (Pp. 21-22)

(Pages 23 and 24 are missing)

ROBERT BAILEY Et Al versus JANE BAILEY Et Al. Allotment of the dower of Jane Bailey. 3 Apr 1866. (Pp. 25-27)

DANIEL S. FORD, Administrator, versus MATHEW DENNIS Et Al. The Clerk is to report if it will be necessary to sell the land in the proceedings. 2 Apr 1866. (P. 28)

FREEMAN & COMPANY and others versus W. H. FISHER & COMPANY. 2 Apr 1866. (Pp. 29-30)

T. W. WOOD, Trustee, versus CREDITORS OF CARMICHAEL ST. JOHN. 2 Apr 1866. (Pp. 30-31)

HIRAM TODD, Administrator of Andrew Burkett deceased, and NANCY TODD versus JOHN BURKETT, JERMIAR BURKETT, and others. Report on the value in money of Nancy Todd's dower interest in the estate of her former husband Anderson Burkett deceased. 2 Apr 1866. (P. 31)

JOHN H. SMITH, Administrator, versus SOPHIA B. MARTIN Et Al. Ivicy Jarrett, Laura Jarrett, Ophelia Jarrett, and Napetian Jarrett are minors without guardian. 2 Apr 1866. (P. 32)

JOHN H. SMITH, Administrator, versus SOPHIA B. MARTIN Et Al. It appears to the court that T. J. Odineal and wife Catherine, J. J. Douglas and wife Rosaline, Frances Martin, Thompson Heriel and wife Elizabeth, William Wright and wife Susan J., Joseph G. Martin, the heirs of Taswell Martin named are unknown citizens of the State of Missouri; Pleasant Laba and the heirs of Elizabeth Laba whose names are unknown are residents of the State of Virgina; Elizabeth J. Gideon, Ophelia, Lana, Napoleon, C. Jarrett; Thomas, William, Josia, and Mary Jane Rucker. The bill is taken for confessed. 2 Apr 1866. (Pp. 32-33)

LUCINDA GRIZZLE and others versus WILLIAM GRIZZLE and others. 2 Apr 1866. (Pp. 33-34)

SARAH E. CARNAHAN versus JESSE GILLEY Et Al. James S. Barton is appointed guardian for Mary, Ann, Jane R., Restora, and Tennessee N. Carnahan, minor heirs of Restora Carnahan. 2 Apr 1866. (P. 34)

JOHN BIGSBY and H. D. NEELEY versus ELIJAH NEELEY. It appears to the court that defendants Elijah, William R., Francis, and Amanda A. Neeley are all minors without guardian. D. L. Elkins is appointed as guardian. 2 Apr 1866. (P. 35)

JOHN RIGSBY and others versus E. NEELEY and others. Petition for partition. Commissioners are appointed to divide the land. 2 Apr 1866. (Pp. 35-36)

A number of causes are continued. (Pp. 36-37)

H. J. ST. JOHN versus ROBERT B. STEPHENS and MARY JANE STEPHENS. On 26 Jun 1863, complainant sold to defendant in consideration of three thousand dollars in Confederate treasury notes a town lot in the town of Woodbury. The Court is to decide the validity of the transaction. 2 Apr 1866. (Pp. 37-38)

MARY CARUTHERS versus W. P. GUTHRIE. John D. Caruthers, Mathew Marth B. Caruthers, Amanda P. Caruthers, and Calvin Caruthers are minors without guardian. W. P. Gaither and wife Sarah A. E., Isaac L. Jarrett and wife Mary E., Ruth J. Caruthers, Edmond J. Caruthers, John D. P. Caruthers have been served with process. Maxwell Caruthers died intestate in 1861, leaving complainant as his widow all all the defendants as his heirs except John P. Gannon. 2 Apr 1866. (Pp. 39-41)

JOHN H. SMITH, Administrator of John C. Martin, versus SOPHIA B. MARTIN Et Al. Defendant Sophia B. Martin is entitled to a dower. 4 Apr 1866. (Pp. 41-42)

T. W. WORD, Trustee, versus FIRM OF CARMICHAEL & ST. JOHN. 4 Apr 1866. (Pp. 43-44)

JAMES B. SUMMER versus IVORY SUMMER. Decree to answer and file a cross bill. Leave is granted until the June Rules. 4 Apr 1866. (P. 44)

R. L. OWEN, Administrator of James S. Odom, versus J. J. ODOM and other heirs and creditors of James S. Odom. 4 Apr 1866. (Pp. 45-47)

EXECUTORS OF JOHN RUSHING versus ANDERSON RUCKER and others. 4 Apr 1866. (Pp. 47-48)

JOHN F. WEEDON versus JOHN H. SMITH, Guardian of Mary B. Sands. The equity is in the complainant's bill. 4 Apr 1866. (P. 48)

ELIZABETH LONG and others versus GEORGE C. BARRETT, Administrator of Israel Long, and others. The administrator is to deliver to the Clerk all the assets in his hands belonging to the estate of the said Israel Long. 4 Apr 1866. (P. 48)

SUSAN A. McFERRIN by her next friend versus A. F. McFERRIN and others. The bill is taken for confessed. 4 Apr 1866. (P. 49)

ROBERT BRYSON, Administrator of George Bogle, and others versus P. G. LEECH. Petition to sell land. 4 Apr 1866. (Pp. 49-50)

J. R. NEELEY, Administrator of William D. Smith, versus AMANDA J., WILLIAM D., AND RUTHA JANE SMITH. Complainant and William D. Smith were partners in trade in a mercantile business at the time of the death of said William D. Smith. Complainant is also the Administrator of said William D. Smith. The Administrator has made settlement with the Clerk. 4 Apr 1866. (Pp. 50-51)

WILLIAM A. CLARK, Administrator of George W. Reed, versus JAMES J. REED, and others. Complainant Sarah Reed is the widow of the said George W. Reed. She is entitled to a dower out of the land of the said George W. 4 Apr 1866. (Pp. 51-52)

WILLIAM A. CLARK, Administrator of Thomas Sisson, and REBECCA SISSON versus MARY A. SISSON and others. The Clerk is to report if the estate is large enough to pay the debts. 4 Apr 1866. (P. 52)

ALLISON heirs versus BOGLE heirs. Harriet A., Nancy P., James W., Miss Eliza, and Timothy P. Allison, minor heirs of Timothy Allison, and Nancy Bogle, Douglas Bogle, minor heirs of M. S. Bogle are infants of tender years without guardian. Moses W. McKnight is appointed as guardian. 4 Apr 1866. (Pp. 54-57)

FOUNTAIN OWEN versus P. G. LEECH. The bill is taken for confessed. 4 Apr 1866. (Pp. 58-59)

C. D. CURLEE versus JUDITH CURLEE and others. All of the defendants are minors without guardian except Judith Curlee who is the widow. 4 Apr 1866. (P. 59)

S. C. HAMBLETON, Administrator of E. A. Kennedy versus SAMUEL KENNEDY, JOSEPHINE KENNEDY, and G. H. KENNEDY. All of the defendants are minors without guardian. James S. Barton is appointed as guardian. The said E. A. Kennedy died in

Wilson County in 1863. The Administrator has exhausted all the personal estate in the payment of debts. It will be necessary to sell thirty acres of land. (Pp. 60-61)

WILLIAM J. SMITH and wife MARTHA versus THOMAS COX and wife ELIZA J. and others. It is necessary to sell a tract of land for the debt. 4 Apr 1866. (P. 62)

LUCINDA MELTON and others versus WILLIAM GRIZZLE and others. 4 Apr 1866. (P. 63)

N. W. SUMMER and J. D. FRANCIS, Administrator of E. Francis, versus NANCY FRANCIS and others. 4 Apr 1866. (P. 64)

LINSLEY HUNTER versus ELLIS WILLIAMS and others. Sale of a tract of land. 4 Apr 1860. (Pp. 64-66)

A number of causes are continued. (Pp. 66-67)

A. R. HAMMER, Administrator of Henry Trott, versus T. J. JELTON and others. 4 Apr 1866. (Pp. 67-68)

Chancery Court met in the town of Woodbury at the Courthouse on the first Monday next after the fourth Monday in Sep, it being the first day of Oct 1866. John P. Steele, presiding. (P. 69)

A number of causes are continued. (Pp. 69-71)

ROBERT BRYSON, Administrator of George Bogle, versus P. G. Leech. Sale of a tract of land. 1 Oct 1866. (Pp. 71-72)

S. C. HAMILTON, Administrator of E. S. Kennedy, versus SAMUEL KENNEDY, JOSEPHINE KENNEDY, and G. W. KENNEDY. Sale of a tract of land. 1 Oct 1866. (P. 73)

HENRY DAUGHERTY, Administrator of T. M. Allison, versus F. S. ANDERSON. Sale of a tract of land. 1 Oct 1866. (Pp. 73-75)

MARY E. CUMMINS versus JAMES H. CUMMINS. This cause is dismissed. 1 Oct 1866. (P. 75)

WARREN CUMMINGS, Administrator, versus R. L. OWEN and others. Construction of the Will of Fountain Owen. The Chancellor decreed that the provisions of the will which gives to the widow, Araminta Owen, all the corn on hand applied to the corn on hand on 7 Mar 1866, the date of the making of the will and not to the growing crops which were not then planted. 1 Oct 1866. (P. 76)

JAMES M. COMER, Administrator of Archebald Hicks, versus SAMUEL E. BURGER and other heirs and distributees of Archebald Hicks. Petition to sell land. A guardian is appointed for Elvira B., Leroy, Eliza, and Tennessee Rose, minor children of Jane A. Rose. 1 Oct 1866. (Pp. 77-78)

FITE, SHEPHERD, & COMPANY versus W. B. NOKES. 1 Oct 1866. (Pp. 78-79)

W. J. McKNIGHT and DAVID RALSTON, Executors of Alexander McKnight, versus J. L. McKNIGHT and other heirs of said Alexander.

All of the heirs are properly before the Court as either complainants are defendants. The bill is taken for confessed.
D. N. Ralston is appointed as guardian for the minor defendants,
to wit, Mary M. Alexander; George C., Maggy, Sallie, and David
M. Ralston. Alexander McKnight died in Cannon County in 1859,
leaving a will. He directed that after the death of his wife,
Anna McKnight, all his estated was to be sold by his executors.
It appears that Anna McKnight is dead. The testator died seized
and possessed of about 400 acres of land in the 1st District.
The land is to be sold. 1 Oct 1866. (Pp. 79-80)

WARREN CUMMINGS, Administrator of F. Owen, versus R. L.
OWEN and other heirs. Fountain Owen died in Cannon County,
leaving a will. R. L. Owen and H. A. Owen were appointed as
executors. A tract of land was sold to satisfy the creditors.
1 Oct 1866. (Pp. 80-81)

ISAAC W. ELLEDGE, Executor of Robert Bailey, versus H. L.
BAILEY Et Al. The bill is taken for confessed. Robert Bailey
left a will in which he conveyed the tract of land in the pleadings to complainants and defendants. He directed that if they
would not live on the land, then it was to be sold. The land
is worth six dollars an acre. 1 Oct 1866. (P. 82)

J. R. NEELEY, Administrator of W. D. Smith, versus AMANDA J.
SMITH Et Al. Petition to sell land. 1 Oct 1866. (Pp. 82-83)

WILLIAM A. CLARK, Administrator of Thomas Scissom, versus
MARY ANN SCISSOM and others. Petition to sell land. 1 Oct
1866. (Pp. 83-84)

WILLIAM A. CLARK, Administrator of G. W. Reed, versus
JAMES J. REED Et Al. The Clerk gives his report. 1 Oct 1866.
(Pp. 84-85)

DALLAS CUMMINGS and others versus P. D. CUMMINGS and other
heirs of William Cummings. Petition to sell land and for dower.
1 Oct 1866. (Pp. 86-87)

JOHN H. SMITH, Administrator of John C. Martin, versus
SOPHIA B. MARTIN Et Al. 1 Oct 1866. (Pp. 87-88)

Jerome S. Ridley gives his bond so as to serve as Clerk &
Master. Among those going on the bond was Broomfield S. Ridley.
1 Oct 1866. (Pp. 89-91)

The Court is adjourned until next regular term. (P. 92)

Chancery Court met at the Courthouse in Woodbury on 7 Nov
1866. (P. 93)

ROBERT BAILEY versus WILLIAM CUMMINGS. Report. 7 Nov
1866. (Pp. 93-94)

CULLEN E. CURLEE, Administrator of John F. Curlee, versus
JUDITH CURLEE, the children and creditors of John F. Curlee.
The widow is the said Judith Curlee. The children are Amanda,
Theodocia, David C., Judith E., Stephen, John, and Forrest Cur-
lee. Petition to sell a tract of land owned by the said John
F. Curlee. 7 Nov 1866. (Pp. 94-96)

JANE B. SUMMERS versus IVORY SUMMERS. Divorce and alimony. Parties have compromised as to alimony. It is agreed that the land is to be a home for the children as well as the said Jane B. and her life estate. If the said Jane B. keeps bad company or permits the children to do so and does not care for her children as a prudent mother should then custody of the children by her is forfeited. 2 Nov 1866. (Pp. 96-98)

T. W. WOOD, Trustee of Carmichael & St. John versus CAR-MICHAEL & ST. JOHN and others. 2 Nov 1866. (Pp. 98-101)

All the files and papers of the office of the Chancery Court at Woodbury were destroyed or done away with in Mar 1863 by authority of the United States service. (P. 100)

JOHN H. SMITH, Administrator of John C. Martin, versus SOPHIA B. MARTIN and others. 2 Nov 1866. (Pp. 102-104)

SARA JANE WARREN versus MARY A. HAILEY and others. Sara Jane Warren, Mary A. Hailey, William B. Hailey, and James A. Hailey enter into an agreement to sell the land mentioned in the pleadings. 2 Nov 1866. (Pp. 104-105)

Warren Cummins is appointed as Deputy Clerk in the Clerk & Master's Office. 2 Nov 1866. (P. 105)

JOHN RIGSBY and H. D. NEELEY versus ELIJAH NEELEY and others. Petition for partition. 2 Nov 1866. (Pp. 106-107)

WILLIAM M. BOWEN, ELLEN BOWEN, JAMES BRADFORD and wife POLLY, MILAS SAFFORD and wife TELETHA, MARTHA E. E. BOWEN, SARAH BOWEN, JAMES R. BOWEN, the last named being minors without guardian; PEYTON LASATER and wife MARY F., ABSOLOM BOWEN, ANN ELIZABETH BOWEN, JOSEPHINE BOWEN, and SALLY BOWEN, the four last named being minors without guardian. Ex Parte. Petition to partition the land of Absolom Bowen deceased. 2 Nov 1866. (Pp. 108-109)

DANIEL S. FORD, Administrator of Henry Dennis, versus MAT-THEW DENNIS and others. Report of the Clerk. 2 Nov 1866. (Pp. 109-112)

GILES S. HARDING versus WILLIAM T. McBROOM; WILLIAM H., ELIZABETH H., JOHN W., MARY A., and GILES H. McBROOM. William T. McBroom has possession of the land described in the pleadings. He sets up no claim thereto. William Barton, one of the defendants is appointed as receiver. He is to hold the land for the benefit of the infant defendants. 2 Nov 1866. (Pp. 113-114)

A. C. MILLIGAN versus BENJAMIN CUMMINS. The demurrer is well taken. The cause should be dismissed. 2 Nov 1866. (P. 114)

MINERVA A. STONE versus HENRY D. STONE. Henry D. Stone is guilty of adultery as charged. The bonds of matrimony are dissolved. 2 Nov 1866. (P. 114)

JEREMIAH BUSH versus JANE BYNUM and others. Defendants Jane, Martha, John, Caroline, Sara, Redmond, and Mary Bynum are minors without guardian. Moses W. McKnight is appointed as guardian.

2 Nov 1866. (P. 115)

MINERVA STONE versus HENRY D. STONE. The bill is taken for confessed. A hearing is set. 2 Nov 1866. (P. 116)

JOHN A. WOOD versus THOMAS TODD. The defendant is indebted to the complainant. A sale of land is necessary to satisfy the debt. 2 Nov 1866. (P. 117)

J. M. ELROD and wife PARALEE versus WILLIAM C. LEECH Et Al. This cause is appealed to the Supreme Court. 2 Nov 1866. (P. 118)

MARY C. MEARS versus WILLIAM MEARS. The bill is taken for confessed. A hearing is set. 2 Nov 1866. (P. 118)

WILLIAM SAULS versus WILEY DAVENPORT and J. W. SUMMERS. The complainant has failed to establish the allegations in his bill. 2 Nov 1866. (P. 119)

AMANDA F. RUSHING versus W. A. RUSHING, M. R. RUSHING, and R. K. HODGES. The said Amanda F. Rushing shall have the custody of her two children, but the defendant William A. Rushing shall have the privilege at all times suitable and convenient to have access to them. The complainant shall have delivered to her immediately the buggy and horses. She is not entitled to alimony in the land or mills for the reason that although the Chancellor is satisfied that the conveyance trade by William A. Rushing to M. R. Rushing, his father, was made with intent to defraud his wife of alimony, it is fraudulent, but still there is no evidence of fraud on the part of M. R. Rushing. 2 Nov 1866. (Pp. 119-120)

A number of causes are continued. (Pp. 120-121)

MARY CARUTHERS versus (   ) and others. 2 Nov 1866. (Pp. 122-124)

ISAAC F. ELLEDGE, Administrator of Robert Bailey, versus H. L. BAILEY and others. Construction of the will of Robert Bailey. 2 Nov 1866. (P. 124)

W. J. McKNIGHT Et Al versus J. P. McKNIGHT Et Al. Construction of the will of Alexander McKnight. The shares should be equalized among the heirs, to wit, Martha E., Caroline, James M., and A. B. McKnight. 2 Nov 1866. (P. 125)

ASA TODD, Administrator of S. P. Gannon versus S. GANNON Et Al. The Clerk is to take proof to ascertain the indebtedness of the estate of S. P. Gannon and if it is necessary to sell land to pay the indebtedness. 2 Nov 1866. (P. 125)

R. W. NEELEY and others versus D. BARKER and others. Elijah Neely, W. R. Neely, B. F. Neely, and Amanda A. Neely are minors without guardian. Petition for partition and sale of land and dower. 2 Nov 1866. (P. 125)

JOHN C. SMITH, Administrator of John C. Martin, versus SOPHIA B. MARTIN Et Al. 2 Nov 1866. (P. 126)

BOGLE heirs versus ALLISON heirs. 2 Nov 1866. (P. 127)

A. OWEN and others versus HORACE OVERALL and others. W. M. Burger and wife Lockey J., John Markham and wife Nancy, Archibald Markham and wife A., and Alfred Owen, a portion of the heirs of Fountain Owen, against Allimenta Owen, the widow of said Fountain Owen and his daughter, Eliza, Richard L. Owen and his wife Mary, and Horace Overall and his wife Mary C., also heirs of Fountain Owen. The parties are willing to settle and compromise. 2 Nov 1866. (Pp. 128-130)

ELIZABETH LONG versus G. C. BARRETT, Administrator of Israel Long. The Master is to take an account and report back at next term. 2 Nov 1866. (Pp. 130-131)

SARA YOUREE versus JOSEPH YOUREE. Bill for divorce and alimony. The complainant is given time to amend her bill. 2 Nov 1866. (P. 131)

R. W. NEELEY and others versus DONELSON BARKER and others. The bill is taken for confessed as to Donelson Barker and wife Polly Jane, formerly Neeley. A. Finley is guardian for the minor heirs, to wit, Elijah Neeley, William R. Neeley, B. F. Neeley, Amanda A. Neeley. It appears to the satisfaction of the court that Elijah Neeley did on 5 Nov 1856 convey land to his children, to wit, Robert Neeley, Nathan L. Neeley, James B. Neeley, Polly J. Neeley (now Barker) in fee simple title reserving life estate to his wife. The wife of the said Elijah Neeley is dead. James B. Neeley is now dead, leaving neither wife nor children. Nathan L. Neeley is dead, leaving his wife Harriet and the petitioners. 2 Nov 1866. (Pp. 131-132)

A number of causes are continued. (Pp. 132-133)

Report of former Clerk & Master Thomas G. Wood. 2 Nov 1866. (Pp. 133-134)

A number of causes are continued. (Pp. 134-135)

J. R. NEELEY, Administrator of W. D. Smith, versus RUTHA JANE SMITH, heirs and creditors. Sale of land. 2 Nov 1866. (Pp. 136-137)

CALVIN SULLIVAN and others versus ANDREW SULLIVAN and others. The Clerk received on 12 Oct 1865 of Warren Cummins and wife Dovey in their own right and in right of Samuel C. Sullivan. Also, received of Jane Sullivan, Administratrix of James Sullivan, in right of Andrew Sullivan. 2 Nov 1866. (Pp. 138-140)

W. C. LEECH versus URIAH JENNINGS and others. The bill is taken for confessed. A sufficient amount of the interest of Uriah Jennings has been attached to pay the judgment. 2 Nov 1866. (P. 141)

Chancery Court met at the Courthouse in Woodbury on the first Monday in Apr, it being 1 Apr 1867. John P. Steele, presiding. (P. 142)

C. B. SUMMER versus S. J. ODOM. 1 Apr 1867. (P. 143)

WILLIAM A. CLARK, Administrator, versus SARAH J. REED. Clerk's report. 1 Apr 1867. (Pp. 144-145)

WILLIAM A. CLARK, Administrator of Thomas Scissom, versus MARY A. SCISSOM Et Al. 1 Apr 1867. (Pp. 145-147)

W. J. McKNIGHT and D. N. RALSTON, Executors of Alexander McKnight, versus JOHN P. McKNIGHT and others. 1 Apr 1867. (Pp. 148-149)

ISAAC W. ELLEDGE, Executor of Robert Bailey, versus H. L. BAILEY and others. 1 Apr 1867. (Pp. 150-153)

R. L. OWEN, Administrator of James S. Odom, versus JOHN J. ODOM and others. 1 Apr 1867. (Pp. 153-157)

HIRAM TODD, Administrator of Andrew Burkett, versus JEREMIAH BUSH, Guardian of Jeremiah Bush. Report. 1 Apr 1867. (Pp. 158-159)

LUCINDA MELTON and others versus WILLIAM GRIZZLE and others. Report of Master. 1 Apr 1867. (Pp. 159-161)

JAMES M. COMER, Administrator of Archebald Hicks, versus SAMUEL C. BURGER and others. Petition to sell land. 1 Apr 1867. (Pp. 161-165)

ULISSIS S. BATES and others versus H. J. ST. JOHN. Report. 1 Apr 1867. (Pp. 165-166)

DALLAS CUMMINGS, Administrator of William Cummings, versus P. D. CUMMINGS and others. Delphia Cummings, widow of William Cummings, is assigned her dower. 1 Apr 1867. (Pp. 166-168)

JANE B. SUMMERS versus IVORY SUMMERS. A decree directing the Clerk to sell the lands of Ivory Summers. 1 Apr 1867. (Pp. 169-171)

DALLAS CUMMINGS versus P. D. CUMMINGS Et Al. Petition to sell land. 1 Apr 1867. (Pp. 173-174)

HENRY DAUGHERTY, Administrator of T. M. Allison, and SARAH M. ALLISON versus SPY ANDERSON and other heirs and creditors of T. M. Allison. Sarah M. Allison, widow of T. M. Allison, is assigned her dower. 1 Apr 1867. (P. 175)

SARAH ANN WARREN versus MARY A. HAILEY. Title to a tract of land is divested out of the heirs of James Warren and vested in Mary A. Hailey. 1 Apr 1867. (P. 176)

JOHN F. WEEDON, Administrator of G. W. Thompson, versus HEIRS and CREDITORS. 1 Apr 1867. (Pp. 177-178)

A number of causes are continued. (Pp. 178-179)

DANIEL S. FORD, Administrator of Henry Dennis, versus MATTHEW DENNIS Et Al. Sale of a tract of land. 1 Apr 1867. (Pp. 179-183)

A. G. MILLIKEN versus S. H. WOOD and others. The bill is taken for confessed. Complainants on 27 Oct 1859 sold by deed to defendant S. H. Wood a tract of land in the 12th District. The land is to be sold to satisfy a judgment. 1 Apr 1867. (Pp. 183-185)

H. OSBORN and wife NAOMI versus JOHN P. GANNON and others. Complainant Naomi P. Osborn is the widow of John A. Travis. She has since the death of the said John A. intermarried with the said H. Osborn. Said Travis departed this life in Cannon County seized and possessed of land in the 1st District. It is bounded on the south by land belonging to the estate of Samuel Travis. The said Naomi P. has never had her dower. She is entitled to the same. The administrator and all of the children of the said Naomi P. are before the Court. Said Naomi P. is assigned her dower. 3 Apr 1867. (P. 185)

ROBERT BAILEY versus WILLIAM CUMMINGS. 3 Apr 1867. (Pp. 186-187)

JEREMIAH BUSH versus JANE BYNUM Et Al. The bill is taken for confessed. 3 Apr 1867. (Pp. 188-190)

JOSEPH SOLOMON versus C. C. HANCOCK and JASPER RUYLE. Defendants to pay the cost. 3 Apr 1867. (Pp. 190-191)

SARAH E. CARNAHAN versus JESSE GILLEY Et Al. Preston Carnahan purchased the lands mentioned in the pleadings in 1859 of defendant Jesse Gilley. He built a valuable house upon the same and made other lasting improvements. He paid the taxes and exercixed other acts of ownership over the property, but had no deed or other written assurance of ownership over the property. Gilley, himself, frequently recognized said Carnahan as owner by refusing to pay the taxes. Carnahan paid the taxes in 1863. Shortly thereafter, Defendant Gilley did dispossess the complainant and her children from the land and took possession of the same except about one acre. Said Sarah E. is the wife of Preston Carnahan deceased and daughter of John McCreasy. The defendants are her children. The Court decrees that the land belonged to the complainant and her children. It was given to her for life, remainder to her children by the deed and will of John McCreasy. 3 Apr 1867. (Pp. 191-192)

MARGARET TODD versus WALTER TODD. Divorce. The bill is taken for confessed. A hearing is set. 3 Apr 1867. (P. 193)

MARGARET TODD versus WALTER TODD. The parties intermarried for two years since. They separated six months since. The defendant has been guilty of adultery as charged, and for this reason the bonds of matrimony are dissolved. 3 Apr 1867. (Pp. 193-194)

A number of causes are continued. (Pp. 194-195)

MARY C. MEARS versus WILLIAM MEARS. Divorce. Defendant has abandoned the compliant who is a woman of good character. The defendant has refused to maintain her and her two children without lawful cause. He has committed adultery on divers times before the instituing of this suit. The bonds of matrimony are dissolved. Complainant is given custody of the two children, to wit, John, about three; and the infant not yet named. 3 Apr 1867. (P. 195)

C. E. CURLEE, Administrator of J. F. Curlee, versus HEIRS and CREDITORS. 3 Apr 1867. (Pp. 196-200)

JOHN F. WEEDON, Administrator of George W. Thompson, versus THE HEIRS and CREDITORS. 4 Apr 1867. (P. 200)

ELLEN BOWER Et Al. Ex Parte. 4 Apr 1867. (Pp. 201-204)

ASA TODD, Administrator of S. P. Gannon, versus JEREMIAH GARRISON and others. The Chancellor is pleased to recommend that the Master be permitted to hear proof touching the matter as to whether complainant by due dilligence could have collected the outstanding debts. 4 Apr 1867. (P. 204)

SARAH YOUREE versus JOSEPH YOUREE. Parties have heretofore been lawfully married. They are hereby divorced from bed and board until the further order of this court. Complainant is restored to the entire and exclusive possession of her dower interest and occupation of the 133 acres where she now lives. Defendant shall remove from the place and shall not molest complainant in the use or enjoyment of the same. Complainant shall retain possession and custody of her daughters Julia Ann, about five, and Eliza Isabel, three, until the further order of the court. 4 Apr 1867. (Pp. 205-206)

JAMES B. THOMAS and others versus ANTHONY OWEN and others. Consolidated by order. 4 Apr 1867. (Pp. 206-207)

BETTY SANFORD, a minor by her guardian William Whorton, versus JOHN F. WEEDON, Administrator of G. W. Thompson, and others. 4 Apr 1867. (Pp. 208-210)

JAMES B. THOMAS and others versus ANTHONY OWEN. 4 Apr 1867. (P. 211)

ALEXANDER MILLIGAN Et Al versus JAMES J. BOGLE and wife JANE. Petition for sale of land. It would be advantageous for the land to be sold rather than partitioned. James Milligan died seized and possessed of the lands mentioned in the petition. The names of the heirs are correctly stated. The widow of James Milligan has had her dower assigned to her. Notice has been given in the UNION & DISPATCH, a Nashville newspaper. James J. Bogle and his wife Jane have failed to answer. The bill is taken as confessed against them. The minor defendants are represented by their guardian except Laura Ann (Murfy) which is represented by her guardian Broomfield L. Ridley. 4 Apr 1867. (Pp. 212-214)

JOHN P. HIGGINS Et Al versus SUSAN HIGGINS Et Al. Petition to sell land. Defendant Susan Higgins is the widow of James Higgins. The administrator has failed to answer. The bill is taken for confessed. James Higgins departed this life intestate in Cannon County in 1859 seized and possessed of the lands mentioned in the pleadings. The name of the heirs are correctly set forth. 4 Apr 1867. (Pp. 214-215)

WILLIAM L. BATES Et Al. Ex Parte. Petition for sale of land. 4 Apr 1867. (Pp. 216-217)

CARMICHAEL & ST. JOHN versus CARMICHAEL & ST. JOHN. 4 Apr 1867. The receiver gives his report to the court. 4 Apr 1867. (Pp. 218-219)

JASPER L. KIMBRO versus ABEL RUSHING. This cause is dismissed. 4 Apr 1867. (P. 219)

A. OWEN Et Al versus HORACE OVERALL Et Al. 4 Apr 1867. (Pp. 220-234)

R. L. OWEN, Administrator of James S. ODOM, versus JOHN J. ODOM, and others. 4 Apr 1867. (Pp. 235-239)

A number of causes are continued. (Pp. 235-239)

Resolution of the Bar at Woodbury. Complimentary to Chancellor John P. Steele. 4 Apr 1867. (Pp. 240-241)

Chancery Court met in the town of Woodbury at the Courthouse on the third Monday in Aug 1867, it being the nineteenth day of the said month. Barclay M. Tillman, presiding. (P. 242)

WILLIAM CUMMINGS' heirs versus WILLIAM STONE. 19 Aug 1867. (Pp. 242-243)

JEMIMA (GRIMES) versus JOHN W. ORAND Et Al. Complainant is a daughter of Britton Grimes and granddaughter of William Grimes. Complainant and her sister, since dead, were born at the date of the execution of the deed from William Grimes to the heirs of Britton Grimes. William Grimes was solvent at the time and Britton Grimes insolvent. Said deed of gift was made and complainant was only 22 years old, the date of commencement of this suit. 20 Aug 1867. (P. 244)

JOHN D. RIGSBY versus IRA HOLLINSWORTH. 20 Aug 1867. (Pp. 244-245)

JEREMIAH BUSH versus JANE BYNUM Et Al. 20 Aug 1867. (Pp. 245-247)

JOHN E. TURNER, Administrator, versus JOHN W. SHIRLEY and wife MARGARET E. William H. Turner, the father of John G., James B., and Melissa Turner, who are minors on 24 May 1862 purchased of defendants a tract of land belonging to the heirs of Joseph Bailey. Said Margaret E. Turner is one of the heirs of one John N. Bailey who was a son and heir of the said Joseph Bailey. Title to a tract of land belonging to the grandfather of the said Margaret E. is divested out of her and vested in the children of William H. Turner. At the time of executing the deed, the said Margaret E. was a minor under 21 years of age. The consideration received from the said William H. was unlawful because it was Confederate money and a mare which at the time was unsound. Therefore, the deed was void. 20 Aug 1867. (Pp. 249-250)

OSLIN ALEXANDER versus MARIA ALEXANDER. The parties were married as stated. The allegations in this bill are not denied. The defendant deserted the premises of complainant and has not returned for more than two years. The bonds of matrimony are dissolved. 20 Aug 1867. (P. 250)

A. G. MILLIKEN versus S. H. WOOD. Sale of a tract of land. 20 Aug 1867. (Pp. 251-252)

C. E. CURLEE, Administrator of I. F. CURLEE, versus HEIRS and CREDITORS. Judith Curlee has received of the property of her husband two mules. 22 Aug 1867. (P. 253)

HENRY OSBORN and wife NAOMI versus JOHN P. GANNON, Administrator of John A. Travis. Naomi Osborn is given her dower out of the estate of John A. Travis. 22 Aug 1867. (P. 254)

A. R. HAMMER, Administrator of Henry Trott, versus T. J. JELTON and others. Petition to sell land. 22 Aug 1867. (P. 255)

S. C. HAMILTON, Administrator of E. A. Kennedy, versus SAMUEL KENNEDY and others. Sale of a tract of land. 22 Aug 1867. (P. 256)

ALEXANDER MILLIGAN Et Al versus JAMES BOGLE and wife and others. Sale of a tract of land. 22 Aug 1867. (Pp. 257-259)

BETTY V. SANFORD by her guardian versus JOHN F. WEEDON, Administrator of George W. Thompson. Harriet C. Neely, Lavisa Summers, Polema S. Summers, Albert C. Summers, Annica C. Summers, Josephine E. Summers, and George Summers, being children of Mary Summers deceased who was a sister of George W. Thompson; John W. Harris, Thomas N. Harris, and Francis Harris, children of Sarah E. Harris who was a sister of George W. Thompson; Mary E. Graham, child of Louisa A. Graham deceased, sister of George W. Thompson; Lafayette Thompson, John W. Thompson, James M. Thompson, Mariah Goforth and husband, George N. Thompson, Louisa Thompson, and Eliza Thompson, children of Pinkney Thompson deceased who was a brother of George W. Thompson; Nancy A. Swink; Frank Thompson and ___ Thompson, a child of Albert G. Thompson who was a brother of George W. Thompson; also Richard Walker, S. C. Slaughter, Elisha Davenport versus HARRIET C. NEWBY and others. 22 Aug 1867. (Pp. 260-262)

LEONARD ADCOCK and wife, SARAH K., and others versus SARAH B. WOOD by her guardian. Defendants Margaret J., Anna E., James B., and Caroline F. Alexander are minors without guardian. John C. Alexander is appointed as guardian. Defendant Sarah B. Wood is also a minor. John K. Rigsby is her guardian. 23 Aug 1867. (Pp. 262-264)

BOGLE heirs versus ALLISON heirs. 23 Aug 1867. (Pp. 265-266)

ALFRED ROBINSON and wife and A. C. THOMAS versus WILLIAM C. LEECH and others. Henry Thomas departed this life in ___. Complainants were a portion of his heirs. The Clerk is to take an account and report to the Court. 23 Aug 1867. (Pp. 266-267)

MARY J. TARPLEY versus J. M. TARPLEY. The bill is taken for confessed. A hearing is set. 23 Aug 1867. (P. 268)

A number of causes are continued. (Pp. 268-269)

R. F. BELL versus JAMES ALLEN. The defendant has absconded to parts unknown. The bill is taken for confessed. 23 Aug 1867.

(Pp. 269-270)

MARY JANE TARPLEY versus JAMES M. TARPLEY. Divorce bill. This cause is continued. 24 Aug 1867. (P. 271)

JOHN P. HIGGINS Et Al versus SUSAN HIGGINS Et Al. Sale of land. 24 Aug 1867. (Pp. 272-276)

JOHN H. SMITH versus A. L. SMITH. The bill is taken for confessed. 24 Aug 1867. (Pp. 276-277)

WARD BARRETT, Administrator of Allen Morgan, versus T. H. BARRETT and wife and others. Defendants Matilda Jane, James A., Robert A., and Rebecca C. Morgan as also Lydia Jane Hayes, Minerva Emaline Hayes are all minors without guardian. Broomfield L. Ridley is appointed as guardian. Defendants F. M. Barrett and wife Mary Ann, David Vance and wife Lydia Elizabeth, William Tenpenny and wife Caroline, John Campbell and wife Josa Emaline, and Serina Morgan not appearing to answer, the bill is taken for confessed. The Clerk is to take a report as to the amount of the indebtedness. 24 Aug 1867. (P. 277)

WARD BARRETT, Administrator, versus MORGAN heirs. 24 Aug 1867. (P. 278)

JOHN F. WEEDON, Administrator of George W. Thompson, versus HEIRS and CREDITORS. 24 Aug 1867. (Pp. 279-280)

JANE B. SUMMERS versus IVORY SUMMERS. Report. 24 Aug 1867. (P. 281)

J. R. NEELEY, Administrator of W. D. Smith, versus AMANDA J. SMITH Et Al. 24 Aug 1867. (Pp. 282-284)

CAROLINE PELHAM, Administratrix of William Pelham versus LEVI PELHAM and others. William Pelham died in Cannon County in 1862, intestate. Complainant Caroline Pelham was appointed as the administratrix. The decedent died leaving no children, but left the said Caroline as his widow who is entitled to a dower out of the lands. 24 Aug 1867. (Pp. 285-286)

JAMES M. COMER, Administrator, versus J. N. YORK Et Al. It is necessary to sell the land to pay the indebtedness. 24 Aug 1867. (Pp. 286-288)

ISAAC W. ELLEDGE, Executor of Robert Bailey, Sr., versus H. L. BAILEY Et Al. All of the debts of the estate have been paid. Robert Bailey, Jr. has purchased the entire interest of his mother Martha E.; William J. John G., and Mary A., now the wife of R. Warren, in the entire estate of Robert Bailey, Sr. 24 Aug 1867. (Pp. 289-290)

LUCY HUNTER versus LYDIA (NUNLEY) Et Al. Eli Turner became the purchaser and executed his note for a tract of land, but since then has departed this life leaving one half of the purchase money unpaid. He left no children, brothers or sisters, and no heirs except his widow. No administrator has been appointed for the estate. 24 Aug 1867. (P. 291)

HORACE OVERALL Et Al versus ALFRED OWEN Et Al. 24 Aug 1867. (P. 292)

Chancery Court was held at the Courthouse in the town of Woodbury, Cannon County, on the third Monday of Feb 1868, it being the seventeenth day of the month. Barclay M. Tillman, presiding. (P. 293)

Barclay Martin was sworn in as a practicing attorney. 17 Feb 1868. (P. 293)

JANE B. SUMMERS versus IVORY SUMMERS. Jane B. Summers and W. G. Summers are indebted to the Estate of John and Ivory Summers. 17 Feb 1868. (Pp. 294-295)

ALEXANDER MILLIGAN, JOHN MILLIGAN, A. P. MULLINAX and wife ELIZA, and JAMES HOLLINSWORTH versus JAMES J. BOGLE and wife JANE, IRA HOLLINSWORTH, WILLIAM HOLLINSWORTH, DILLARD HOLLINS-WORTH, ELIZABETH HOLLINSWORTH, SUSAN HOLLINSWORTH, and LAURA ANN MURPHY. The tract of 168 acres belonging to the Estate of James Milligan failed to sell. It was sold to John Milligan at a later sale. Title to the land was divested out of the heirs of James Milligan and vested in John Milligan. 17 Feb 1868. (Pp. 296-297)

J. R. NEELY, Administrator of W. D. Smith, versus AMANDA JOSEPHINE SMITH and W. D. SMITH, Guardian for Rutha J. Smith. Final Decree. 17 Feb 1868. (Pp. 298-300)

CAROLINE PELHAM, Administratrix of William Pelham, versus LEVI PELHAM and others. Caroline Pelham was the purchaser of the tract of land ordered sold. 17 Feb 1868. (Pp. 300-301)

WARD BARRETT, Administrator of Allen Morgan, versus W. M. BARRETT and wife and other heirs of Allen Morgan. Thomas Campbell was the purchaser of the tract of land ordered sold. The land excludes the widow's dower. 17 Feb 1868. (Pp. 301-302)

LEONARD ADCOCK Et Al versus SARAH B. WOOD Et Al. Sale of a tract of land. 17 Feb 1868. (Pp. 303-304)

C. B. SUMMERS, Administrator of Anthony Summer, versus S. J. ODOM. Decree. Sale of a tract of land. 17 Feb 1868. (P. 305)

W. A. CLARK, Administrator, versus M. A. SCISSOM. Petition to sell land. 18 Feb 1868. (Pp. 306-307)

S. C. HAMILTON, Administrator of E. A. Kennedy, versus SAMUEL KENNEDY Et Al. (Pp. 307-308)

W. L. ODOM, Administrator of J. L. Odom, versus WILLIAM F. ODOM. The Special Commissioner directed the widow to pay over to Henry Daugherty the amount due. 18 Feb 1868. (P. 308)

W. J. McKNIGHT and D. M. RALSTON, Executors of Alexander McKnight, versus JOHN P. McKNIGHT Et Al. 18 Feb 1868. (P. 309)

JAMES M. COMER, Administrator of William York, versus J. N. YORK. Sale of a tract of land. 18 Feb 1868. (Pp. 310-311)

E. A. (LEACH) versus E. A. ALEXANDER and others. All the heirs of Abner Alexander were made defendants to this cause. 18 Feb 1868. (P. 312)

HENRY DENNIS' Administrator versus MATTHEW DENNIS and others. The Clerk is to pay the debts and distribute the residue to the heirs. 18 Feb 1868. (Pp. 313-316)

C. E. CURLEE, Administrator, versus WIDOW CURLEE'S heirs. P. B. Curlee was the purchaser of one tract of land. 18 Feb 1868. (Pp. 316-319)

BOGLE heirs versus ALLISON heirs. 18 Feb 1868. (Pp. 319-321)

JOHN H. SMITH, Administrator of John C. Martin, versus SOPHIA B. MARTIN and others. 18 Feb 1868. (Pp. 321-323)

J. W. McADOO versus J. H. SMITH and others. 18 Feb 1868. (P. 324)

HENRY DENNIS' Administrator versus MATTHEW DENNIS Et Al. 18 Feb 1868. (P. 325)

MARY J. TARPLEY versus JAMES M. TARPLEY. The defendant could not be found. The bill is taken for confessed. A hearing is set. 20 Feb 1868. (P. 326)

WILLIAM PHILLIPS versus NANCY ANN PHILLIPS. The bill is taken for confessed. A hearing is set. 20 Feb 1868. (P. 326)

C. B. SUMMERS versus ZACHARIAH SMITH'S heirs. Zachariah Smith died seized and possessed of one half of a tract of land. He was the husband of Complainant Susan C. Smith who now occupies the land. The complainant is entitled to her dower. 20 Feb 1868. (Pp. 327-329)

MARTHA CUMMINS versus WARREN CUMMINS, JR. Complainant and defendant were intermarried in Jan 1862. One child, a daughter, Della Jane, has been the offspring of said marriage. She is now some four or five years old. The character of the complainant is good. Defendant without cause abandoned and deserted the complainant and refused to cohabit with her or recognize her as a wife. He has refused and neglected to furnish her and her child with a house or to maintain them. The bonds of matrimony are dissolved. 20 Feb 1868. (Pp. 329-330)

JAMES M. ROBERTS versus JOHN W. SUMMERS, WILLIAM BARTON, D. M. JARRETT, J. D. FRANCIS, and N. W. SUMMERS, Administrator of E. Francis. Sale of a tract of land. 20 Feb 1868. (Pp. 330-331)

WILLIAM PHILLIPS versus NANCY ANN PHILLIPS. Defendant has been guilty of adultery with Alex Moore as charged in the bill. The bonds of matrimony are dissolved. 20 Feb 1868. (Pp. 332-333)

J. B. THOMPSON and wife versus HENRY DAUGHERTY and others. 20 Feb 1868. (Pp. 334-335)

ALSA JONES versus ALFORD OWEN and others. The demurrer is well taken. 20 Feb 1868. (P. 335)

ASA TODD, Administrator, versus SUSANNAH GANNON and others. Master's report is confirmed. 20 Feb 1868. (Pp. 335-336)

JAMES B. THOMAS and others versus ANTHONY OWEN and others. 21 Feb 1868. (Pp. 336-340)

R. F. BELL versus JAMES ALLEN. The bill is taken for confessed. 21 Feb 1868. (P. 341)

ALLISON heirs versus BOGLE heirs. 21 Feb 1868. (P. 342)

ELIZA ENOS versus CHARLOTTE BARRETT Et Al. Defendant has leave to answer complainant. 21 Feb 1868. (Pp. 342-343)

ABEL RUSHING versus TRUSTEES OF LAWRENCE ACADEMY. It appears that the complainant has built the house according to the contract with said trustees which was satisfactory to them. The lot on which the Academy was built is within the corporate limits of Woodbury. The trustees took possession of the lot in 1843 or 1844. The Court rules that the house and lot are liable for the debts of the trustees. 21 Feb 1868. (Pp. 343-344)

A number of causes are continued. (Pp. 344-346)

WILLIAM L. BATES and others versus A. BURGER and others. Affidavit. 21 Feb 1868. (Pp. 346-348)

R. L. ODOM, Administrator, versus JOHN J. ODOM Et Al. Report of Special Commissioner. 21 Feb 1868. (Pp. 348-352)

MARY J. TARPLEY versus JAMES M. TARPLEY. The defendant has wilfully abandoned the complainant and refused to provide for her. The bonds of matrimony are dissolved. 21 Feb 1868. (P. 353)

C. B. SUMMERS, Administrator of Anthony Summers, versus L. SMITH Et Al. 22 Feb 1868. (P. 354)

SUSAN A. McFERRIN versus A. F. McFERRIN Et Al. Complainant intermarried with the defendant in 1854. At the time of their marriage, defendant had no means except a horse, saddle, and bridle. The complainant had in the hands of her guardian (she being a minor) $2000 from the estate of her father and grandfather. The tract of Solomon Spear's and the tract of William McGill's were bought and paid for out of the money of the complainant. The land is to be under the control of the complainant free from the control of her husband. 21 Feb 1868. (P. 355)

A. OWEN Et Al versus HORACE OVERALL Et Al. The personal assets of Fountain Owen are insufficient to pay the debts. Land is to be sold to satisfy the indebtedness. 22 Feb 1868. (P. 356)

CLEM R. WATERS and wife versus WILLIAM BARTON, Executor of Joshua Barton. 22 Feb 1868. (Pp. 357-360)

Chancery Court met at the Courthouse in the town of Woodbury on the third Monday in Aug 1868, it being the seventeenth day of the month. Barclay M. Tillman, presiding. (P. 361)

JAMES M. COMER, Administrator of Archibald Hicks, versus SAMUEL BURGER and others. Petition to sell land for distribution. 17 Aug 1868. (Pp. 361-362)

ELIZABETH LONG and others versus G. C. BARRETT and others.
The Clerk is to take proof as to the reasonable compensation
for the defendant as Administrator of Israel Long. 17 Aug 1868.
(P. 363)

LEONARD ADCOCK and wife SARAH B., and others versus SARAH
B. WOOD and others. Sale of a tract of land. 17 Aug 1868.
Title to a tract of land is divested out of the heirs and dis-
tributees of William Wood, to wit, John B. Wood, James H. Wood,
Thomas J. Wood, William W. Wood, Leonard Adcock and wife Sarah B.,
A. B. Womack and wife Elizabeth G., David Grizzle and wife
Margaret J., Nancy Ann Elledge, Sarah B. Wood, Margaret J.
Alexander, Anna E. Alexander, James B. Alexander, and Caroline
L. Alexander. 17 Aug 1868. (Pp. 364-368)

A number of causes are continued. (Pp. 368-369)

C. B. SUMMERS, Administration of Anthony Summers, and others
versus ANNA LANSDEN, JOHN E. FLANAGAN and wife LEONA, and others.
Sale of a tract of land subject to the dower of Susan C. Smith.
Title to a tract of land is divested out of the heirs and distributees of Anthony Summers, to wit, C. B. Summers, J. W.
Williams and wife Martha, Thomas Stanley and wife Jane, E. B.
Summers, A. B. Summers, Andrew See and wife Nancy, S. L. Summers, D. W. Summers, Eliza Jane Bogle, John E. Flanegan and wife
Leona, George Bogle, F. Young and wife Teresy, Nancy Summers,
Jefferson Summers and the children and heirs of Elijah Summers
and Lurana Summers deceased whose names are unknown. Also, the
interest of Anna Lansden and Susan C. Smith. 17 Aug 1868. (Pp.
369-371)

ELIZA ENOS versus CHARLOTTE BARRETT and others. Henry Enos,
father of complainant has been gone from the country and un-
heard of for upwards of twenty years. They suppose him to be
dead. Complainant is the only child and heir at law of said
Henry Enos. She is now twenty-three years of age. Said Henry
Enos was the owner of all the land set forth in the pleadings.
Defendant now has the land set forth in their possession. It
appears to the court that complainant is entitled to the said
land. There is no relation of the land to the Estate of William
Barton deceased. 17 Aug 1868. (Pp. 371-373)

PETER MAXEY versus WILLIAM M. KEY and others. Articles of
Agreement between John Tenpenny and Peter Maxey. Parties are
in possession of a tract of land. John Tenpenny is satisfied
that his title to a tract of land is no good. He transfers his
interest to Peter Maxey. He had been claiming title from
Granville Young. 19 Aug 1868. (Pp. 373-375)

JAMES KING, Administrator of William B. Kelly, and TOM KING
in his own right versus BETHEL A. KELLY and others. Defendants
Bethel A. Kelly, Samuel T. Kelly, Alaminta J. Kelly, Mary P.
Kelly, William R. Kelly, and Lydia A. Kelly are all minors without guardian. William Kelly died seized and possessed of a
tract of land. The Clerk is to determine whether the widow has
had her dower assigned to her. He is to determine the amount for
the children. 19 Aug 1868. (P. 376)

A number of causes are continued. (P. 377)

ABEL RUSHING versus TRUSTEES OF LAWRENCE ACADEMY. Clerk was ordered to sell the Lawrence Academy and lot in Woodbury. It was sold to A. F. Todd. 19 Aug 1868. (Pp. 378-379)

JAMES KING, Administrator, Et Al versus BETHEL KELLY Et Al. William B. Kelly died seized of one half of the land set forth in the pleadings. It is a joint deed to the decedent and William King. Morning Kelly by deed executed to her by William B. Kelly and William King on 11 Mar 1850 is entitled for life to the house and yard where she now lives with privilege of having access to the spring. Complainant Lucinda Kelly is the widow of William B. Kelly. She has not been endowed of his lands. Defendants are the only children and heirs of the said decedent. Owing to the number of heirs, it will be necessary to sell the land. 19 Aug 1868. (Pp. 379-380)

C. B. SUMMERS, Administrator of A. Summers, and others versus CHESTER F. BETHEL and others. 19 Aug 1868. (Pp. 381-383)

L. W. MILES versus ULYSSES BATES and others. Decree. 19 Aug 1868. (Pp. 383-384)

STEPHEN ROBINSON versus URIAH JENNINGS and others. Consolidated cases. Attachment. 19 Aug 1868. (Pp. 385-387)

ELIZABETH SPARKS versus WILLIAM R. SPARKS. The bill is taken for confessed. Defendant is an able bodied man who has abandoned his wife and child and refuses to labor and supply his family with the comforts and necessities of life. He is indolent and trifling and will not even work to gain sustenance for his wife and child. He has turned them out of doors without home, food, or rainment. The bonds of matrimony are dissolved. Complainant is to have custody of the child. 19 Aug 1868. (P. 388)

P. D. CUMMINGS versus WARREN CUMMINGS. The death of P. D. Cummings is suggested. The suit is revived in the name of H. J. St. John who is the administrator of said Cummings. 19 Aug 1868. (P. 389)

JAMES B. THOMAS and others versus ANTHONY OWEN. Report. Sale of a tract of land. 19 Aug 1868. (Pp. 389-393)

JOHN P. HIGGINS and others versus SUSAN HIGGINS and others. John P. Higgins is the purchaser of a tract of land. He is one of the heirs of James Higgins. He is desirous to have the interest coming to him out of the proceeds coming on the use of the land mentioned. 19 Aug 1868. (P. 393)

OWEN heirs versus OWEN heirs. 19 Aug 1868. (Pp. 390-391)

MINOR HEIRS OF A. G. ODOM versus P. C. TALLEY and others. Account of the funds for the benefit of R. L. Odom, M. M. Odom, J. H. Odom, and John S. Odom, minor heirs of A. G. Odom. 21 Aug 1868. (Pp. 395-397)

A number of causes are continued. (P. 397)

ALEXANDER MILLIGAN and others versus JANE BOGLE and others.

John Milligan, the purchaser of land mentioned in the pleadings and one of the heirs of James Milligan deceased, is desirous to have the notes executed by him and securities for the payment of the purchase money credited with the amount of interest that he has in said notes as one of the heirs of said deceased. Alexander Milligan, one of the heirs of said deceased, appeared in open court and stated that he had agreed with John Milligan to let him have his interest in the notes. 21 Aug 1868. (P. 398)

A. G. ADAMS versus J. F. WEEDON. Motion to file amended bill making J. L. Fare and Elizabeth A. Weedon as defendants. 21 Aug 1868. (P. 399)

WILLIAM L. BATES and others versus A. BURGER and others. The Clerk is to ascertain the charges against the complainants as the heirs of William Bates deceased. 21 Aug 1868. (Pp. 399-400)

MINOR HEIRS OF ARMSTEAD ODOM versus R. L. ODOM, Administrator of J. S. Odom, and others. James S. Odom was appointed as guardian of complainants John S., Matthew, Rufus, and James H. Odom, children of Armstead Odom deceased. He executed a bond with Robert Bryson and ___ Ramsey which person is dead and not sued in suit as his security. 21 Aug 1868. (Pp. 401-402)

WILLIAM L. BATES Et Al versus A. BURGER Et Al. Process has been served on Eliza Smith and Arthur W. Smith, heirs of complainant Elizabeth Smith whose death has heretofore been suggested. It appears to the court that Ann Eliza and Arthur W. Smith are minors without guardian. Complainant Nancy Ann Bates has intermarried with John Shockley. The said John is desirous of becoming a party to the suit. 21 Aug 1868. (Pp. 402-403)

MOORE & ASHLEY versus BERRY BUSH and JOSEPHUS FINLEY as Clerk and Commissioner. Defendant Berry Bush is indebted to the complainants Moore and Ashley by note. Defendant Josephus Finley, Clerk of the County Court, has funds in his hands belonging to said Berry Bush, it being his distributive share of a tract of land sold by said Clerk that belonged to Lucinda Bush, now deceased, who was the mother of said Berry Bush which was sold for distribution among the heirs. 21 Aug 1868. (P. 403)

GILES S. HARDING versus JOHN D. McBROOM, Administrator of William L. McBroom; Robert Carter and wife Elizabeth H., William H. McBroom, John W. McBroom, Mary A. McBroom, and Giles H. McBroom. Thomas M. Harding by his will, executed in 1857, bequeathed a portion of his estate to his sister, Amy McBroom, with directions to complainant who was named as trustee to secure the same to the children of said Amy, to wit, defendants Elizabeth H. Carter, William H. McBroom, John W. McBroom, Mary A. McBroom, and Giles H. McBroom. The said Amy died on 8 Oct 1858 purchase of William Barton the tract of land mentioned in the pleadings. Said Barton was trustee of Mrs. Sarah A. McBroom and her children. That is, he executed two notes. William T. McBroom, the husband of Sarah Amy agreed verbally to pay the deficit, but died without doing so, leaving the same unpaid. The Court rules that the transaction was a valid purchase. The money due Barton is a lien. Land is to be sold to satisfy the debt. 22 Aug 1868. (Pp. 404-405)

JOSEPH BOGLE versus C. H. HAMMONS and others. It appears to the court that complainant made and executed a deed to defendants Elisha R. Hammons and Larkin W. Hammons on 8 Dec 1862. Said Elisha R. and Larkin W. Hammons were small boys and minors at the date of the deed. Defendant C. H. Hammons is the father of Elisha R. Hammons and Larkin W. Hammons. The trade of the land was effected by fraudulent means of defendant Hammons. By undue force of fear and by threats of military officers made by Defendant Hammons against complainant in case he refused to receive the Confederate money which was the consideration paid for the land, thereby through force of fear caused complainant to receive said Confederate money against his will. The allegations of the complainant's bill are well founded. The deed of bargain is declared null and void. 22 Aug 1868. (Pp. 405-406)

JAMES ALLEN versus L. D. STAR. Defendant is indebted to complainant by a promissory note dated 5 Nov 1862. Defendant is the owner as tenant in common of an undivided interest or distributive share as heir in a tract of land in Cannon County which has been levied on by an attachment. 22 Aug 1868. (Pp. 407-408)

L. M. KEEL and others versus NANCY E. KEEL. The demurrer of the defendant is not well taken. The bill is dismissed. 22 Aug 1868. (P. 409)

HENRY A. WILEY versus WILLIAM L. COVINGTON and wife FRANCES ANN. The tract of land known as the Vance tract cannot be partitioned advantageously. It is ordered to be sold. William L. Covington was paid the amount agreed to as the value of his life estate. 22 Aug 1868. (Pp. 410-411)

W. R. BOGLE and others versus WOMACK and others. 22 Aug 1868. The sale of the land by Bogle to T. A. Womack in May of 1861 was a bona fide transaction. The said T. A. Womack is dead and A. S. McKnight is insolvent. Land is ordered to be sold. (Pp. 411-413)

JAMES J. PRATER Et Al versus BRINKLEY LASATER and others. An injunction is issued. 22 Aug 1868. (P. 414)

JAMES H. WOOD versus E. W. and MATILDA VAUGHAN. Defendants are indebted to the complainant. It is the opinion of the court that the charge of fraud against complainant are negative. 22 Aug 1868. (Pp. 415-416)

JESSE JERNIGAN versus J. W. JERNIGAN, Administrator of Levi Todd; L. D. Todd and wife Melvina, C. W. Todd, Elizabeth Todd, Jane Todd, and James H. Todd. Levi Todd in his lifetime on 26 Jan 1860 purchased a tract of land of J. W. Jernigan. A debt is owed. Title to the land is transferred from the heirs of Levi Todd to Jesse Jernigan. 22 Aug 1868. (Pp. 417-418)

DALLAS CUMMINS versus P. B. CUMMINS. 22 Aug 1868. (P. 418)

JEMIMA GRIMES versus JOHN W. ORAND and others. Elizabeth
J. Davis; Nancy Ann, William H., and Susan Grimes; Britter
Grimes; Idle and wife Mary; Grief, Jane, William Franklin,
and Rachael, children of John Grimes deceased who was a son
of said William Grimes; William Redman and wife Nancy; Tempe
Grimes; William Grimes; Henry Hays, Susan Hays; James Cole-
man and wife Elizabeth; James Bright and wife Sarah; Fanny
Grimes; Jemima Morgan; and J. Brogan against T. B. Smith and
T. B. Brevard, A. C. Taten, and Stanford Smith, defendants.
In 1845, William Grimes, the paternal grandfather of complai-
nant Jemima made his deed of gift to the heirs of his son,
Britton Grimes, of a tract of land in the 6th District of Cannon
County. At the date of the execution of the deed that Britton
Grimes, had but one child, the complainant Jemima, and one other
son who was soon thereafter born alive and died after a short
life time. The said Britton had born to him afterwards the
following other children, to wit, the defendant Elizabeth J.
David, Mary, Nancy Ann, William H., and Susan Grimes who are
minors. In 1846, William Grimes and Britton Grimes joined in a
deed of the same land to T. B. Smith with notice to him of the
previous conveyance to complainant. The said Jemima is entitled
to recover in this suit half of the 52 acres conveyed by her
grandfather, William Grimes, and an equal share with her other
brothers and sisters of the other half which belonged to the
deceased brother. The other brothers and sisters each, Elizabeth J. Davis, Mary, Nancy Ann, William H., and Susan Grimes
are entitled to one seventh of one half. 22 Aug 1868. (Pp.
419-421)

A number of causes are continued. (Pp. 421-424)

HENRY DAUGHERTY, Administrator of T. M. Allison, Et Al versus THE HEIRS and CREDITORS. 22 Aug 1868. (Pp. 424-429)

The resignation of J. S. Ridley as Clerk & Master was this
day tendered in open court. Alexander F. McFerrin was appointed
as the new Clerk. He then took the oath of office. 22 Aug 1868.
(Pp. 429-431)

JAMES M. COMER, Administrator of Archibald Hicks, versus
S. W. BURGER Et Al. 22 Aug 1868. (Pp. 432-433)

ALEXANDER MILLIGAN and others versus BOGLE and others. It
appears to the Court that the note executed by John Milligan and
securities is past due. 22 Aug 1868. (Pp. 433-434)

R. L. OWEN, Administrator of James Odom, versus THE HEIRS
and CREDITORS. 22 Aug 1868. (Pp. 435-437)

WILLIAM L. BATES versus S. N. BURGER. 22 Aug 1868. (Pp.
437-444)

TAYLOR THOMPSON and wife and others versus DAVID SUMMER
and others. The motion is well taken. The Clerk is directed to
take proof. 22 Aug 1868. (Pp. 444-445)

McFARLAND and others versus THOMAS G. WOOD and others.
A receiver is appointed. 22 Aug 1868. (Pp. 446-447)

ST. JOHN and FINLEY versus SAMUEL PHILLIPS and others.
22 Aug 1868. (P. 448)

DALLAS CUMMINGS versus P. D. CUMMINGS and others. 22 Aug
1868. (P. 449)

JOHN S. ODOM and others versus RICHARD LAFAYETTE OWEN,
Administrator of James S. Odom, and others. 22 Aug 1868. (Pp.
450-452)

It appears from the official returns of an election held
in Coffee, Cannon, White, DeKalb, Warren, Franklin, Grundy,
and Putnam Counties on 27 May 1869 for the purpose of electing
a Chancellor of the Twelfth Chancery Division that B. M. Tillman received the highest number of votes polled in said election.
(Pp. 452-453)

A number of causes are continued. (Pp. 453-454)

On this the 17th day of Aug 1869, James S. Barton announced
in open court the death of Honorable Broomfield L. Ridley which
occurred at his residence in Murfreesboro on 11th past. He
moved that members of the Bar in attendance take suitable proceedings in reference to the lamented event. The Chancellor
was appointed to act as chairman of the meeting. A resolution
was passed. (Pp. 454-456)

TAYLOR THOMPSON and wife and others versus DAVID SUMMERS
Et Al. It appears to the court that the complainants, except
Taylor Thompson who is husband of one of the children of James
Allman, and the defendants Ephraim Allman and other children
of James Allman are entitled to a legacy of $900 from the will
of their uncle, Harden Allman. 18 Aug 1869. (P. 456)

SARAH HOLLINSWORTH versus JOSIAH HOLLINSWORTH. The Clerk
will proceed to sell the property. 18 Aug 1869. (P. 457)

A. G. ODOM'S heirs versus P. C. TALLEY and others. Matthew,
R. L., and James H. Odom are minor heirs of A. G. Odom and are
without guardian. 18 Aug 1869. (Pp. 458-460)

ABEL RUSHING versus TRUSTEES OF LAWRENCE ACADEMY at Woodbury. Sale of the house and lot. 18 Aug 1869. (Pp. 461-462)

MARTIN PEEBLES & COMPANY versus THOMAS G. WOOD. Complainants move to strike the demurrer of the defendants because it
is improperly filed. 19 Aug 1869. (P. 463)

AMANDA C. LEECH versus W. C. LEECH and others. Defendant
moves that the Court demand additional security. The motion
is continued. 19 Aug 1869. (P. 464)

A. R. HAMMER, Administrator of Henry Trott, versus T. J.
JELTON and others. Petition to sell land. 19 Aug 1869. (Pp.
464-467)

HENRY A. WILEY and others versus WILLIAM L. COVINGTON
and others. 20 Aug 1869. (Pp. 468-469)

L. H. LEECH and wife E. A. versus EZEKIEL ALEXANDER and
others. 20 Aug 1869. (Pp. 469-470)

A number of causes are continued. (Pp. 470-471)

NANCY PITMAN versus JAMES M. PITMAN. Divorce. Process
has been served. The bill is taken for confessed. A hearing
is set. It appears to the court that the defendant has been
guilty of adultery as charged. The bonds of matrimony are
dissolved. Complainant is to have all the property mentioned
in the pleadings. 20 Aug 1869. (Pp. 472-473)

JANE B. SUMMERS versus IVORY SUMMERS. Report of the Clerk.
20 Aug 1869. (Pp. 473-476)

MILTON WARD and others versus ROBERT PATERSON and others.
Final Decree. There is now in the hands of Robert Patterson,
Administrator of John Patterson the sum of $888.43. The several
complainants recover of the said Robert Patterson. 21 Aug
1869. (Pp. 477-478)

J. B. HAWKINS and others versus MILES GEORGE and others.
The Clerk gives his report. 21 Aug 1869. (P. 479)

WILLIAM L. BATES and others versus S. N. BURGER, A. BURGER,
and others. Decree confirming report of indebtedness of William Bates deceased. 21 Aug 1869. (Pp. 479-485)

J. A. and NATHAN PETTY versus SARAH BUCY. The allegations
of complainant's bill are not sustained by the evidence. The
cause is dismissed. 21 Aug 1869. (P. 485)

C. P. BROWN, Administrator of Joseph Spurlock, versus
J. F. WEEDON, Administrator. Joseph Spurlock was the security
of G. W. Thompson for the tract of land. Complainant recovers
of the defendant. 21 Aug 1869. (P. 486)

H. J. ST. JOHN versus MARY WILLIS. Defendant Mary Willis
is a person of unsound mind and wholly incapable of attending
to her own business for want of mental capacity. The said Mary
is the legal owner of a tract of land and some little personal
effects. She is the mother of a son, now about three years
old, named William Willis who would be the legal heir of the
defendant in case of her death. Blake Sagely is named as temporary guardian. 21 Aug 1869. (P. 487)

S. H. McKNIGHT, Administrator of Alexander McKnight versus
JAMES M. McKNIGHT and others. 23 Aug 1869. (Pp. 488-489)

ELIZA WOODS, Administratrix of James Woods, versus JOHN F.
WOODS. Petition to sell land. The bill is dismissed. 23 Aug
1869. (P. 489)

H. J. ST. JOHN, Administrator, versus JAMES SULLIVAN and
others. Report of the Clerk. There has never come into the
hands of H. J. St. John any of the personal effects belonging
to the estate of John E. Sullivan. It will be necessary to
sell some land to pay the debts. 23 Aug 1869. (Pp. 490-492)

WILLIAM D. KELLY'S Administrator versus BETHEL A. KELLY
and others. Assignment of dower to Lucinda Kelly, the widow
of William D. Kelly. 23 Aug 1869. (Pp. 493-496)

R. L. OWEN, Administrator of James S. Odom, versus J. J. ODOM and others. 23 Aug 1869. (Pp. 496-504)

C. B. SUMMERS versus J. J. BRANDON and others. 23 Aug 1869. (P. 504)

D. S. FORD, Administrator of Henry Dennis, versus MATTHEW DENNIS Et Al. 23 Aug 1869. (Pp. 504-505)

A number of causes are continued. 25 Aug 1869. (Pp. 506-507)

IRA HOLLINSWORTH versus WARREN CUMMINS, Administrator of F. Odom. Complainant's amount of profits is not sufficient enough to justify a general reference. 25 Aug 1869. (P. 507)

A. OWEN and others versus H. A. OVERALL and others. Petition to sell land. 25 Aug 1869. (Pp. 508-509)

A. R. HAMMER, Administrator, versus T. J. JELTON and others. 25 Aug 1869. (Pp. 509-513)

WILLIAM B. STOKES versus ASA SMITH. The Minutes book concerning the decree is destroyed. Complainant's bill is taken for confessed. 25 Aug 1869. (Pp. 514-515)

BOGLE heirs versus ALLISON heirs. 25 Aug 1869. (Pp. 515-517)

ELIZABETH LONG and others versus G. C. BARRETT. Comfirming report of the Clerk & Master. 25 Aug 1869. (Pp. 518-519)

PETER MAXEY Et Al versus WILLIAM McKEY Et Al. Final Decree. 25 Aug 1869. (P. 519)

C. B. SUMMERS versus R. L. OWEN and the CLERK & MASTER. The interest of R. L. Owen in the estate of his father, Fountain Owen, is settled upon his wife and co defendant Mary Owen. 25 Aug 1869. (Pp. 520-521)

WILLIAM P. STEPHENS and wife versus RICHARD HOLT Et Al. A. F. Todd is appointed as the administrator of the Estate of Fielding Holt. 25 Aug 1869. (Pp. 521-522)

J. A. PETTY Et Al versus SARAH BUCY. Complainants insist that the proof shows that they purchased and paid for the Wallace land. They are thrown upon the tender mercies of Mrs. Bucy as to whether she will under any circumstances give them a title to the Wale land. 25 Aug 1869. (Pp. 522-523)

WARREN CUMMINS, Administrator, versus C. B. SUMMERS and others. Final Decree. 25 Aug 1869. (Pp. 524-525)

HENRY A. WILEY versus WILLIAM L. COVINGTON and wife. Commissioners were appointed to partition the land between said Wiley and said Covington and wife, Frances Ann. 25 Aug 1869. (Pp. 525-527)

DAVID TODD versus Z. L. BREVARD. Complainant purchased from the defendant on 26 Apr 1855 the land specified in the pleadings. Said Brevard has no title. The contract between the parties is cancelled. 25 Aug 1869. (Pp. 527-528)

LEONARD ADCOCK and wife versus SARAH B. WOOD and others. On 23 Sep 1840, John H. Wood recovered a judgment against William Wood and Archebald Stone for $997. The said John H. Wood is entitled to satisfaction out of the personal estate in the hands of James H. Wood, Administrator of William Wood. 25 Aug 1869. (P. 529)

DALLAS CUMMINS, Administrator, versus P. D. CUMMINS and others. 25 Aug 1869. (Pp. 529-532)

McFARLAND and others versus T. G. WOOD and others. 26 Aug 1869. (Pp. 533-534)

ELIZA A. WEEDON versus JOHN F. WEEDON. 26 Aug 1869. (P. 534)

A number of causes are continued. (Pp. 534-535)

JOHN L. ODOM and the minor heirs of Armstead G. Odom versus PETER C. TALLEY and others. 26 Aug 1869. (Pp. 535-537)

ODOM heirs versus P. C. TALLEY. Decree confirming report of the Master. 26 Aug 1869. (P. 537)

HENRY DAUGHERTY, Administrator of T. M. Allison, versus THE HEIRS and CREDITORS. 26 Aug 1869. (Pp. 538-541)

PRATER and MARY L. ELKINS versus B. LASATER and others. Motion for receiver. 26 Aug 1869. (P. 542)

It is ordered by the Court that all cases finally disposed of and required by law to be enrolled by the Clerk & Master and thereupon the Court adjourned till court in course. BAR-CLAY M. TILLMAN, Chancellor of the 12th Division. (P. 543)

Chancery Court met in the town of Woodbury, Cannon County, on the sixteenth day of May 1870. Samuel M. Fite, presiding. (P. 541)

H. J. ST. JOHN, Administrator of John E. Sullivan, versus JAMES SULLIVAN Et Al. The Master would beg leave that he went upon the premises of the land mentioned in the pleadings on 7 Oct 1869 and sold the same to James Champion, the highest bidder. 17 May 1870. (Pp. 544-545)

S. SPICER versus CALVIN SULLIVAN. Complainant Spicer obligated himself by deed of writing since the filing of this bill of complaint to prosecute this cause. 17 May 1870. (Pp. 545-546)

R. L. OWEN, Administrator of James S. Odom, versus J. J. ODOM'S heirs and creditors. 17 May 1870. (Pp. 546-550)

MELISSA J. SPURLOCK versus E. P. BROWN, Administrator, and others. This cause is continued. 17 May 1870. (P. 550)

JAMES HELTON versus A. G. MILLIKEN. The Clerk will ascertain by proof how much the complainant was paid by the defendant in consequence of the purchase of the piece of land mentioned in the pleadings. He will also report the value of the rents of the land. 17 May 1870. (P. 551)

J. P. HIGGINS and others versus SUSAN HIGGINS and others. 17 May 1870. (Pp. 552-554)

ALEXANDER MILLIGAN Et Al versus JANE BOGLE and C. C. ODOM, Guardian. 17 May 1870. (Pp. 554-555)

WARREN CUMMINS, Administrator of F. Owen, and CHRISTOPHER OWEN versus A. OWEN Et Al. 17 May 1870. (Pp. 556-557)

A number of causes are continued. (Pp. 558-559)

WILLIAM PHILLIPS and J. FINLEY versus J. R. NEELY. One of complainant's securities has moved to the State of Arkansas out of the jurisdiction of this court. 17 May 1870. (Pp. 559-560)

BLAKE SAGELY, Guardian of Mary Willis and WILLIAM VAPER. Petition for confirmation of sale of land. 18 May 1870. (Pp. 561-562)

HUGH CRAFT versus E. J. LAWRENCE. This is a proper cause for a cross bill. 18 May 1870. (P. 561)

MARY WILLIS by her guardian Blake Sagely. The Court confirms that it is in the interest of the complainant that the land be sold. 18 May 1870. (P. 562)

HUGH CRAFT versus E. J. LAWRENCE. The defendant agrees that the complainant is entitled to $200. 18 May 1870. (P. 563)

A. F. McFERRIN versus J. L. JARRETT and others. Complainant recovers of the defendant. 18 May 1870. (P. 564)

A number of causes are continued. (P. 565)

JOHN S. ODOM Et Al versus F. S. ANDERSON. The name of Hannah E. is ordered to be strickened as a defendant and that she and her husband, Henry, be made complainants. (P. 565)

B. L. McFERRIN versus JOHN WOOD, Executor, and others. 19 May 1870. (P. 566)

The Honorable S. M. Fite having retired from the bench, Chancellor B. M. Tillman took his seat and proceeded to dispatch the business of the court. 19 May 1870. (P. 567)

W. T. HART versus LAURA HART. The bill is taken for confessed. A hearing is set. 19 May 1870. (P. 568)

A. J. BRYSON and others versus P. G. LEACH, Administrator of Lehanna Summers and others. Defendants Johite Bogle and wife A. L., Sarah Bogle, James R. Vasser, Mary M. Vasser, Lovie Vasser, and Thomas L. Vasser are non residents of the state. Defendants Z. T. Summers, Elizabeth Summers, James Summers, F. M. Willard and husband Francis, Alcena E. Milligan and husband Henry, William Robinson who is the guardian of Foster Robinson, Lehanna Robinson, Francis C. Robinson, James G. Robinson, and Richard Robinson , also minors; Polly Duggin, William H. Duggin, Charles Duggin, Thomas Duggin, Richard Duggin, Nancy Duggin, Sarah Duggin, A. Owen, P. C. Talley, and

Security of Lahanna Summers, Executrix of James B. Summers, have been served. The bill is taken for confessed. 19 May 1870. (Pp. 569-570)

A. R. WOOD versus JOHN BOYETT and others. It appears to the court that John A. Moore, Administrator of William Arnold, has filed his answer. Harvey Arnold and Betty Arnold are minors without guardian. A. F. McFerrin is appointed as their guardian. 19 May 1870. (Pp. 569-570)

JAMES KING, Administrator of W. B. KELLY, versus BETHEL A. KELLY Et Al. Sale of a tract of land. 19 May 1870. (Pp. 570-571)

W. R. BOGLE and others versus MARTHA J. WOMACK and others. Consolidated cases. 19 May 1870. (Pp. 571-573)

ALEXANDER MILLIGAN and others versus IRA HOLLINSWORTH, Guardian of Dillard, Elizabeth, and Susan Hollinsworth and others. Petition for sale of land. 19 May 1870. (Pp. 574-575)

ALEXANDER MILLIGAN Et Al versus IRA HOLLINSWORTH and others. C. C. Odom, age 40 years, gives his deposition. He states that he is satisfied that the land could not be partitioned. 19 May 1870. (Pp. 575-577)

J. R. CARTER and wife ELIZABETH H. versus WILLIAM L. McBROOM and others. Charles Ready states that he has been acquainted with the land for many years having been raised from childhood to manhood on adjoining land. He states that it would be best to sell the whole land rather than for the said Elizabeth H. to receive her share from it. 19 May 1870. (Pp. 577-579)

JOSEPH DILL versus ELIZA WOOD and others. It appears to the court that James G. Wood is a minor without guardian. Thomas G. Wood is a suitable person to serve as guardian. 19 May 1870. (P. 579)

STEPHEN ROBINSON, Trustee, versus URIAH JENNINGS and others. Defendants James Francis, Sarah Ann Francis, Margaret Francis, and Elizabeth Francis are all non residents of the State. The bill is taken for confessed. 20 May 1870. (P. 580)

R. L. OWEN, Administrator of James S. Odom, versus J. J. ODOM and others. Creditor's bill. 20 May 1870. (Pp. 581-582)

WILLIAM SAULS versus WILEY DAVENPORT. The defendant has leave to take the deposition of Thomas H. Smith, a citizen of the State of Missouri. 20 May 1870. (P. 583)

N. W. SUMMERS versus J. A. and S. S. JARRETT and others. Final Decree. 20 May 1870. (Pp. 583-584)

A number of causes are continued. 20 May 1870. (P. 585)

JAMES PETTY, Administrator, versus GUY and wife. Complainant fails to give sufficient security. Therefore, the cause is dismissed. 20 May 1870. (P. 586)

LEONARD ADCOCK and others versus SARAH B. WOOD and others. Title to a tract of land is divested out of the said Leonard Adcock and the heirs of William Wood and vested in L. G. Batten. 20 May 1870. (P, 586)

Chancery Court, Cannon County, continued to Book E.

ELIZA SANDRIDGE and others versus THOMAS G. WOOD and others. This suit will stand dismissed. 20 May 1870. (P. 1)

S. B. SPURLOCK and others versus WILLIAM GOAD and others. The bill is taken for confessed. It appears to the court that the deed of the 20th of Sep 1865 from defendant William Goad to his son in law, Robert Patterson, for the tract of land described in the pleading was more to hinder and delay the creditors of William Goad. 20 May 1870. (Pp. 1-2)

DANIEL GRIGG and others versus W. W. WOOD and others. John H. Wood is a non resident of the state. The bill is taken for confessed. 20 May 1870. (P. 2)

HEIRS OF WILLIAM SHELTON versus JACOB THOMAS and others. Warren Cummins is appointed as receiver. 20 May 1870. (P. 2)

J. T. D. WALE versus SARAH BUCY. Final Decree. Sale of a tract of land. 20 May 1870. (P. 3)

A number of causes are continued. (P. 4)

A. E. McKNIGHT, Guardian of Odum heirs. It appears to the court that Rufus Odum is about nineteen years old. He is a prudent, careful young man and needs some funds to pay for a horse and saddle. 20 May 1870. (Pp. 4-5)

B. B. COOPER versus JOSEPHUS FINLEY, Executor, Et Al. The controversy has been amicalbly solved. 20 May 1870. (P. 5)

T. J. JELTON versus R. R. BOGLE and others. Robert Bryson, Administrator of George and Margaret Bogle; R. R. Bogle in his own right and as trustee; Thomas Bogle; Thomas B., Jr., George Bogle; H. C. Odum and wife Hannah; Josephine Bogle; John S. Odum; Mathew M. Odum, R. L. Odum, and James H. Odum have been served with process. James Francis, Sarah, Ann Francis, Margaret Francis, Elizabeth Francis are all non residents of the State. The bill is taken for confessed. 21 May 1870. (P. 6)

E. A. LEECH Et Al versus EZEKIEL ALEXANDER Et Al. The said Ezekiel Alexander is executor of Abner Alexander. He has in his hands a sum of money belonging to the legatees. 21 May 1870. (P. 7)

W. C. SWOPE versus A. J. McNABB. 21 May 1870. (P. 8)

J. S. MARCUM Et Al versus BRINKLEY LASSITER Et Al. This is a proper cause for a reference. 21 May 1870. (Pp. 8-9)

W. P. STEPHENS and wife versus RICHARD HOLT and others. George ( ) and wife Matilda, Elizabeth Haley, Labner Goacher and wife Fannie, James H. Dickings, W. F. Dickings, J. F. Holt and wife Fannie, Joseph Johnson and wife have been served with process. The bill is taken for confessed. The unknown heirs of Green M. and Caroline Haley; Harrod Holt; James D. Holt; the unknown heirs of (Maxey) Glascock and wife Millie; the unknown heirs of George Long and wife Matilda are all non residents of the State. The bill is taken for confessed. 21

May 1870. (Pp. 9-10)

McFARLAND and others versus THOMAS G. WOOD and others. 21 May 1870. (Pp. 10-11)

A number of consolidated causes. 21 May 1870. (Pp. 11-12)

DANIEL ( ) versus NANCY DODD and others. It appears to the court that Elizabeth Vanhooser, Lenard Vanhooser, and William Vanhooser are minors without guardian. John S. Dodd is appointed guardian. 21 May 1870. (P. 13)

SARAH WEEDON versus CALVIN SULLIVAN. 21 May 1870. (P. 14)

A. G. ODOM'S minor heirs versus PETER C. TALLEY and others. Report. 21 May 1870. (Pp. 15-17)

DALLAS CUMMINS and others versus P. D. CUMMINS and others. 23 May 1870. (Pp. 17-18)

PETER MAXEY Et Al versus WILLIAM McKEE Et Al. 23 May 1870. (P. 19)

ALFRED ROBINSON and wife MARY J. and A. C. THOMAS versus WILLIAM CHEEK and J. W. SUMMERS. The bill is taken for confessed. 23 May 1870. (Pp. 19-20)

JAMES J. PRATER Et Al versus BRINKLEY LASATER Et Al. 23 May 1870. (Pp. 20-21)

A. J. BRYSON Et Al versus P. G. LEECH, Administrator, and others. Decree of sale. 23 May 1870. (Pp. 22-23)

H. A. WILEY versus W. S. COVINGTON and wife FRANCES A. The original suit pertaining to the partitioning of land has been settled. 23 May 1870. (Pp. 23-24)

ST. JOHN and FINLEY versus SAMUEL PHILLIPS and others. 23 May 1870. (Pp. 25-27)

M. M. GANN versus NATHAN GANN. Final Decree. It appears to the satisfaction of the court that defendant and complainant were married in Cannon County in Mar 1868. Defendant abandoned complainant without any reasonable cause in Oct 1868 and left her without any means of support. The bonds of matrimony are dissolved. 23 May 1870. (Pp. 27-28)

R. L. BELL versus JAMES ALLEN. 23 May 1870. (P. 28)

W. P. STEPHENS and wife versus RICHARD HOLT and others. The bill is taken for confessed. The Clerk is ordered to sell the land. 23 May 1870. (Pp. 29-30)

BENJAMIN BAILEY versus ROBERT BAILEY Et Al. Defendants are ordered to pay the Clerk. 23 May 1870. (P. 31)

STEPHEN ROBINSON, Trustee, versus URIAH JENNINGS and others. Sale of a tract of land. 23 May 1870. (P. 32)

DANIEL TRAVIS versus NANCY DODD. Complainant is entitled to the relief sought. 23 May 1870. (P. 33)

L. J. HOUSE versus IVORY SUMMERS and JACOB HOOVER. The notes are to be paid to the Clerk & Master for the use of Jane B. Summers and children. 24 May 1870. (P. 35)

JAMES M. COMER, Administrator of Archebald Hicks, versus S. E. BURGER and others. Final Decree. The Clerk reports on the real estate of Archebald Hicks deceased. 24 May 1870. (P. 36)

A. OWEN and others versus H. A. OVERALL and others. Petition to sell land. 24 May 1870. (Pp. 37-38)

JOHN D. McBROOM, Administrator of W. T. McBroom, versus B. T. McBROOM Et Al. Petition to sell land. 24 May 1870. (Pp. 38-41)

T. J. JELTON versus JOHN R. SULLIVAN and others. Complainant is the assignee of A. Burger and is subject to all the rights which the said Burger has in the premises. 24 May 1870. (Pp. 42-43)

D. S. FORD, Administrator of Mathew Dennis. The Master is to take an account with the administrator to ascertain whether the administrator is entitled to a credit. 24 May 1870. (P. 43)

DALLAS CUMMINS and others versus P. D. CUMMINS and others. 24 May 1870. (Pp. 44-46)

JAMES M. COMER versus I. N. YORK. Petition to sell land to pay the debts. 24 May 1870. (P. 47)

HARVY DAUGHERTY, Administrator of T. M. Allison, versus CREDITORS and HEIRS. 24 May 1870. (P. 48)

(There are no pages 49-52)

JOHN F. WEEDON, Administrator of G. W. Thompson, versus CREDITORS and HEIRS. 24 May 1870. (P. 53)

Chancery Court met in the town of Woodbury, Cannon County on the twenty-first day of Nov 1870. Albert S. Marks, presiding. (P. 54)

J. P. HIGGINS and others versus SUSAN HIGGINS and others. 24 May 1870. (P. 54)

PLEASANT CAWTHON versus S. CAWTHON. Leave is granted defendant until the January Rules. 21 Nov 1870. (P. 55)

ELIZA SANDRIDGE versus MICHAEL BARNS and others. The defendant has failed to give security. 21 Nov 1870. (P. 56)

MALISSA J. SPURLOCK versus C. P. BROWN, Administrator of Joseph Spurlock, S. B. SPURLOCK and others. The bill has been compromised. 8 Sep 1870. (P. 57)

A number of causes are continued. (P. 58)

J. T. D. WALE versus SARAH BUCY. Final Decree. Report of sale. 22 Nov 1870. (Pp. 59-60)

ALEXANDER MILLIGAN, JOHN A. MILLIGAN, A. P. MILLIGAN and

wife, ELIZA MULLINAX, JAMES G. HOLLINSWORTH, and JANE BOGLE, versus JOHN HOLLINSWORTH, WILLIAM HOLLINSWORTH, DILLARD HOLLINS- WORTH, ELIZABETH HOLLINSWORTH, SUSAN HOLLINSWORTH, LUCY ANN MURPHY, and IRA HOLLINSWORTH, the guardian. On 6 Aug 1870, the Court ordered John A. Milligan to sell a tract of land. The land was transferred to Elizabeth Milligan, now deceased, by a decree of the County Court of Cannon County. Said Eliza- beth is the widow of James Milligan. 22 Nov 1870. (Pp. 60- 61)

JOHN S. ODOM, MATHEW M. ODOM, R. L. ODOM, and JAMES H. ODOM, the last three are minors, E. A. McKNIGHT, NANCY C. BOGLE, UNIS BOGLE, DOUGLAS by their guardian, THOMAS M. BOGLE, minor, HENRY C. ODOM, JOHN W. SUMMERS, GEORGE R. BOGLE, J. B. THOMAS, THOMAS W. BOGLE, HENRY C. ODOM and wife HANNAH E. versus F. S. ANDERSON, Guardian of Josephine Bogle, minor. The Clerk gives his report, stating that on 8 Aug 1870, the 161 acre tract was sold to W. A. Groom. 22 Nov 1870. (Pp. 62-63)

LYDIA ST. JOHN versus THOMAS D. CUMMINS and others. Final Decree. It appears to the court that all the equity set up in the bill has been met. The proof does not sustain the bill. Complainant's bill is dismissed. 22 Nov 1870. (Pp. 64-65)

ALEXANDER MILLIGAN Et Al versus IRA HOLLINSWORTH, Guardian. It does not appear to the court what would be a reasonable fee for each of the solicitors. 22 Nov 1870. (Pp. 65-66)

L. J. HOUSE versus IVORY SUMMERS. It appears to the court that the complainant has paid the amount decreed on the bill. 22 Nov 1870. (Pp. 66-67)

JOSEPH McCRARY and wife versus HEIRS OF YOUNG WHITFIELD and others. The parties have reached a compromise. Complai- nants have agreed to dismiss their bill. 22 Nov 1870. It is decreed by the court that defendants Malinda Whitfield, (Silus) Robinson, Elizabeth Robinson, and Alfred Whitfield pay the costs. Special commissioners are appointed to lay off the dowery to Melinda Whitfield. 22 Nov 1870. (P. 68)

W. P. BALTIMORE and wife and others versus EMANUEL BURKS and others. Emanuel Burks has died since the last term of court. George Burks is his administrator. The land in the suit has descended to his children, to wit, Martha Williams and husband John Williams, Jane Earls and husband Nathaniel Earls, Richard Burks, Mary Herrod and husband H. Herrod, George Burks, Elizabeth Burks, R. F. Burks, John Burks, Elza Burks, Verice Burks, and Rebecca Burks. Also that he left out one Caroline. A sci fi is to be served on the said Caroline, John Williams and wife, Nathan Earls and wife. 22 Nov 1870. (P. 69)

DALLAS CUMMINS, Administrator of William Cummins, versus P. D. CUMMINS and others. 22 Nov 1870. (Pp. 70-71)

LEONARD ADCOCK and wife SARAH B., and others versus SARAH B. WOOD and others. 22 Nov 1870. (Pp. 71-73)

S. B. SPURLOCK and others versus WILLIAM GOAD. The defendant has not paid any money nor filed any receipts. The land is ordered to be sold. 22 Nov 1870. (P. 73)

JOHN STARR and others versus JOSEPH STARR and others. Gabriel Elkins, one of the defendants has not been served. It is necessary for a receiver to take charge of the land. 22 Nov 1870. (Pp. 74-75)

J. D. McBROOM, Administrator, versus B. T. McBROOM and others. The Master reports that he sold the lands described in the pleadings on 3 Oct 1870. 22 Nov 1870. (Pp. 75-76)

C. B. SUMMERS, Administrator of Anthony Summers, versus ANNA LANSDON, JOHN FLANAGAN and wife LEVISA and others. Sale of a tract of land. 22 Nov 1870. (P. 77)

A. F. McFERRIN, Clerk & Master, versus JAMES A. CHAMPION, JAMES W. CHAMPION, and SARAH J. HARRISON. Defendants executed a promissory note to the Master for the use of the heirs and creditors of John E. Sullivan. The note is now due. Land is ordered sold to satisfy the debt. 22 Nov 1870. (Pp. 77-79)

WILLIAM PHILLIPS and J. FINLEY versus J. R. NEELY. The exceptions are sustained. 22 Nov 1870. (Pp. 80-81)

J. T. WOODRUFF and others versus BLAKE SAGELY, Guardian. 22 Nov 1870. (P. 81)

J. W. HILL versus McBROOM Et Al. Final Decree. The cross bill is dismissed. 23 Nov 1870. (Pp. 82-83)

THOMAS L. BRYAN versus ELMIRA F. BRYAN. A hearing is set. 23 Nov 1870. (P. 84)

A. J. BRYSON Et Al versus P. G. LEECH Et Al. Decree confirming sale. 23 Nov 1870. (Pp. 84-85)

J. R. CARTER and wife ELIZABETH H. versus WILLIAM T. McBROOM, JOHN W. McBROOM, MARY AMY McBROOM, GILES McBROOM. The Master reports that he sold the land in the pleadings. 23 Nov 1870. (P. 86)

G. S. HARDING versus W. T. McBROOM Et Al. The Court is pleased to order that counsel be paid. 23 Nov 1870. (P. 87)

J. T. WOODRUFF Et Al versus BLAKE SAGELY, Guardian. The Special Commissioner reports that he has not yet collected all the money in the doubtful claims. 23 Nov 1870. (P. 88)

JAMES ALLEN versus L. D. STARR. The Master reports that he sold the interest of L. D. Starr in a tract of land to James Allen. 23 Nov 1870. (Pp. 89-90)

S. H. McKNIGHT versus JAMES H. McKNIGHT Et Al. Petition to sell land of Alexander McKNIGHT. 23 Nov 1870. (Pp. 90-91)

JAMES KING, Administrator of W. B. Kelly, versus BETHEL A. KELLY. Title to the land mentioned in the pleadings have been divested out of the heirs of W. B. Kelly and vested in J. S. B. Hall. 23 Nov 1870. (P. 92)

JOHN A. WOOD versus B. L. and W. H. McFERRIN and others. It appears to the court that John S. Wood is the surety of John A. Wood. 23 Nov 1870. (Pp. 93-94)

BURGER and wife versus WARREN CUMMINS, Administrator of Fountain Owen. Decree confirming report. 23 Nov 1870. (Pp. 94-98)

T. J. JELTON versus R. P. BOGLE Et Al. Final Decree. 23 Nov 1870. (Pp. 99-101)

JAMES B. THOMAS and others versus ANTHONY OWEN and others. It appears to the court that James Hawkins, one of the pur-chasers of the lands mentioned in the pleadings executed his note to the Clerk. The note is due and unpaid. 23 Nov 1870. (P. 101)

JOHN P. HIGGINS versus SUSAN HIGGINS Et Al. On 6 Jul 1867, A. Milligan and J. P. Milligan executed their note to the Clerk & Master with John Milligan and Ira Hollinsworth as securities. The notes were for the use of the heirs of James Higgins deceased. It is decreed that the heirs of James Higgins recover against said Milligan and Hollinsworth. 23 Nov 1870. (P. 102)

SARAH F. MELTON versus THOMAS F. WEST and others. The complainant has intermarried since the filing of this bill with one Pleasant Turner. It is ordered that he be made party com-plainant with his said wife. 23 Nov 1870. (Pp. 102-103)

H. L. BATES and others versus S. N. BURGER and others. It appears to the court that William Bates in his lifetime was seized and possessed of two tracts of land containing eight thousand acres of land. The said William Bates has the following living heirs, to wit, Abigal Smith, wife of F. M. Smith; Analiza Smith, a granddaughter whose mother was an heir and is dead; Ulissis S. Bates; William Bates; Lucy A. Shacklett, wife of John Shacklett; Martha St. John, wife of Harmon St. John, all of whom are before the court either as complainants or defen-dants. The minor, Analiza Smith, is represented by her guar-dian. Sewell and wife have sold their interest in said land to Arthur W. Smith who is also a party to the proceedings. William Bates has sold his interest to Ulissis S. Bates. It appears to the court that the land should be partitioned. 23 Nov 1870. (Pp. 103-104)

ELIZABETH LONG and others versus G. C. BARRETT, Adminis-trator of Israel Long and others. The administrator has turned over all the debts due the estate to the Clerk & Master. 23 Nov 1870. (Pp. 104-105)

This day, the Court appointed W. J. Wood as Clerk & Master for the constitutional period of six years from the present time of this court. Bond is made. 23 Nov 1870. (Pp. 105-107)

A. R. WOOD versus JOHN BOYETT and others. Decree confirm-ing Clerk's report. It is ordered by the court that the in-terest of John Boyett, W. F. Jacobs, A. R. Wood, and the heirs of William Arnold deceased, to wit, Betsy Arnold, John Arnold, Lee Dye and wife Polly Ann, Harry Arnold, and Betty Arnold to a tract of land be divested out of them and vested in John A. Moore. 23 Nov 1870. (Pp. 108-109)

Chancery Court was held at the Courthouse in the town of Woodbury, Cannon County on the third Monday, it being the 15th day of May 1871. Albert S. Marks, presiding. (P. 110)

JAMES B. THOMAS and others versus A. OWEN and others. The Master reports that on 27 Jan 1871 he received from Jacob B. Hawkins on a judgment rendered against him. 15 May 1871. (P. 110)

JOHN P. HIGGINS and others versus SUSAN HIGGINS and others. The Master reports that in Dec 1870, he received from Alexander Milligan on a judgment rendered against him. 15 May 1871. (P. 111)

WARD BARRETT, Administrator, and others versus F. M. BARRETT and others. The Clerk is to report at next term of court. 15 May 1871. (P. 112)

D. S. FORD, Administrator of Henry Dennis, versus MARTHA DENNIS and others. The Master's report is confirmed. The Master is ordered to pay out the money to the distributees of Henry Dennis. 15 May 1871. (P. 113)

R. L. ODOM, Administrator of James S. Odom, versus JOHN J. ODOM and others. Report. 15 May 1871. (Pp. 113-116)

LEONARD ADCOCK and wife versus SARAH B. WOOD and others. Report of Warren Cummins, Receiver. 15 May 1871. (Pp. 117-118)

BETTY V. SANFORD versus CREDITORS OF G. W. THOMPSON. 15 May 1871. (Pp. 118-120)

W. C. BARNES Et Al versus L. J. HOUSE. Sale of a tract of land. 15 May 1871. (Pp. 121-122)

J. A. COLLIER and others versus M. FRANCIS and others. The death of M. Francis is suggested. The suit is revived against Robert Bryson, administrator of said M. Francis. 15 May 1871. (P. 222)

HIRAM KIRKLAND Et Al versus JAMES HARE and wife and others. Petition to sell land. Process has been served on Thomas D. Stephens, Joanna C. Stephens, Samuel Kirkland, Newton Petty, Frances C. Petty, and Enola C. J. Williams. James Hare and wife Minnie are non residents of Tennessee. The bill is taken for confessed. 15 May 1871. Petition to sell land. 15 May 1871. (Pp. 122-133)

DALLAS CUMMINS, Administrator of William Cummins, versus P. D. CUMMINS. Commissioner's report. 15 May 1871. (Pp. 123-126)

HUGH CRAFT versus E. J. LAWRENCE and J. B. BELL. Defendant executed the note as charged in the bill for the land upon which defendant Lawrence now lives. There was a deficiency in the quantity of the land. Defendants have a credit on the note. 15 May 1871. (Pp. 126-127)

E. A. LEECH Et Al versus EZEKIEL ALEXANDER. The Master is ascertaining the additional interest to be charged against the defendant. 17 May 1871. (P. 127)

E. L. C. WITTY Et Al versus G. W. SUMMERS and others. The Master is to take and state an account showing the amount due from E. J. Summers to the Price heirs for which said Witty is bound. 17 May 1871. (P. 128)

FRANK WEST and others versus ROBERT CANTRELL Et Al. The court is pleased to decree that the sale from Robert Cantrell to H. J. St. John of the house and lot be ratified and confirmed. 17 May 1871. (P. 128)

ROBERT F. BELL versus JAMES ALLEN. Defendant is indebted to complainant. Said defendant is a non resident, but owns land in Cannon County. The land is ordered sold to pay the debt. 17 May 1871. (P. 129)

WILLIAM SHELTON'S heirs versus JACOB THOMAS and others. By consent of the parties this cause is continued till the next term of court. 17 May 1871. (P. 129)

J. T. DICKENS and wife versus T. E. PRAITOR Et Al. The bill is taken for confessed against James M. Praitor, T. E. Praitor, and Thomas P. Praitor. John H. and Martha Praitor are minors. T. E. Praitor is their guardian. 17 May 1871. (P. 130)

J. T. MARCUM Et Al versus BRINKLEY LASATER, PETER REED, WILLIAM H. WOODS, E. C. CURLEE, LUKE LASATER, WILLIAM McGILL, JOHN DUNCAN, Administrator of Irvin Cherry, WARREN CUMMINS, BENJAMIN CUMMINS, and C. C. AKERS. Alfred Cummins, Constable, on 22 Feb 1862 collected for said Lasater the sum of $65.87. There is no evidence to show that the money was ever paid over. The court is of the opinion that the administrator and sureties should be held liable. Complainants recover of the defendants. 17 May 1871. (P. 131)

HENRY DAUGHERTY, Administrator of T. M. Allison, versus T. M. ALLISON'S heirs and creditors. 17 May 1871. (Pp. 131-133)

KESSY EMELINE McKNIGHT by her next friend versus WILLIAM A. McKNIGHT AND A. S. McKNIGHT. The proof does not sustain the allegation. Title to the land belongs to the defendant William A. McKnight free from any trust or right of the complainant. She is not entitled to recover the same. 17 May 1871. (P. 133)

WILLIAM PHILLIPS versus J. R. NEELY. Final Decree. Settling the rights of the parties. Said Neely is entitled to collect the balance of the money due him. 17 May 1871. (Pp. 133-134)

JAMES PETTY, Administrator, versus JAMES GUY and wife NARCISSA. Complainant recovers of the defendant. Land is ordered sold to pay the debt. 17 May 1871. (Pp. 134-135)

JAMES HELTON versus A. G. MILLIKEN. The Chancellor decrees that complainant recover of the defendant the sum of $26.64. The Chancellor is satisfied that the said sum is the balance due to complainant for money paid by him for the land in controversy. Defendant has six months to pay. If it is not paid, then the land will be sold. 17 May 1871. (P. 135)

R. L. ODOM, Administrator of James S. Odom, versus JOHN J. ODOM and other heirs and distributees. 17 May 1871. (Pp. 136-138)

A number of causes are continued. (Pp. 138-139)

JOSEPH McCRARY and wife versus ALFRED WHITFIELD and others. Decree settling dower. The commissioners, chosen by Malinda Whitfield, widow of T. Y. Whitfield, have gone on the premises and in accordance to a compromise made by the parties to a suit brought in Chancery Court by Joseph McCrary and wife against the heirs of Young Whitfield and others. They have laid off to the said Malinda her dower. 17 May 1871. (Pp. 139-140)

J. T. WALE versus SARAH BUCY. Decree confirming report. Title to a tract of land is divested out of J. T. Wale and be vested in A. F. McFerrin. 17 May 1871. (P. 140)

SARAH F. TURNER and husband PLEASANT T. versus T. F. WEST and others. James S. Gribble as attorney for complainant became the purchaser of a tract of land. Title to the land is divested out of Thomas F. West and vested in the said Pleasant Turner, Sarah Turner, and Jarratt Melton, the minor child of the said Sarah F. after the termination of her life estate. 17 May 1871. (P. 141)

JAMES M. CHAMPION versus H. J. ST. JOHN, Administrator of John E. Sullivan and others. The court is pleased to decree that the injunction is dissolved. 17 May 1871. (P. 142)

ROBERT BRYSON, Administrator of G. Bogle, versus P. G. LEECH. Report of T. J. Jelton. 17 May 1871. (Pp. 143-144)

BETTIE V. SANFORD versus JOHN F. WEEDON Et Al. 17 May 1871. (Pp. 144-147)

JOHN STARR and others versus CALINDA PARTON and others. Aaron Hutchen and wife Sarah, John Tubb and wife Elizabeth Crider, M. G. Elkins, and John Starr have been served with process. The bill is taken for confessed. 17 May 1871. (P. 147)

JAMES H. REED and others versus B. S. RING and others. It appears to the court that by the will of James H. Reed all the land known as the family ridge was included in the devises made to John Young and Hugh Reed except that part embraced in the deed from said George W. Reed to James Reed and belonged to said George W. Reed at his death and was sold by his administrator to pay the debts. Defendants Allen Thomas and B. S. Ring did not purchase any part of the land at said sale. 17 May 1871. (Pp. 148-149)

DANIEL GRIZZLE Et Al versus W. W. WOOD Et Al. Order referring cause for an account. This cause is referred to the Master will take an account as between the several heirs as to the amount of advancements made to each of them by William Woods in his life time. 17 May 1871. (Pp. 150-151)

M. L. YOUNG versus J. F. SMITHSON. The injunction is dissolved. 17 May 1871. (P. 151)

WILLIAM PHILLIPS versus G. W. PETTY and wife. In this cause, the papers have been misplaced and not in court. This cause is continued. 17 May 1871. (P. 151)

LEONARD ADCOCK and wife SARAH versus SARAH B. WOOD and others. 17 May 1871. (P. 152)

A number of causes are continued. (Pp. 153-155)

WILLIAM L. STONE versus ROBERT MASON. Final Decree. The sale is ratified. 17 May 1871. (P. 155)

B. L. McFERRIN versus A. D. FUGITT Et Al. The bill is taken for confessed as to defendants H. D. Fugitt, J. B. Young, L. F. Smalling, J. B. Clardy, John Webb, and H. A. Wiley. 17 May 1871. (Pp. 155-156)

B. L. and W. H. McFERRIN versus GREEN SUMMERS. This is a proper cause for a reference. 18 May 1871. (P. 156)

WILLIAM SAULS versus WILEY DAVENPORT. The said Wiley Davenport recovers against the said William Sauls. 18 May 1871. (Pp. 157-158)

JOSEPH BOGLE versus C. A. HAMMER Et Al. The Supreme Court ruled that there is no error in the decree of the Chancellor. 18 May 1871. (P. 159)

A. J. BRYSON and wife SUSAN and other heirs of James B. Summers and also heirs of Lahanna Summers versus Z. T. SUMMERS, A. OWEN, and others. The Clerk is to take an account of the administrator of the estate of James B. Summers by his executrix Lahanna Summers taking her settlement. 18 May 1871. The Clerk will also report what would be reasonable compensation to A. J. Bryson for keeping the idiot, David D. Summers, and how much he received for the same. (Pp. 160-161)

A number of causes are continued. (Pp. 161-162)

SOLOMON SPICER versus J. A. GARRETT and CALVIN SULLIVAN. 18 May 1871. (P. 162)

JAMES H. WOODS versus E. H. and MALINDA VAUGHN. This cause will be referred to the Clerk to take an account. 18 May 1871. (P. 163)

C. B. SUMMERS, Administrator of A. Summers, and others versus ANNA LANSDON AND OTHERS. 18 May 1871. (P. 164)

IVORY SUMMERS versus J. S. RIDLEY. Final Decree. 18 May 1871. (Pp. 164-167)

McFARLAND and others versus THOMAS G. WOOD. 18 May 1871. (P. 167)

JAMES M. ROBERTS versus J. D. FRANCIS and others. The sale of the land is confirmed. 18 May 1871. (P. 168)

W. C. SWOPE versus A. J. McNABB. Modification of the report. 18 May 1871. (Pp. 169-170)

A number of causes are continued. (P. 171)

E. A. LEECH Et Al versus EZEKIEL ALEXANDER Et Al. The Court is of the opinion said Alexander ought to be allowed to file his petition for a rehearing. The Clerk is to take proof as to the circumstances under which said Alexander took Confederate money, if at all, and whether it should be credited to him in said estate. 18 May 1871. (Pp. 172-173)

J. R. NEELY, Surviving partner of SMITH & NEELY, versus NATHAN A., CHARLES, and JAMES A. PETTY. The Complainant will recover of the defendants. 18 May 1871. (P. 173)

S. J. ODOM versus JOSEPH CARTER. Complainant Carter is entitled to recover from defendant. 18 May 1871. (P. 174)

HIRAM KIRKLAND and others versus JAMES HARE and wife and others. The Court decrees that it is in the interest of the parties that the land be sold. 18 May 1871. (Pp. 175-176)

HIRAM KIRKLAND, HIRAM TODD and wife PARMELIA, WILLIAM ROBINSON and wife EMELINE, JOANNAH KIRKLAND, ALEX PETTY, and JOHN F. WILLIAMS versus JAMES HARE and wife MILLIE E., SAMUEL KIRKLAND, NEWTON PETTY, NANCY C. PETTY, ENOLA E. J. WILLIAMS, THOMAS STEPHENS, and JOSHUA STEPHENS. It appears to the court that Isaac Kirkland died in Cannon County in the year 186_, intestate. Hiram Todd is his administrator. There is sufficient property to pay the debts. Petitioners and defendants are all of the heirs of the said Isaac Kirkland. It is in their interest that the land be sold. 18 May 1871. (Pp. 176-177)

The Court is adjourned until the next regular term. 18 May 1871. (P. 178)

Chancery Court met at the Courthouse in the town of Woodbury, Cannon County, on the third Monday of November, it being the 20th day 1871. Albert S. Marks, presiding. (P. 179)

BOGLE heirs versus ALLISON heirs. The Special Commissioners report that there is due from the Allison estate to the Bogle heirs. 20 Nov 1871. (Pp. 180-182)

ROBERT BELL versus JAMES ALLEN. Final Decree. The land was sold at the Courthouse to J. L. Fare, attorney for B. F. Bell. 20 Nov 1871. (Pp. 183-184)

W. C. BARNES versus L. J. HOUSE. The lot on which the defendant lives was sold to William A. McKnight. 20 Nov 1871. (Pp. 185-186)

J. B. THOMAS and others versus A. OWEN and others. It is suggested by the court that there is a mistake in the taxation. 20 Nov 1871. (Pp. 186-187)

A number of causes are continued. (P. 188)

E. A. LEECH and others versus EZEKIEL ALEXANDER, Executor of Abner Alexander, and HENRY DAUGHERTY, Administrator of W. C. Donnell. The said Ezekiel Alexander as the executor of Abner Alexander has in his hands $3568 which is due to the complainants as devisees of Abner Alexander. S. J. Odom and Henry Daugherty are his securities and are liable jointly with him. 20 Nov 1871. (Pp. 188-189)

LEONARD ADCOCK and wife versus SARAH B. WOOD. 20 Nov 1871. (Pp. 190-191)

J. P. FLOYD versus HENRY DAVENPORT. It was suggested to the Court that Defendant Davenport has paid since the filing of this report a portion of the debt, it not appearing how much is yet due. The Clerk will take an account. 20 Nov 1871. (P. 191)

JOHN S. ODOM versus F. S. ANDERSON. The land and slaves belonging to the estate of Joseph H. Bogle, except the widow's dower, was sold by the former Clerk & Master on the 2nd day of Jan 1858. (See Minutes Book, pages 220 and 222) He also sold the dower land on 3 Dec 1858. (Pp. 192-198)

JOHN S. ODOM Et Al versus F. S. ANDERSON Et Al. 20 Nov 1871. (Pp. 199-206)

S. B. SPURLOCK Et Al versus WILLIAM GOAD. Sale of a tract of land. 20 Nov 1871. (Pp. 206-207)

J. S. WOMACK Et Al versus P. G. LEECH. The heirs of Matthew Bogle are minors without guardian. 20 Nov 1871. (P. 207)

A number of causes are continued. 20 Nov 1871. (P. 208)

JAMES HELTON versus A. G. MILLIKEN. Sale of one acre in the 6th District about three fourth's of one mile south east of the town of Woodbury. Bounded: west by the lands of defendant A. G. Milliken. 20 Nov 1871. (P. 209)

HUGH CRAFT versus E. J. LAWRENCE. Sale of a tract of land. 20 Nov 1871. (P. 210)

WARD BARRETT, Administrator of Allen Morgan, versus F. M. BARRETT and others. Report. 20 Nov 1871. (P. 211)

DALLAS CUMMINS versus P. D. CUMMINS and others. 20 Nov 1871. (Pp. 212-213)

DAVID DODD versus Z. T. BREVARD. 20 Nov 1871. (P. 214)

HIRAM KIRKLAND and others versus JAMES HARE and others. 20 Nov 1871. (Pp. 215-217)

LEWIS MILES and wife ELIZA versus ULISSIS S. BATES and others. Title to a tract of land shall be divested out of the executors of Russell Brewer and vested in Eliza Miles, wife of Lewis Miles. 20 Nov 1871. (Pp. 218-219)

J. R. CARTER and wife versus W. T. McBROOM and others. 20 Nov 1871. (P. 219)

ALEXANDER MILLIGAN and others versus IRA HOLLINSWORTH Et Al. The Clerk received a note, payable one year after date executed, from John A. Milligan with Ira Hollinsworth and A. Milligan as securities. It was received for the use of the heirs of James Milligan. The Clerk moved the Court for a decree against the said John A. Milligan, Ira Hollinsworth, and A. Milligan for the debt and interest. 20 Nov 1871. (Pp. 219-220)

DALLAS CUMMINS, Administrator of William Cummins, versus P. D. CUMMINS. It appears to the Court that the note is due and is unpaid. 20 Nov 1871. (P. 222)

W. P. BALTIMORE versus GEORGE BROOKS, Administrator, and others. John Smith, Thomas Smith, Margaret Stone have been served with process. The bill is taken for confessed. A hearing is set. 20 Nov 1871. (P. 222)

LEONARD ADCOCK and wife SARAH and others versus SARAH B. WOOD and others. 20 Nov 1871. (P. 223)

H. J. ST. JOHN versus MARY WILLIS. The Clerk will proceed to take and state an account touching the amount of means belonging to his ward which is in the hands of B. Sagely as guardian. 20 Nov 1871. (P. 224)

ALSA JONES versus ALFORD OWENS Et Al. The defendant, Alford Owen died. The cause was revived against his children in the Supreme Court. J. L. Fare was appointed as their guardian. The children are Lafayette Owen, Josiah Owen, and Cancie Owen. 20 Nov 1871. (P. 225)

J. C. OWEN and others versus JAMES B. THOMAS and others. Sale of a tract of land. 20 Nov 1871. (Pp. 226-227)

JOSIAH M. CRANE versus WEST & ACRES. William West by his guardian, William Acres, about the 28th of Jun 1856 recovered a judgment against Josiah Crane for $160.11 besides costs. The Clerk will sell a tract of land to satisfy the judgment. 20 Nov 1871. (Pp. 227-228)

DALLAS CUMMINS, Administrator of William Cummins, versus P. D. CUMMINS. 20 Nov 1871. (P. 229)

WILLIAM SHELTON and others versus OWENS' heirs. 20 Nov 1871. (P. 230)

ELIJAH NEELY versus ROBERT W. NEELY and others. Elijah Neely, William R. Neely, B. F. Neely, and Anna Neely are the minor defendants. B. F. Vinson is their guardian. 20 Nov 1871. (P. 231)

DANIEL TRAVIS versus NANCY DODD and others. This cause is continued. 20 Nov 1871. (P. 231)

C. B. SUMMERS, Administrator, versus ANNA LANSDEN and T. SMITH. The Special Commissioner has the honor to report that he has made settlement with the County Court of Warren County. 20 Nov 1871. (Pp. 232-235)

LARKIN KEATON versus JOHN P. HALE, Administrator of Thomas Hale. Complainant is indebted to the defendant. 20 Nov 1871.

(P. 236)

JAMES R. FUSON and others versus SARAH FUSON and others.
It appearing to the satisfaction of the court from the affidavit
of defendant Sarah Fuson that Peter A. Keaton is not sufficient
security for costs for the prosecution of complainant's suit.
20 Nov 1871. (P. 236)

W. P. BALTIMORE and wife versus GEORGE BURKS, Administrator of Emanuel Burks Et Al. Jane Earles, formerly Jane Burks,
has since the last term of court departed this life intestate.
J. E. Cawthon, William G. Earles, D. J. Earles, and Joseph R.
Earles are heir heirs. 20 Nov 1871. (P. 237)

LOCKEY J. BURGER and others versus MARY TASSY. Process
has been served on the defendant. The bill is taken for confessed. It has been suggested that a portion of the debt of
complainants has been paid. The Clerk is to take an account
and report back. 20 Nov 1871. (Pp. 237-238)

SOLOMON SPICER versus J. A. JARRATT, S. S. JARRATT, and
JOHN WOODS, Executor of D. M. Jarratt. The complainants bill
is illegal. Defendants recover of the complainants. 20 Nov
1871. (P. 238)

GILES S. HARDING versus W. T. McBROOM and others. B. C.
Carter, wife of complainant J. R. Carter, appeared privately
before the Chancellor stating that her husband stated her wishes
as to her proposition of the money arising from the sale of the
lands in this cause. The commissioner is to pay over to the
said J. R. Carter the money due to his wife, the said Elizabeth
H. (The name of the wife is stated differently in two places.)
22 Nov 1871. (Pp. 239-240)

B. L. and W. H. McFERRIN versus GREEN SUMMERS. The defendant is indebted to the complainant. 22 Nov 1871. (P. 241)

ROBERT BRYSON, Administrator of George Bogle, versus P. G.
LEECH. 22 Nov 1871. (P. 242)

WILLIAM PHILLIPS versus G. A. PETTY and wife. Defendant
G. A. Petty is justly indebted to the complainant in the sum
of $126.62. It further appears that he purchased the land with
his own means from one Thomas Charick and procured a deed to
be made to his wife, the defendant Frances Petty at which time
defendant G. A. Petty was indebted to complainant by promissory
notes. If the debt is not paid, then the land will be sold for
the debt. 23 Nov 1871. (P. 243)

J. H. DICKENS versus ASA LEMONS and others. It appears to
the court that the land in controversy was bought of J. J. Owen
and paid for by Isaac Lemons and James Lemons. While James
Lemons was in the army, Asa Lemons, his father, procured a deed
to be made to himself and Isaac, instead of to James and Isaac.
Asa Lemons had no interest whatsoever in said land. 23 Nov
1871. (Pp. 244-245)

P. CAWTHON versus W. P. CAWTHON and others. It appears to
the court that H. R. Cawthon, the father of the defendants, to wit,

102

William Cawthon, M. E. J. Cawthon, Sarah H. Cawthon, H. R. Cawthon, Mary S. Cawthon, Cinthia Cawthon and husband of Adaline Cawthon made an agreement with complainant by which he was to assist complainant in the redemption of the land mentioned in the pleadings for which he was to be compensated. 23 Nov 1871. (Pp. 245-246)

R. D. SMITH versus HENRY TIDWELL. It appears to the court that the defendant was justly to the complainant by a judgment. Land is to be sold to satisfy the judgment. 23 Nov 1871. (P. 246)

ANDERSON KEELE versus MARIAH KEELE. Process has been served. The bill is taken for confessed. A hearing is set. 23 Nov 1871. (P. 247)

W. P. STEPHENS and wife versus RICHARD HOLT. In the year 1860, Fielding Holt deeded to Joseph Holt the land mentioned in the pleadings. The same was as an advancement. The court is of the opinion that Joseph P. Holt received and used some gold belonging to Fielding Holt and that he should be charged with the same. The Master will report to the next term of court the amount of gold used by the said Joseph P. from the time he went to live with Fielding Holt up to the death of said Fielding. The court disallows Richard Holt's account against the estate of Fielding Holt. 23 Nov 1871. (Pp. 247-249)

SARAH E. CARNAHAN versus JESSIE GILLEY and others. Process has been served on defendants Jessie Williams and wife Sarah, Joseph McCrary and wife Mary Ann. A. L McCrary, Administrator of Preston Carnahan. The bill is taken for confessed. Jane R. Carnahan, Peterson A. E. Carnahan, and Tennessee L. Carnahan are minors without guardian. J. S. Barton is appointed as guardian. 23 Nov 1871. (P. 250-251)

ROBERT CANTRELL versus H. J. ST. JOHN. Robert Cantrell, receiver of H. J. St. John, the amount of purchase money due from St. John to said Robert Cantrell for a house and three lots known as the Asa Smith Tavern house and lots where the said St. John now lives in the town of Woodbury. There is a lien on the property. If the lien is not paid, then the property will be sold. 23 Nov 1871. (P. 251)

A. J. BRYSON and wife SUSAN and other heirs of James B. Summers and the heirs of Lanahan Summers versus P. C. TALLEY and others. 23 Nov 1871. (Pp. 252-258)

WILLIAM SHELTON'S heirs versus J. B. THOMAS and others. The death of William Shelton, one of the complainants, was suggested. 23 Nov 1871. (P. 258)

JAMES M. ROBERTS versus J. D. FRANCIS. A tract of land was sold to complainant Roberts. 23 Nov 1871. (Pp. 259-260)

R. F. BELL versus JAMES ALLEN. Sale of a tract of land. 23 Nov 1871. (P. 261)

WILLIAM GOODING versus PARALEE GOODING. The defendant has been guilty of acts of adultery as charged in the bill.

The bonds of matrimony are dissolved. 23 Nov 1871. (Pp. 262-263)

Clerk & Master's report of funds on hand. 23 Nov 1871. (P. 263)

J. F. DICKENS and wife M. J. versus F. E. PRATOR and others. 23 Nov 1871. (Pp. 264-265)

HENRY C. ODOM and wife versus F. S. ANDERSON and others. 23 Nov 1871. (Pp. 265-266)

ZACHARIAH THOMASON Et Al versus R. H. HANCOCK Et Al. 24 Nov 1871. (P. 267)

A number of causes are continued. (Pp. 268-269)

A. KEELE versus MARIAH KEELE. It appearing that complai-nant's character is not very good for chastity, the Court dis-misses the bill but without prejudice to complainant's rights. 24 Nov 1871. (P. 270)

A number of causes are continued. (Pp. 271-272)

BETTY V. SANFORD versus JOHN F. WEEDON. 24 Nov 1871. (Pp. 272-273)

DAN GRIZZLE and others versus W. W. WOOD and others. Final Decree. The said W. W. Wood is charged with pasturing three head of stock upon the premises at the rate of 8/12 per head for 14 months. 24 Nov 1871. (Pp. 274-277)

JOHN A. WOOD versus B. L. and W. H. McFERRIN. Final Decree. 24 Nov 1871. (Pp. 277-278)

ALFRED ROBINSON and wife versus W. C. LEECH and others. 24 Nov 1871. (Pp. 278-282)

JOHN STARR and others versus CELINDA PARTON and others. The Clerk will give an account and report back. 24 Nov 1871. (Pp. 282-283)

Chancery Court met at the Courthouse in the town of Wood-bury, Cannon County, on the third Monday in May 1872, it being the 20th day of the same. Albert S. Marks, presiding. (P. 284)

J. B. THOMAS Et Al versus A. OWEN Et Al. 20 May 1872. (Pp. 284-285)

E. A. LEACH Et Al versus EZEKIEL ALEXANDER Executor. The Master reports that Abner Alexander willed to each of the lega-tees, to wit, J. M. Alexander, Catherine L. Dickens, Mark Alexander, and E. A. Leach. 20 May 1872. (Pp. 285-290).

M. L. ELKINS and J. J. PRATOR versus B. LASATER Et Al. The parties have entered into a compromise agreement. 20 May 1872. (Pp. 290-291)

JOSIAH M. CRANE versus WEST & AKERS. 20 May 1872. (Pp. 292-293)

J. P. FLOYD versus HENRY DAVENPORT Et Al. It appears to the court that the debt has been paid. 20 May 1872. (P. 293)

B. L. and W. H. McFERRIN versus GREEN SUMMERS. Green Summers tract of land was sold at the Courthouse to the complainants. 20 May 1872. (P. 294)

JOHN C. OWEN Et Al versus JAMES B. THOMAS. Decree confirming sale. 20 May 1872. J. W. Bryant and Christopher Owen became the purchasers of the land. (Pp. 294-295)

A. J. BRYSON Et Al versus P. G. LEECH Et Al. A note was executed to P. G. Leech, Administrator of the estate of James B. Summers, by M. L. Duggin with W. H. Duggin as security. 20 May 1872. (P. 296)

A. J. BRYSON versus P. G. LEECH. Judgment on note. 20 May 1872. (P. 297)

LOCKEY J. BURGER versus MARY TASSEY. Defendant executed to complainant her two promissory notes. 20 May 1872. (Pp. 298-299)

JOHN STARR Et Al versus CALINDA PARTON Et Al. Decree confirming sale. It is ordered by the court that the several heirs of Lewis Starr be divested of their interest in the land and be vested in J. and J. B. Hawkins. 20 May 1872. (Pp. 300-301)

S. H. McKNIGHT, Administrator, versus J. M. McKNIGHT Et Al. This cause is referred to the Clerk to take an account. 20 May 1872. (Pp. 302-303)

NANCY MATTHEWS versus FRANK NEELY Et Al. This cause is continued. 20 May 1872. (P. 304)

J. D. McBROOM versus B. T. McBROOM Et Al. A note was issued to the Clerk by J. D. McBroom, B. T. McBroom, and Henry McBroom. 20 May 1872. (P. 305)

A. J. BRYSON and others versus P. G. LEECH and others. 20 May 1872. (P. 306)

J. T. BLAIR Et Al versus J. C. HENEGER Et Al. Report of the Master. The Clerk finds that Paralee York has received certain property named. He finds from the statement of James York that he received after the death of his father from his mother certain property. Sarilda Foster shows the advancements to be made out of her mother's exempt property. J. N. York received by way of advancement certain property. Ann Eliza Blair received her advancements. Jeremiah York received his advancements. J. H. York received his advancements. John Henegar received his advancements. This is the Master's report on the settlement of the estate of William York deceased. 20 May 1872. (Pp. 307-310)

SARAH WEEDON Et Al versus CALVIN SULLIVAN. The defendant has recently had an unusual family affliction and for this reason, he is not prepared for trial. This cause is continued. 20 May 1872. (P. 310)

R. L. ODOM versus E. A. McKNIGHT. Report. 20 May 1872. (Pp. 311-312)

A number of causes are continued. (Pp. 313-316)

S. M. WOMACK versus S. E. BURGER. Defendants S. E. Burger, George Woods, and Mary Jones have been served. The bill is taken for confessed. 20 May 1872. (Pp. 316-317)

A number of causes are dismissed or continued. (P. 318)

JOHN S. ODOM Et Al versus F. S. ANDERSON. Report of the Clerk & Master. 20 May 1872. (Pp. 319-321)

BLAKE SAGELY Et Al. Petition to incorporate high school. on 21 May 1872, petitioners filed their petition for Bradyville High School. 20 May 1872. (Pp. 321-324)

AMANDA E. LEECH versus W. C. LEECH. This cause will stand as dismissed. 20 May 1872. (P. 324)

J. A. COLLIER and others versus M. FRANCIS Et Al. Final Decree. R. Bryson, intestate, was the owner of a note against the estate of J. S. Odom which was due 1 Jan 1860. The several complainants recover from the defendants. 20 May 1872. (P. 325)

HENRY C. ODOM and wife versus F. S. ANDERSON. Consolidated causes. 20 May 1872. (Pp. 326-339)

DANIEL BRYSON, Executor of Mary Alexander, versus F. C. ALEXANDER and others. Defendants Emily Bryson and Mary Alexander have since the last term of court intermarried with William Myers and Christopher Ready. Their husbands are made parties to the suit. 20 May 1872. (P. 339)

HENRY C. ODOM versus F. S. ANDERSON. 20 May 1872. (Pp. 339-340)

R. D. SMITH versus HENRY TIDWELL. R. D. Smith was the purchaser of a tract of land sold at the Courthouse. Title to the land is divested out of Henry Tidwell and vested in the complainant R. D. Smith. 20 May 1872. (Pp. 341-342)

WILLIAM SAULS versus WILEY DAVENPORT. Defendant Wiley Davenport was the purchaser of a tract of land for $586.79. A writ of possession shall be issued by the Sheriff to dispossess the complainants from the land. 20 May 1872. (Pp. 342-343)

P. CAWTHON versus W. P. CAWTHON. Sale of a tract of land. 20 May 1872. (P. 343)

MARTHA HAMILTON versus MICAJAH HAMILTON. This cause is compromised. 20 May 1872. (P. 344)

J. M. BAIRD versus C. P. CURLEE. Final Decree. The Clerk is to take proof and report back to the next term of court. 20 May 1872. (Pp. 345-346)

H. J. ST. JOHN versus MARY WILLIS. Mary Willis is a person of unsound mind. The Clerk gives a report on her estate. 20 May 1872. (Pp. 346-348)

The Clerk & Master gives his report of the funds on hand to May Term. 20 May 1872. (Pp. 348-349)

JOHN P. McBROOM versus B. T. McBROOM Et Al. 21 May 1872. (P. 350)

JAMES A. CHAMPION versus H. J. ST. JOHN. Parties enter into an agreement in which the suit is dismissed. 21 May 1872. (Pp. 351-352)

Chancery Court met at the Courthouse in the town of Wood-bury, Cannon County, on the third Monday in Nov 1872, it being the 18th day of said month. Albert S. Marks, presiding. (P. 353)

W. L. BATES and others versus A. BURGER and others. Division of the lands of William Bates deceased to U. S. Bates, Lucy A. Shacklett, Martha St. John, Abigal Sewell, W. S. Bates, Analiza Smith. 18 Nov 1872. (Pp. 354-359)

A. J. BRYSON versus P. G. LEECH Et Al. There is a note executed by Elizabeth Summers which is for the use of the heirs and creditors of James B. Summers. 18 Nov 1872. (Pp. 360-361)

J. B. THOMAS Et Al versus A. OWEN Et Al. Report of the Clerk. 18 Nov 1872. (Pp. 361-362)

SARAH B. MELTON versus T. F. WEST Et Al. Report of the Clerk. 18 Nov 1872. (Pp. 361-362)

(The next page is page 365)

J. A. JARRATT versus J. L. JARRATT. Final Decree. The petitioner agrees to dismiss the petition filed by him. 18 Nov 1872. (P. 366)

A. J. BRYSON Et Al versus P. G. LEECH Et Al. The Clerk will make a report as to who has rented the lands since the death of James B. Summers until the same was sold. 18 Nov 1872. (P. 367)

J. D. McLIN versus W. B. WILLARD. Complainant recovers of the defendant. The defendant is the owner of one interest in the tract of land that he acquired by purchase from one G. W. McLin which has been attached. 18 Nov 1872. (P. 368)

R. L. ODOM versus E. A. McKNIGHT. Report of the Clerk. 18 Nov 1872. (Pp. 369-372)

NANCY C. HILL and widow versus SAMUEL M. HILL, CADY F. HILL, and LETTICE J. HILL, minor children and heirs of J. H. Hill. A guardian is appointed. 18 Nov 1872. (P. 372)

JOHN STARR and others versus CELINDA PARTON and others. The Clerk in his report finds that the taxes were unpaid at the date of the purchase, but has now been paid by J. B. Hawkins. 18 Nov 1872. (Pp. 373-374)

ELIZABETH CUMMINS versus J. H. CUMMINS. Leave is given to the defendant. 18 Nov 1872. (P. 374)

T. J. BLAIR and others versus J. C. HENEGER and others. Report is given. 18 Nov 1872. (Pp. 374-375)

JOHN S. ODOM versus F. S. ANDERSON Et Al. Josephine B.

Odom (formerly Bogle), wife of Sam C. Odom, appeared privately before the Chancellor to state her desire that her portion of the money arising from the sale of the lands in this cause be paid to her said husband. It is so ordered. 18 Nov 1872. (P. 375)

ROBERT BELL Et Al versus JOHN FERGUSON Et Al. Process has been served in Rutherford County on John O. Furguson, Harriet Furguson, R. B. Furguson, and Martha E. Dillin. They are minors without guardian. 18 Nov 1872. (Pp. 376-377)

THOMAS L. BRYAN versus E. L. BRYAN. This cause is continued. 18 Nov 1872. (P. 378)

L. S. BROWN versus JAMES P. FORD. Defendant purchased the tract of land from complainant on 20 Apr 1867. Notes were held on the land. The land was ordered sold to pay the debt. 18 Nov 1872. (Pp. 378-379)

ISAAC GAITHER and wife versus D. F. BRAGG and others. The Clerk is to take an account with the administrator of William Bragg. 18 Nov 1872. (P. 379)

DANIEL GRIZZE Et Al versus J. B. WOOD Et Al. Process has been served on Amanda E. Alexander and James B. Alexander. Process has also been served on Caroline F. Alexander and Margaret J. Alexander Denby. The bill is taken for confessed. B. M. Webb is appointed as guardian. 18 Nov 1872. (P. 380)

P. D. CUMMINS versus WARREN CUMMINS. 19 Nov 1872. (Pp. 380-381)

NANCY C. HILL, Administratrix, versus SAMUEL HILL. Order appointing counsel. Counsel is appointed to represent Samuel M., Kedy F., and Lottie J. Hill who are minors. 18 Nov 1872. (P. 382)

T. B. BRISON Et Al versus SOPHIA B. MARTIN Et Al. A guardian is appointed for the unknown heirs of L. Martin. 19 Nov 1872. (P. 383)

W. B. BYNON Et Al versus JOHN BYNON Et Al. Application for a writ of injunction is sustained. 18 Nov 1872. (P. 383)

JOSEPH BOGLE versus C. A. HAMMONS. The Chancellor is pleased to allow complainant's exceptions to so much of said report as charges him with $945 on account for confederate money. At the time the complainant received $800 in confederate money from the defendant, he should have then added twelve per cent to the $266 being the difference between gold and national currency commonly called Greenbacks. 18 Nov 1872. (Pp. 384-385)

SARAH E. WEEDON and others versus CALVIN SULLIVAN. 18 Nov 1872. (Pp. 385-386)

A. E. McKNIGHT, Guardian. Ex Parte. A. E. McKnight is the guardian of James H. Odum who is now in his 19th year. He has an estate of some $2500 or $3000. He has recently married and needs some funds to purchase necessities. The Court not being satisfied as to whether said Odom was an industrious and saving young man, referred this cause to the Clerk & Master to take proof and report upon this point. 20 Nov 1872. (P. 386)

A. E. McKNIGHT, Guardian. Ex Parte. The Clerk reports that he finds James Henry Odom is an industrious, sober, and equinomical young man. The court authorizes the guardian to pay over $300 to said Odom. 20 Nov 1872. (P. 387)

ROBERT BELL, Administrator, versus JOHN O. FURGUSON Et Al. Process has been served. The bill is taken for confessed. 21 Nov 1872. (P. 388)

T. B. BREVARD Et Al versus SOPHIA B. MARTIN. Process has been served on Sophia B. Martin, John A. Herrod and wife Frances, T. J. Oatried and wife Catherine, Joseph G. Martin, William B. Wright and wife Susan J. The bill is taken for confessed. 20 Nov 1872. (P. 388)

JOHN S. ODOM and others versus F. S. ANDERSON. 20 Nov 1872. (P. 389)

ROBERT BELL, Administrator, Et Al versus JOHN O. FURGUSON Et Al. Petitioners and defendants are the owners of the town lots described in the pleadings. It is to their interest that the said lots be sold. 21 Nov 1872. (Pp. 389-390)

L. P. GOFF versus AMANDA GOFF. Process has been served. The bill is taken for confessed. A hearing is set. 21 Nov 1872. (Pp. 390-391)

A number of causes are continued. (Pp. 391-392)

C. C. BROWN versus BETTY ANN WILSON. Motion of complainant for the appointment of an administrator on the estate of _____ Wilson. It appears to the satisfaction of the court that said Wilson had been dead for more than six months before the bill was filed. C. C. Brown is appointed as administrator of said estate. 21 Nov 1872. (Pp. 392-393)

GILES HARDING VERSUS W. T. McBROOM and others. Report. 21 Nov 1872. (Po. 394-396)

JAMES H. WOOD versus J. S. WOOD, Administrator. Defendant Malissa Vaughan prays an appeal of this cause to the Supreme Court. 21 Nov 1872. (Pp. 396-397)

M. L. YOUNG versus J. H. SMITHSON. There is a defect or flaw in the title of the land in controversy. It would be inequitable for the complainant to accept such a title. 21 Nov 1872. (P. 397)

ROBERT BRYSON, Administrator of T. A. Womack, versus MARTHA J. WOMACK. It is necessary to sell the land to pay the debts against the estate of T. A. Womack. Said Martha J. is the widow of the said T. A. Womack. It appears to the court that T. A. Womack died in Cannon County several years since and Robert Bryson was appointed his administrator. Defendants Sarah J. B., Margaret, J. B., and Cicero Womack are his children. 21 Nov 1872. (Pp. 398-399)

B. S. McFERRIN versus JAMES TODD, Trustee of J. B. Young, JOHN WEBB, H. A. WILEY, A. D. FUGITT, L. F. SMALLING, J. B. CLARDY, and N. L. CLARDY. Defendant Young executed a trust deed to said Todd conveying to him his real estate in Cannon County. Said Webb and Wiley purchased the real estate conveyed in said trust. In 1870, McBroom recovered a judgment against said Young and McFerrin as surety. If the debt is not paid, the land will be sold. 21 Nov 1872. (Pp. 399-402)

DANIEL BRYSON, Executor of Mary Alexander, versus C. C. ALEXANDER and others. It appears to the court that defendants John Alexander, Emily C. Bryson, A. A. Bryson, H. T. Bryson, F. T. Bryson; and Robert W., Cam Broils, and Martha A. Alexander, children of B. B. Alexander deceased of Hardin County and perhaps some of the children of John M. C. Alexander of Texas, all of whose names are unknown are minors without guardian. John W. Harris is appointed as their guardian. The bill is taken for confessed. The Clerk is to take proof as to the debts of the estate of Mary Alexander. 21 Nov 1872. (Pp. 402-404)

WILLIAM SHELTON'S heirs versus JACOB THOMAS. Process is to be served on Martha Shelton, Elbert Shelton, Mary L. Shelton, and James Shelton who reside in Gibson County. 21 Nov 1872. (P. 405)

J. B. MATHIS versus MARTHA HOLLAN Et Al. The bill is taken for confessed. 21 Nov 1872. (P. 405)

JOHN W. PAGE versus A. G. MILLIKEN. This cause is reinstated. 21 Nov 1872. (P. 406)

The Court, having dispatched it business on the docket, adjourned until next regular time. (P. 407)

Chancery Court met at the Courthouse in the town of Woodbury on the third Monday in May, it being the 19th day of said month. Albert S. Marks, presiding. (P. 408)

JOHN STARR Et Al versus CELINDA PARTON Et Al. 19 May 1873. (P. 408)

B. L. McFERRIN versus JAMES TODD and others. Agreed decree. 19 May 1873. (Pp. 409-411)

S. R. FUSON versus SARAH FUSON. Proceeds from the sale of the land will be equally divided between the widow of Joseph Fuson and his children. 19 May 1873. (Pp. 412-413)

G. B. HIPP versus WILLIAM PHILLIPS. Sale of a tract of land to satisfy a debt. 19 May 1873. (Pp. 413-414)

JOHN H. SMITH versus A. A. FANN and J. H. GILLAM. Sale of a tract of land to satisfy a debt. 19 May 1873. (Pp. 414-415)

ROBERT BELL and others versus JOHN O. FERGUSON and others. Report. Tennessee McFerrin was the purchaser of the lots. 19 May 1873. (Pp. 415-416)

W. L. BATES versus A. BURGER. 19 May 1873. (P. 416)

A number of causes are continued. (Pp. 416-417)

NANCY C. HILL versus SAMUEL M. HILL, KADY HILL, and LETTY HILL. Samuel M. and Kady F. Hill are minors over the age of fourteen. The Clerk is to report as to whether the land is susceptible of partition. 19 May 1873. (P. 417)

J. D. McLIN versus W. B. WILLARD. Sale of a tract of land to J. D. McLin. The land was previously owned by W. B. Willard. 19 May 1873. (Pp. 418-419)

ALSA JONES versus ALFRED OWEN Et Al. J. L. Fare is appointed as guardian for the minor heirs of Alfred Owen. 20 May 1873. (P. 420)

L. S. BROWN versus JAMES P. FORD. Complainant became the purchaser of the land mentioned in the pleadings. The complainant has failed to comply with the terms of the sale. The land is to be sold. 20 May 1873. (P. 421)

JAMES JAMISON VERSUS MARGARET JAMISON. Complainant James Jamison has died since the instituting and during the pending of this suit, leaving his two children, W. A. Jamison and Sarah A. Jamison. Margaret Jamison is his widow. 20 May 1873. (Pp. 421-424)

P. CAWTHON versus H. S. CAWTHON. Articles of agreement. 20 May 1873. (Pp. 424-426)

McFARLAND and others versus THOMAS G. WOOD and others. 20 May 1873. (Pp. 427-428)

J. W. PAGE versus A. G. MILLIKEN. The Clerk is ordered to take an account and report back to the court. 20 May 1873. (Pp. 428-429)

W. C. HILL, the widow and administratrix of John H. Hill, versus SAMUEL M. HILL, KADY F. HILL, and LETTIE HILL. 20 May 1873. (Pp. 429-431)

WILLIAM SAULS versus WILEY DAVENPORT. By an oversight on the Master's part, he failed to advertize the tract of land. 20 May 1873. (Pp. 432-433)

ISAAC GAITHER and wife versus D. F. BRAGG Et Al. The Master will determine what will be reasonable compensation for H. J. St. John as guardian for the minor in this cause. 20 May 1873. (P. 434)

BETTY V. SANFORD versus JOHN F. WEEDON, Administrator. Decree confirming report. 20 May 1873. (Pp. 435-436)

I. W. DUNCAN versus LEWIS CANNON Et Al. All of the defendants, namely, Lewis Cannon, Nancy J. Cannon, Louisa Cannon, and James Cannon are non residents of the State of Tennessee. The bill is taken for confessed. A hearing is set. 20 May 1873. (P. 437)

A number of causes are continued. (Pp. 437-438)

DANIEL BRYSON, Executor, versus C. C. ALEXANDER and others. 20 May 1873. (Pp. 438-439)

J. S. WOMACK and others versus P. G. LEECH and others. The bill is taken for confessed. 20 May 1873. (Pp. 440-441)

S. H. McKNIGHT, Administrator, and others versus JAMES M. McKNIGHT and others. The Clerk, as required by law, took an account in his office on 21 Apr 1873. The last previous account was taken in 1871. 20 May 1873. (Pp. 441-444)

MARY STARR versus JOSEPH STARR. Money from the sale of land comes into the hands of the Master. 20 May 1873. (P. 444)

A number of causes are continued. (Pp. 445-446)

C. C. BROWN versus BETTY ANN WILSON and others. The Clerk is to determine whether the personal assets of the estate of A. J. Wilson have been exhausted. 20 May 1873. (P. 446)

JOHN W. D. DUNCAN versus WILLIAM LOUIS CANNON Et Al. It appears to the court that one Ruford Cannon on 20 May 1850 made and executed a deed to the complainant. Before the conveyance had been proven, the late war broke out and by the casualties of war, the papers of the office and said deed was lost or destroyed and cannot now be found. The said Cannon has purduced a substantially true and correct copy of the original deed. 20 May 1873. (Pp. 447-449)

T. B. BREVARD Et Al versus SOPHIA B. MARTIN Et Al. Sale of land. 20 May 1873. (Pp. 449-450)

E. L. C. WITTY versus E. J. SUMMERS and G. W. SUMMERS. Final Decree. The court is of the opinion that the land purchased from Hopkins was purchased with the means of defendant Eli J. Summers and that he fraudulently procured the deed to be made to his son, Defendant W. G. Summers, and that the title to the same in equity belonged to Defendant Eli J. Summers. 20 May 1873. (Pp. 450-451)

ISAAC GAITHER versus D. F. BRAGG Et Al. The guardian is allowed ten dollars for his services as guardian for the minor defendant in this cause. 20 May 1873. (Pp. 451-452)

The Court having dispatched all the business on the docket, it adjourned until the next regular term. (P. 453)

Chancery Court met at the Courthouse in the town of Woodbury, Cannon County, on the third Monday in Nov 1873, it being the 17th day of said month. Albert S. Marks, presiding. (P. 454)

B. H. COOK & COMPANY versus J. W. PAGE and others. Master's report. D. B. Vance, one of the defendants in this cause, became the purchaser of the tract of land mentioned in the proceedings. Title to the land is divested out of the complainants and vested in the said Vance. 17 Nov 1873. (Pp. 454-455)

W. L. BATES and others versus A. BURGER and others. 17 Nov 1873. (Pp. 455-456)

ANN SULLIVAN versus JOHN R. SULLIVAN. The parties enter into an agreement. Defendant relinquishes all his rights to to complainant's dower land. She is to have full and complete control of said land during her lifetime and at her death to her children. Filed 14 Oct 1873. (Pp. 457-458)

J. B. MATHIS versus MARTHA WALLACE. The purchaser has failed to comply with the terms of the sale. 17 Nov 1873. (P. 459)

J. R. FUSON and others versus SARAH FUSON and others. Jessie McGee became the purchaser of a tract of land. All the interest of the complainants and defendants to the land is divested out of them and vested in the said McGee. 17 Nov 1873. (P. 460)

JOHN D. McBROOM, Administrator, versus B. T. McBROOM and others. Report. 17 Nov 1873. (Pp. 461-462)

JOHN H. SMITH versus A. A. FANN and others. All the interest of the said A. A. Fann and J. H. Gillman is divested out of them and vested in the said John H. Smith. 17 Nov 1873. (Pp. 462-463)

ISAAC GAITHER versus D. F. BRAGG and others. Report. 17 Nov 1873. (Pp. 464-469)

WILLIAM PHILLIPS versus GEORGE PETTY. Decree confirming report of sale. 17 Nov 1873. (Pp. 469-470)

ELIJAH NEELY versus ROBERT W. NEELY and others. Motion of Sarah E. Neely, the widow of Elijah Neely in her own right and as the next friend of Elijah Neely, Jr., Thomas L. Neely, and Isaiah Neely, minor children and heirs of Elijah Neely, to revive the suit. 18 Nov 1873. (P. 474)

T. J. JELTON versus R. R. BOGLE and others. 18 Nov 1873. (Pp. 471-473)

DANIEL BRYSON, Executor, versus C. C. ALEXANDER and others. Sale of a tract of land. 18 Nov 1873. (Pp. 473-475)

ALFORD ROBINSON and wife versus W. C. LEECH and others. Report. 18 Nov 1873. (Pp. 475-476)

A number of causes are continued. (Pp. 476-477)

C. C. BROWN versus BETTY ANN WILSON and others. It appears to the court that there are no personal assets of the estate of A. J. Wilson for the payment of bona fide debts against the estate. The said A. J. Wilson died seized and possessed of an undivided interest in a tract of land in the 4th District. It will be necessary to sell the same. 18 Nov 1873. (Pp. 477-478)

L. P. GOFF versus ANN C. GOFF. The allegations in the bill are sustained by the proof. The bonds of matrimony are dissolved. 18 Nov 1873. (P. 478)

ROBERT BRYSON, Administrator, and others versus J. W. SUMMERS and others. The Clerk is to ascertain the amount of the personal effects which came into the hands of said J. W. Summers as Executor of B. D. Summers. 18 Nov 1873. (Pp. 478-479)

W. W. BURGER versus E. L. JORDAN. The papers in this cause have been lost or mislaid. Trial will be at next term of court. 18 Nov 1873. (P. 480)

W. B. CAMPBELL versus A. J. GANNON and others. Process has been served for the defendant, A. J. Gannon, who was a non resident of the State. The bill is taken for confessed. It appears that the defendant, A. J. Gannon, is justly indebted to the complainant by promissory note. The Clerk will taken an account of funds now in the hands of defendants Vance and McBroom belonging to the said Gannon. 18 Nov 1873. (P. 481)

N. G. MADDOX versus A. A. WARE and others. Defendant Delia Ware has been served with process. She is a minor without guardian. 18 Nov 1873. (P. 482)

E. L. C. WITTY versus E. J. SUMMERS and others. Report. 18 Nov 1873. (Pp. 482-484)

WILLIAM SHELTON'S heirs versus JACOB THOMAS and others. The death of F. M. Shelton, one of the complainants, was suggested. Process is ordered against the heirs, to wit, Martha E. Shelton, Elbert Shelton, Mary L. Shelton, and James Shelton who reside in Gibson County. 18 Nov 1873. (P. 484)

JOHN W. ST. JOHN versus H. A. WILEY. Sale of a tract of land. 18 Nov 1873. (Pp. 485-486)

S. H. McKNIGHT, Administrator of Alexander McKnight, versus JAMES M. McKNIGHT and others. Report. 18 Nov 1873. (Pp. 487-489)

T. J. WOODRUFF versus B. SAGELY, Guardian. Motion to make Mary Willis a party to this suit. 18 May 1873. (P. 490)

A number of causes are continued. (P. 491)

McFARLAND and others versus THOMAS G. WOOD and others. 18 Nov 1873. (P. 492)

E. L. C. WITTY versus E. J. SUMMERS Et Al. Report. 18 Nov 1873. (Pp. 493-495)

JANE WALLS and others versus BENJAMIN FUGITT and others. Benjamin Fugitt, E. T. Dillon and wife Sallie presented their cross bill in open court. The Court is of the opinion that it is a proper case for a cross bill. 18 Nov 1873. (P. 495)

DANIEL GRIZZLE and others versus J. R. WOOD and others. Margaret J. Grizzle, one of the complainants, died since the last term of court. She left the following children, to wit, William Grizzle, Sarah E. Tassey who has intermarried with Ed Tassey, John R. Grizzle, and George Grizzle, the last three being minors. By consent, the Master will sell the lands to the highest bidder. 18 Nov 1873. (P. 496)

H. J. ST. JOHN versus MILES WILLIS. It is ordered that Blake Sagely, guardian of Miles Willis, pay the cost of this cause. This cause will be retired for the purpose of settlement with the guardian. 18 Nov 1873. (P. 497)

J. L. JARRATT versus JOHN WOODS Et Al. The Court must rule as to whether Chancery Court in Cannon County or Rutherford County has jurisdiction. 18 Nov 1873. (P. 497)

JOHN N. MITCHELL versus B. H. COOK Et Al. Complainant is entitled to the relief sought. The land mentioned in the pleadings will be sold by the Master for $1707, the amount due by said J. N. Mitchell as guardian for David Elrod, and G. W. Costner and wife Rachael. The Court further decrees that J. H. Mitchell is entitled to homestead. 18 Nov 1873. (P. 498)

ELIJAH NEELY versus R. W. NEELY Et Al. Sale of a tract of land. 18 Nov 1873. (Pp. 498-499)

J. R. FUSON and others versus SARAH FUSON. Report. 18 Nov 1873. (P. 499)

WILLIAM A. CLARK, Administrator, versus LIDIA J. REED Et Al. The Master is directed to make a deed to A. J. Thomas and B. A. Ring for the tract of land sold. Title is divested out of the heirs of George Reed and vested in the purchasers. Said Ring and Thomas then sold their interest in the land to William Tolbert. 18 Nov 1873. (Pp. 501-502)

SARAH E. WEEDON and JACK M. WEEDON versus CALVIN SULLIVAN. 18 Nov 1873. (Pp. 502-504)

J. W. McADOO Et Al versus JOHN H. SMITH Et Al. The matters of equity are met. Complainant's bill is dismissed. 18 Nov 1873. (Pp. 504-505)

HIRAM KIRKLAND and others versus JAMES HARE and wife MILLIE D. and others. Report. 18 Nov 1873. (Pp. 506-508)

J. M. DUNN, Administrator of Thomas W. Brewer, versus J. R. NEELY. The former complainant, T. W. Brewer deceased, and the defendant, J. R. Neely, were engaged in the tanning business in Cannon County as equal partners for several years prior to the year 1870. It appears that the partnership was dissolved and a settlement had between the parties on 27 Jan 1870. A balance of $109 was due Brewer. The Court decrees that the complainant recover of the defendant. 18 Nov 1873. (Pp. 509-510)

N. C. HILL, Administrator of John H. Hill, versus SAMUEL M. HILL and the other minor heirs. 18 Nov 1873. (Pp. 510-513)

T. B. BREVARD and others versus SOPHIA B. MARTIN and others. 18 Nov 1873. (Pp. 513-520)

The Court having dispatched business adjourned until Court in course. (P. 520)

Chancery Court met at the Courthouse in the town of Woodbury, Cannon County, on the third Monday in May 1874, it being the 18th day of said month. Albert S. Marks, presiding. (P. 521)

SARAH E. WEEDON versus CALVIN SULLIVAN. 18 May 1874. (P. 521)

ALEXANDER MILLIGAN and others versus IRA HOLLINSWORTH and others. 18 May 1874. (Pp. 522-523)

W. L. BATES versus A. BURGER and others. Master's Report. 18 May 1874. (Pp. 523-526)

PETER ADAMS versus T. P. MASON. Complainant recovers of the defendant. 18 May 1874. (Pp. 527-528)

A number of causes are continued. (Pp. 528-529)

J. B. MATHIS versus MARTHA WALLACE and others. Title to a tract of land is divested out of the parties and vested in Hannah B. Foster. 18 May 1874. (Pp. 529-530)

ISAAC GAITHER versus D. F. BRAGG and others. James Gribble became the purchaser of the lands belonging to the estate of William Bragg. 18 May 1874. (Pp. 531-532)

R. L. ODOM versus E. A. McKNIGHT. E. A. McKnight's ward, R. L. Odom, has attained his majority. 18 May 1874. (Pp. 532-535)

ELIJAH NEELY versus R. W. NEELY and others. Fifteen barrels of corn are sold to C. M. Rankhorn. 18 May 1874. (Pp. 533-534)

J. H. ODOM by his guardian E. A. McKnight. Ex Parte. 18 May 1874. (Pp. 536-541)

T. B. BREVARD versus SOPHIA B. MARTIN and others. 18 May 1874. (Pp. 541-542)

W. P. STEPHENS and wife versus RICHARD HOLT and others. Fielding Dickens as surety of Richard Holt will jointly with the said Richard pay the cost of the said Richard in the court. 18 May 1874. (Pp. 543-545)

STEPHENS and wife versus HOLTS. The decree as to Joseph Holt is probably as near the court result as could be arrived at upon the record unless as to the gold. As to Richard, the decree refusing to allow his account for $500 for services rendered his father is correct. The question of doubt is as to the gold. The old man had gold and silver probably from $700 to $1000. It is not certain what became of it although it is reasonably certain that Richard and Joseph Holt both got part of it. The decree will be against Richard and Joseph Holt each for one half of $900 of gold and the costs of the court. 18 May 1874. (Pp. 546-547)

WARREN CUMMINS versus W. H. GOAD and others. Sale of a tract of land. 18 May 1874. (Pp. 547-548)

A number of causes are continued. (Pp. 548-549)

L. W. BREWER versus J. L. BREWER. John A. Collier and wife Susan, E. G. Brewer, Joseph Pinkerton and wife Nancy, a portion of the heirs of T. W. Brewer whose death was suggested at the last term of court ask the court to be made complainants. It is further decreed that D. H. Vance and wife Bettie, William Brewer of Cannon County, and Robert Brewer of Texas, the heirs of

116

T. W. Brewer deceased returnable to the second rule day commanding them to show cause, if any, they have why this suit should not be prosecuted to final termination by such of the heirs of the said T. W. Brewer deceased who wish so to do. 19 May 1874. (P. 549)

JOHN N. MITCHELL versus B. H. COOK. Master's report. 19 May 1874. (Pp. 549-552)

MARY R. CRANK versus G. W. CRANK. The bill is taken for confessed. Complainant is entitled to the relief prayed for. The bonds of matrimony are dissolved. Complainant is restored to her maiden name. 19 May 1874. (P. 552)

NARCISSA DeLONG versus W. J. DeLONG. The bill is taken for confessed. Complainant is entitled to the relief prayed for. The bonds of matrimony are dissolved. Complainant is to have the care and custody of her children and all the property attached. 19 May 1874. (Pp. 553-554)

J. L. JARRATT versus JOHN WOODS and others. A written agreement between the complainant and defendants J. A. and S. S. Jarratt. J. L. Jarratt states that during the Spring of 1873, he filed a bill in Chancery Court against the executors and legatees of his father, D. M. Jarratt. The complainant was against the executors, Snow S. and J. A. Jarratt for allowing a tract of land purchased by them for the said J. L. under the direction of D. M. Jarratt to be resold for the unpaid purchase money and to Sophia Linch and who purchased the same for $4000. It is hereby stipulated and agreed between the said J. L. Jarratt, Snow S. Jarratt, and J. N. Jarratt that the bill filed by J. L. Jarratt be dismissed. 19 May 1874. (Pp. 554-555)

H. C. McBROOM Et Al versus ANNY and SOPHIA GANDY. Ruth McBroom died in Cannon County the owner of the lands described in the bill. Complainant and defendants are her heirs. The Clerk is ordered to take proof as to whether the lands should be partitioned or sold. 19 May 1874. (Pp. 556-558)

GEORGE PATTERSON Et Al versus T. B. BREVARD Et Al. The Court is of the opinion that this is a proper case for a receiver. 19 May 1874. (P, 558)

ANALIZA GUNTER by next friend versus W. C. and SARAH TODD. The demurrer is sustained. 19 May 1874. (P. 558)

(Page 559 is blank)

S. C. ODOM versus JOHN S. ODOM. This cause will be referred to the Master to take proof and report back to the court. 19 May 1874. (P. 560)

JAMES JAMISON Et Al versus MARGARET JAMISON Et Al. The sale of the lands to H. L. Elam is confirmed. 19 May 1874. (Pp. 561-562)

A. J. BRYSON versus P. G. LEECH and others. 20 May 1874. The fund devised between the nineteen heirs. Two of the distributees, David D. Summers and James M. Summers, departed this life since the death of their father and died intestate and without issue and their interest descended to their brothers and sisters. Elizabeth Summers is the owner by purchase of four shares in the land. She purchased the interest of M. P. G. Summers, W. H. H. Summers, and Z. T. Summers. P. L. Duggin, the husband of M. S. Duggin, was the owner at the time of his death by purchase of eight shares in the James B. Summers lands which interest descended to his wife and children who are all set out in the bill as defendants, four of the children are minors. The land belonging to the deceased brothers descended to seventeen surviving heirs. They are A. J. Bryson and wife Susan, Dan Travis and wife, Robert Brandon and wife, J. W. Summers, William Blanks and wife, J. J. Bryson and wife, H. C. Summers, T. R. Summers, J. R. Summers, John Bogle and wife, William Vassar's heirs, W. M. Robison, Robert J. Summers, Sarah Bogle, Z. T. Summers, W. H. H. Summers, and M. P. G. Summers. 20 May 1874. (Pp. 563-572)

ROBERT BRYSON, Administrator, versus JOHN W. SUMMERS Et Al. 20 May 1874. (Pp. 572-579)

A number of causes are continued. (Pp. 580-581)

JOHN M. BARRETT and wife versus M. C. NEELY Et Al. 21 May 1874. (Pp. 581-582)

J. D. McBROOM, Administrator, versus B. T. McBROOM and others. Sale of a tract of land. 21 May 1874. (Pp. 582-583)

W. M. BURGER, Administrator of Abraham Burger, versus E. L. JORDAN. The papers in this cause have been lost. The bill is dismissed. 21 May 1874. (P. 584)

ANALIZA GUNTER versus W. C. and SARAH TODD. Analiza Gunter is a person twenty-one years of age and for this reason, Summers has no right to prosecute this suit as next friend. This cause will stand dismissed. 21 May 1874. (Pp. 585-586)

GEORGE W. DAVENPORT versus JOHN W. PAGE Et Al. Complainant Davenport is to have one third of the produce of the land during his life and at his death the property is to belong to F. F. Page and her heirs by J. W. Page. J. W. Page is to have free access to spring. 21 May 1874. (P. 586)

JOHN N. MITCHELL versus MARY MITCHELL. The Court is pleased to decree that complainant in her cross bill be allowed a sufficient amount of means out of the estate of defendant for her support until the suit is settled by this court. The said John N. Mitchell will pay into the hands of the Clerk & Master the sum of fifteen dollars per month until this suit is ended. 21 May 1874. (Pp. 587-588)

ALICE CAMPBELL by next friend J. R. Wheeler versus ANDERSON RUCKER. Defendants are allowed until July to respond. 21 May 1874. (P. 588)

JOHN S. ODOM versus F. S. ANDERSON. The Clerk gives his report. 21 May 1874. (Pp. 589-597)

WILLIAM J. JUSTICE versus HENRY McBROOM and BENJAMIN Mc-
BROOM. Complainant has sustained the charges in his bill.
Defendants by the erection of their mill dam, mentioned in the
pleadings, have caused the water in the river above said mill
to overflow the springs of said Justice and to back up upon
his mill "wheel" and have thereby created a nuisance by the
obstruction of said river. The defendants' dam is declared a
nuisance. The same is ordered to be reduced ten inches lower
than it now is so as to remove the obstruction. 21 May 1874.
(Pp. 597-599)

ALFRED ROBINSON Et Al versus W. C. LEECH Et Al. 21 May
1874. (Pp. 600-601)

JOHN M. BARRETT and wife versus M. C. NEELY Et Al. The
bill is without equity. Complainants bill will be dismissed.
21 May 1874. (Pp. 601-602)

MARY SUTTON, Executrix of Edmond Sutton, and others versus
WILLIAM H. MOSES and wife ALEY and others. There are promissory
notes to be for the use of Mary Sutton, widow of Edmond Sutton.
21 May 1874. (Pp. 602-603)

W. B. BYNUM and others versus JOHN BYNUM and others. The
Court is of the opinion that this is a case for a receiver. 21
May 1874. (P. 603)

W. R. NOKES versus JAMES S. GRIBBLE, Administrator of Asa
Smith; $\overline{W}$. C. AKERS, Administrator of William West; and GEORGE
W. SMITH. The bill is taken for confessed as to George W.
Smith. Complainant Stokes at the Oct term of this court in
1861 recovered a judgment against Asa Smith, George W. Smith,
and William West for $611. Judgment has been discharged or des-
troyed together with all the papers and records connected with
the same. Asa Smith is dead. James Gribble is his administrator. The estate is insolvent. Said West is dead. W. C. Akers
is his administrator. He has suggested the insolvency of said
estate. Said estate is in the McMinnville Chancery Court as an
insolvent estate. 21 May 1874. (Pp. 603-605)

Report on the funds in the Clerk's Office. 21 May 1874.
(P. 606)

J. W. PAGE versus A. G. MILLIKEN. The Court is of the
opinion that the reference in this cause was improvidentially
made became the defendant in his answer set up a final settlement. Said settlement is substantially established by the
evidence. 21 May 1874. (P. 607)

J. S. WOMACK and others versus P. G. LEECH and others. 21
May 1874. (Pp. 608-609)

THOMAS F. WEST in his own right as next friend FRANCES
LANCE, MARY JANE LANCE, and THOMAS H. LANCE; WILLIAM (HENNESSEE)
and wife MARTHA ANN: WILLIAM C. WEST: WILLIAM CUMMINS and wife
MINERVA ANN: and MARGARET WEST versus H. J. ST. JOHN, ROBERT
CANTRELL, S. H. GRAY and MATILDA GRAY. Consolidated causes.
21 May 1874. (Pp. 609-610)

TURNER VAUGHAN versus JAMES H. WOOD. Turner Vaughan on 14 Feb 1860 secured a judgment in Circuit Court against Asa Smith and George W. Smith for $3986.29. On 17 Mar 1860, said Vaughan filed his attachment bill attaching the property of said Smiths. 21 May 1874. (Pp. 611-614)

SUSAN C. BETHEL versus NELSON BRYAN and E. B. SUMMERS. The bill is taken for confessed. Defendant Bryan executed his promissory note to his co-defendant Summers. The note since endorsed to complainant. 21 May 1874. (Pp. 614-615)

A. J. BRYSON versus P. G. LEECH. Report. 21 May 1874. (Pp. 615-616)

JAMES JAMISON versus (MARIAH) JAMISON. 21 May 1874. (Pp. 617-618)

The Court having dispatched all the business ready for hearing adjourned the Court until Court in course. (P. 618)

Chancery Court met in the town of Woodbury, Cannon County, at the Courthouse on the third Monday in Nov 1874. Albert S. Marks, presiding. (P. 619)

JOHN N. MITCHELL and others versus B. H. COOK & COMPANY. Nov 1874. (Pp. 620-622)

JOHN C. OWEN and others versus J. B. THOMAS. Nov 1874. (Pp. 623-624)

A number of causes are continued. (Pp. 624-625)

J. S. WOMACK Et Al versus P. G. LEECH Et Al. Master's Report. Nov 1874. (Pp. 625-626)

JOHN W. ST. JOHN versus H. A. WILEY. 16 Nov 1874. (P. 626)

R. L. ODOM versus E. A. McKNIGHT. Master's Report. 16 Nov 1874. (Pp. 627-628)

ALEXANDER MILLIGAN and others versus IRA HOLLINSWORTH and others. Master's Report. 16 Nov 1874. (Pp. 628-630)

ALEXANDER MILLIGAN and others versus JANE J. BOGLE and others. Master's Report. 16 Nov 1874. (Pp. 630-634)

A number of causes are continued. (Pp. 634-635)

W. P. STEPHENS and wife versus RICHARD HALL and others. 16 Nov 1874. (Pp. 636-637)

W. R. CAMPBELL versus A. J. GANNON and others. Master's Report. A judgment was rendered in favor of complainant. 16 Nov 1874. (Pp. 638-639)

WILLIAM SUMMERS versus JAMES SUMMERS. The parties have compromised. 16 Nov 1874. (Pp. 639-640)

SUSAN C. BETHEL versus NELSON BRYAN and others. Master's Report. 16 Nov 1874. (P. 640)

The proceedings of this day have been carried to Minutes Book F.

Chancery Court met at the Courthouse in the town of Woodbury, Cannon County, on the third Monday in May 1875, it being
the 17th day of said month. Albert S. Marks, presiding. (P. 1)

B. L. and W. H. McFERRIN versus A. D. FUGITT Et Al. R. B.
Bingham was the purchaser of a tract of land. 17 May 1875. (P.
2)

A number of causes are continued. (Pp. 3-4)

DANIEL GRIZZLE and others versus JOHN B. WOOD and others.
Master's Report. William W. Wood became the purchaser of a tract
of land. 17 May 1875. (Pp. 4-5)

A. J. BRYSON and others versus P. G. LEECH and others. 17
May 1875. (Pp. 6-8)

WARREN CUMMINS versus W. H. GOAD and others. Master's Report. 17 May 1875. (Pp. 9-10)

JANE YOUNG versus JOSEPH YOUNG, THOMAS RIGSBY and wife
MARJORIE, SARAH FRANCES YOUNG, and others. A. Finley, as guardian for the minor defendants, is allowed ten dollars for serv-
ing them. 17 May 1875. (P. 10)

ELIJAH NEELY versus R. W. NEELY Et Al. Master's Report.
17 May 1875. (Pp. 10-13)

MARY E. JONES versus HENRY EASON. Process has been served
on the defendant. This bill is taken for confessed. Defendant
executed a promissory note to the complainant. The note is due.
If it is not paid, then Clerk will sell the house and lot. 17
May 1875. (Pp. 13-14)

W. R. CAMPBELL versus A. J. GANNON and others. Master's
Report. 17 May 1875. (Pp. 14-16)

R. W. NEELY Et Al versus D. BARKER Et Al. Sale of a tract
of land. 17 May 1875. (Pp. 16-18)

S. P. POWELL and others versus JAMES A. WOOD Et Al. The
house and lot described in the pleadings belonged to the parties as stated. There is a lien on it. It appears to the
Court that complainant H. A. Overall has a deed to four shares
in said house and lot purchased by John A. Wood from H. O. Wood,
M. E. St. John and wife Helen, T. W. Wood, and the share the
said John A. held under the will of John Wood deceased. 17
May 1875. (Pp. 18-19)

S. P. POWELL and wife PARALEE, W. J. WOOD, G. G. WOOD,
IRA HOLLINSWORTH and wife SARAH, JOHN A. McFERRIN and wife
TENNESSEE, B. L. McFERRIN, H. A. OVERALL, and PAYNE versus
JOHN A. WOOD and M. J. SPURLOCK. Master's Report. The property is so situated that partition cannot be made to an advantage of all the parties. There is but one improvement on
the town lot but one well and no cistern or spring and the
out buildings and lots are so arranged as to render it fit
only for one residence. 17 May 1875. (Pp. 20-21)

H. C. McBROOM Et Al versus ANNY GANDY Et Al. A. C. Tatum

became the purchaser of a tract of land. 18 May 1875. (Pp. 21-22)

(Parts of pages 23 and 24 are torn out.)

J. A. GOODING versus J. L. CAWTHON. The bill is taken for confessed. A hearing is set. 18 May 1875. (Pp. 25-26)

SARAH B. HUDSPETH versus (CERTIN) HUDSPETH. Complainant and her securities will pay the costs. 18 May 1875. (P. 26)

J. R. FUSON versus SARAH FUSON. The Master reports that the administrator has exhausted all of the personal assets of his intestate's estate. There is yet outstanding debts. 18 May 1875. (Pp. 26-28)

JOHN STARR versus CELINDA PARTON. Report. There is a failure of title to 93¼ acres of the tract of land sold in this cause to John and J. B. Hawkins. 18 May 1875. (Pp. 28-29)

JANE YOUNG versus JOSEPH YOUNG, THOMAS RIGSBY and wife MARGARET, SARAH FRANCES YOUNG and others. Commissioners were assigned to lay off to complainant, Jane Young, widow of John Young, a homestead and dower out of the 138 acre tract of land mentioned in the pleadings. 18 May 1875. (Pp. 30-33)

A number of causes are continued or dismissed. (P. 33)

PETER C. TALLEY versus HENRY A. WILEY and others. Samuel Wharton's name is substituted for William Wharton. 18 May 1875. (P. 34)

Z. THOMASON versus LARKIN KEATON. This cause is revived in the name of Matilda Thomason, B. D. Thomason, John Thomason, Charles Thomason, and Willis Thomason, the last four being minors without guardian. The suit is revived against the heirs of Larkin Keaton whose names are as follows, to wit, William Keaton, Sarah King, Mary Hale, L. J. Keaton, Caroline Keaton, and Barbara Keaton. 18 May 1875. (P. 34)

WILLIAM SWANN versus MARY SWANN. Process has been served on the defendant. The bill is taken for confessed and set for hearing. The Court is of the opinion that the complainant is entitled to the relief sought. The bonds of matrimony are dissolved. 18 May 1875. (P. 35)

JOHN STARR Et Al versus CELINDA PARTON Et Al. The Clerk is to take proof and report back. 18 May 1875. (P. 36)

JAMES H. WOOD versus SAM ALEXANDER. The bill is taken for confessed. Complainant is entitled to the relief sought. 18 May 1875. (Pp. 37-38)

N. G. MATTOX versus A. A. WARE. Master's report. It is necessary to sell the land to reimburse the complainant for money paid out for the benefit of the estate of J. W. Ware deceased because the administrator has exhausted the assets in the payment of debts. 18 May 1875. The $300 bequeathed to defendant Delia for her education has never been paid to her. (Pp. 38-40)

JANE YOUNG versus JOSEPH YOUNG. The surveyor is allowed an allowance for laying off the homestead in this cause. 18 May 1875. (P. 41)

HIRAM KIRKLAND versus JAMES HARE Et Al. Master's Report. 18 May 1875. (P. 42)

J. B. HAWKINS versus MARY and L. E. FITZPATRICK. The Court is satisfied from the proof that a case is made in which it is to the interest of complainant's wards that a reasonable amount of the corpus of the guardian's funds, now in the hands of the complainant, be encroached upon for the purpose of enabling the guardian to educate the defendants. 18 May 1875. (P. 43)

S. S. JARRATT versus J. L. JARRATT. A. G. Milliken is appointed guardian for J. L. Jarratt. 18 May 1875. (P. 44)

TOWNSEND FUGITT Et Al for the use of B. Fugitt, Sr. versus GEORGE ST. JOHN. The defendant recovers against B. Fugitt. 18 May 1875. (P. 45)

JOHN STARR versus CELINDA PARTON. The Clerk will take an account and ascertain the amount belonging to each heir and pay them the same. 18 May 1875. (P. 46)

J. A. GOODING, Administrator of William J. Leigh, MARY ANN LEIGH, DELALA A. LEIGH, LOUELA LEIGH, and WILLIAM LEIGH versus J. L. CAWTHON, JOSEPHUS FINLEY, and SAMUEL A. SWOPE. On 12 Feb 1869, complainant William Leigh conveyed to William J. Leigh, intestate of complainant Gooding, husband of complainant Mary Ann and father of complainant Deliah A. and Louela a certain tract of land in the 4th District of Cannon County containing 408 acres. A mistake was made in the description of the said land. The Court is of the opinion that the parties are entitled to the relief prayed for. 18 May 1875. (Pp. 47-48)

ALEXANDER MILLIGAN versus JANE J. BOGLE and IRA HOLLINS-WORTH. 18 May 1875. (P. 49)

R. W. NEELY Et Al versus D. BARKER Et Al. A tract of land is ordered sold. 18 May 1875. (Pp. 50-51)

SARAH WHITLOCK versus JOHN W. WHITLOCK. Costs of suit is adjudged against complainant. 18 May 1875. (P. 51)

The Court adjourned having dispatched all the business ready for hearing. 18 May 1875. (P. 52)

Chancery Court was held at the Courthouse in the town of Woodbury, Cannon County on the fourth Monday in Oct 1875, it being the 25th day of said month. Albert S. Marks, presiding. (P. 53)

JOHN C. OWEN and others versus J. B. THOMAS and others. 25 Oct 1875. (P. 53)

W. R. CAMPBELL versus A. J. GANNON. The Master is ordered to collect the funds attached in the hands of D. B. Vance due the defendant. 25 Oct 1875. (P. 54)

BILLY YOUNG versus W. C. TODD and others. W. J. Bailey is the statutory guardian of William B., Louis, and Mary Parton. 25 Oct 1875. (P. 55)

J. R. FUSTON versus SARAH FUSTON. It is ordered by the Court that funds in the hands of the Clerk & Master be paid to the Fuston heirs. 25 Oct 1875. (P. 55)

T. W. BREWER versus W. L. SULLIVAN and others. If the defendants do not pay the balance due, then the land will be sold. 25 Oct 1875. (Pp. 56-57)

S. S. JARRATT versus J. L. JARRATT. John H. Smith is appointed as guardian for defendant J. L. Jarratt. 25 Oct 1875. (P. 58)

A number of causes are continued. (Pp. 58-59)

G. W. SMITH versus A. G. PETTY. Master's Report. Defendant is indebted to Cantrell & Gribble. 25 Oct 1875. (Pp. 59-61)

S. P. POWELL and others versus JOHN D. WOOD and others. James S. Gribble and J. C. Webb became the purchasers of 114 acres, it being the remaining unsold portion of the original tract of land owned by James Wood deceased. 25 Oct 1875. (Pp. 61-62)

N. G. MADDUX versus A. A. WARE Et Al. Master's Report. Sale of a tract of land. 25 Oct 1875. (Pp. 62-63)

R. L. OWEN and wife versus W. J. OWEN and others. The Master reports that the title to the Warren County land contracted for as set out in the pleadings is clear and unencumbered for the following reasons shown by the title papers. The land was entered by Jeremiah Neely Nov. 26, 1826. The grant was issued to Richard Hancock, assignee of said Neely Aug. 21, 1838. Richard Hancock owned and claimed said land under said grant to some time in 1840 and gave it to C. C. Hancock who held and claimed it till some time in 1867 and then deeded it to A. L. Hancock who held and claimed it until 1871 under said deed and then sold it to Alaminta Owen. 29 Sep 1875. (Pp. 64-65)

J. R. NEELY and others versus G. W. SMITH. A note was issued for a tract of land. If the note is not paid, then the land will be sold. 25 Oct 1875. (Pp. 66-67)

J. R. NEELY Et Al versus M. C. NEELY Et Al. Complainant recovers of the defendant. 25 Oct 1875. (Pp. 67-68)

(ALMAN) RIGSBY versus JOHN K. RIGSBY. 25 Oct 1875. (P. 69)

J. H. YORK and others versus DANIEL S. FORD, Administrator. The Clerk will take proof and show how much is due from said Ford to the heirs of the intestate. 25 Oct 1875. (P. 70)

LUCINDA OWEN versus ALAMINTA OWEN and others. Complainant's security is insolvent. Complainant is ordered to give other security. 25 Oct 1875. (P. 71)

JOHN C. HAYES versus H. C. McBROOM and others. 25 Oct 1875. (P. 71)

ANN ELIZA GUNTER by next friend versus W. C. and SARAH TODD, Executors of A. F. Todd. The relief prayed for in complainant's bill is not well founded under the proof. The bill is dismissed. The Confederate money filed in this cause $3501 will be transmitted to the Supreme Court with the transcript in the case. 26 Oct 1875. (P. 72)

W. R. AKERS versus M. R. DUNCAN. The demurrer is not well taken. 26 Oct 1875. (Pp. 72-73)

W. P. BALTIMORE and others versus RICHARD BURKS and others. William Driver and wife Kezie, Louisa Hopkins, J. N. Darby and wife Elizabeth are non residents of the State. Defendant Richard Keele's residence is unknown. John Fletcher and wife Sarah have been served with process. The bill is taken for confessed. A hearing is set. 26 Oct 1875. (P. 74)

LAURA A. SUMMERS versus JOHN W. SUMMERS. The court is pleased to overrule the demurrer. 26 Oct 1875. (P. 74)

McFARLAND and others versus THOMAS G. WOOD and others. The Court rules that Thomas G. Wood is not answerable for any part of the funds drawn by him from the Planter's Bank of Tennessee. 26 Oct 1875. (P. 75)

R. W. NEELY and others versus D. BARKER and others. The Clerk is to report what would be a reasonable fee for B. F. Vinson, guardian of the minor heirs of N. L. Neely. 26 Oct 1875. (Pp. 76-77)

GEORGE W. DAVENPORT and others versus T. F. PAGE and others. Defendants Bettie and Nellie Page are minors without guardian. J. H. Cummins is appointed as guardian. 26 Oct 1875. (P. 77)

J. S. WOMACK Et Al versus P. G. LEECH Et Al. The Clerk will distribute the balance of the funds among the six heirs of Joseph H. Bogle deceased. 27 Oct 1875. (Pp. 78-79)

NELSON and SPERRY versus J. M. WILLIAMS and others. Defendant S. E. Williams was the creditor of her husband in the sum of $2000. The conveyance of the house and lot described in the bill so far as it conveys a life estate to defendant Jane Williams was voluntary and therefore void as to complainants. 27 Oct 1875. (Pp. 79-80)

H. A. WILEY and others. Charter of incorporation for the McMinnville & Smithville Turnpike Company for the purpose of constructing a turnpike road from Woodbury two miles in the direction of McMinnville two miles up Stone's River in the direction of Smithville. 27 Oct 1875. (Pp. 81-88)

E. L. C. WITTY versus E. J. SUMMERS. 27 Oct 1875. (Pp. 88-91)

JOHN STARR versus CELINDA PARTON. Master's Report. 27 Oct 1875. (Pp. 91-92)

(Pages 93-96 are blank)

Chancery Court met at the Courthouse in the town of Woodbury on the fourth Monday in Apr 1876, it being the 24th day of

125

said month. Albert S. Marks, presiding. (P. 97)

J. A. TENPENNY versus R. B. BRANDON Et Al. J. A. Tenpenny became the purchaser of 135 acres in the 11th District, his being the only bid made. 21 Mar 1876. (Pp. 97-98)

E. L. C. WITTY versus SARAH R. ROSS. Defendant is a minor without guardian. B. M. Webb is appointed as guardian. 24 Apr 1876. (P. 98)

T. W. BREWER versus W. L. SULLIVAN Et Al. J. M. Dunn, Administrator of T. W. Brewer, became the purchaser of one acre in the 6th District. It was purchased for the use of the estate. 24 Apr 1876. (Pp. 99-100)

J. R. NEELY versus G. W. SMITH. Master's Report. John H. Smith became the purchaser of 103 acres, it being a half interest only. 8 Mar 1876. (Pp. 100-102)

J. R. NEELY Et Al versus M. C. NEELY Et Al. Master's Report. John H. Smith became the purchaser of a tract of land in the 4th District formerly owned by complainant J. R. Neely and T. W. Brewer deceased which Complainant J. R. Neely conveyed to Defendant M. C. Neely by deed on 12 Aug 1870. 24 Apr 1876. (Pp. 102-104)

ALMON RIGSBY versus JOHN K. RIGSBY. Compromise decree. The Court decrees that the defendant execute to the complainant a quit claim deed for all the land described in the pleadings except 104 acres sold to George Melton. 24 Apr 1876. (Pp. 104-105)

JOHN HAMMONS versus R. F. BELL, FRANCES HALPAIN and her attorney Joseph Clark, and WILLIAM VICKERS. A tract of land is ordered sold. The purchase money is to be divided equally between complainant and defendant. 24 Apr 1876. (Pp. 105-106)

N. C. HILL, Administrator, versus SAMUEL M. HILL Et Al. 24 Apr 1876. (Pp. 107-108)

A number of causes are continued. (Pp. 109-110)

S. S. JARRATT versus J. L. JARRATT. Master's Report. 24 Apr 1876. (Pp. 110-112)

NELSON and SPERRY versus JAMES WILLIAMS Et Al. Master's Report. Nelson and Sperry became the purchasers of the life interest of Jane Williams in a tract of land. 24 Apr 1876. (Pp. 112-113)

THOMAS D. CUMMINS versus RICHARD SPIDELL. Mariah and E. J. Justice are minors without guardian. James A. Jones is appointed as guardian. 24 Apr 1876. (P. 114)

J. P. FLOYD versus JAMES M. ROBERTS. Master's Report. James M. Roberts became the purchaser of a tract of land. Title was divested out of the said J. P. Floyd as assignee of J. H. Summers and vested in the said Roberts. 24 Apr 1876. (Pp. 114-115)

A number of causes are continued. (Pp. 115-117)

M. B. MILLIKEN versus J. P. MILLIKEN. The complainant recovers of the defendant. It is decreed by the Court that the
complainant have a lien on the land described in the pleadings.
25 Apr 1876. (Pp. 117-118)

DANIEL BRYSON, Administrator, versus C. C. ALEXANDER Et Al.
Master's Report. The Master reported that he sold the land
mentioned and described in the pleadings in two tracts. 25 Apr
1876. Lot No. 1 was sold to A. P. Cooper who married the daughter of Nancy Bryson, formerly Nancy Alexander, one of the
original heirs of the estate of Mary Alexander. The said
Nancy Alexander was the mother of eight children which would
entitle the said Cooper to one eighth interest in said estate.
Said Cooper is the guardian of several of the minor heirs of
said estate. The Master reports that he finds said Cooper entitled to credit for the interest of seven wards as follows,
to wit, John McCoy Alexander died leaving nine children;
Benjamin Alexander died leaving four heirs; Abner Alexander
died leaving four children; Nancy Bryson, formerly Alexander,
died leaving eight heirs. The said Cooper purchased the interest of Mary A. Ready, daughter of Abraham Alexander deceased, who died leaving four children. He credited by purchase with the interest of E. P. Bryson, son of Nancy Bryson,
it being one eighth of her original share. Said Cooper credited with the interest of Emily S. Mears, M. J. Bryson, and
Margaret F. Cooper, heirs of Nancy Bryson. Credited with interest in part of Abraham Bryson, being also an heir of Nancy
Bryson. (Pp. 118-123)

ZACHARIAH BAWLEY versus SUSAN J. BAWLEY. The bill is taken
for confessed. The complainant is entitled to the relief sought.
The bonds of matrimony are dissolved. 25 Apr 1876. (P. 123)

A number of causes are continued. (Pp. 123-125)

J. R. FUSON versus SARAH FUSON. Master's report. 25 Apr
1876. (Pp. 125-128)

W. B. BYNUM versus MARY BYNUM and JOHN BYNUM Et Al. The
dower land of the widow was rented out. The tenant hindered
and delayed the collection of the rents. In all probability,
the Receiver will be unable to collect the rents. 16 Mar 1876.
(P. 128)

ANN SULLIVAN versus CALVIN SULLIVAN. The complainant dismisses her bill. 25 Apr 1876. (Pp. 128-129)

ELIJAH LYON versus W. B. LILLARD, Administrator. The
costs of this cause will be taxed to W. B. Lillard as the
administrator of William Summerhill. 26 Apr 1876. (P. 130)

S. B. SPURLOCK versus B. A. HANCOCK. Order of reference.
The Master is to ascertain what amount, if any, the sureties
of John F. Weedon, administrator of the estate of G. W. Thompson, are liable. 26 Apr 1876. (Pp. 130-131)

ADAM WEAVER versus L. N. WOODSIDE. The Clerk will pay
one hundred dollars to the attorney of Adam Weaver. 26 Apr
1876. (P. 131)

I. N. FULLER, Administrator, versus H. C. McBROOM and others. The motion to dismiss this cause is disallowed. 26 Apr 1876. (Pp. 131-132)

E. J. BYNUM and P. C. PATTON for the use of J. C. Harris versus JOHN A. SUMMERS. Defendant John A. Summers purchased of E. J. Bynum on 15 Jan 1872 a tract of land in the 4th District. There was a lien placed on the land which has not been paid. If not paid, then the land is to be sold. 26 Apr 1876. (Pp. 132-133)

E. L. C. WITTY versus SARAH R. ROSS Et Al. Process has been served. The bill is taken for confessed. Complainant and defendants Robert Pain, Sarah R. Ross, and W. C. Edwards are the owners of the land described in the pleadings. The Clerk will take an account as to whether the land should be partitioned or sold. 26 Apr 1876. (Pp. 133-134)

THOMAS CUMMINS and wife VERSUS KENEDY Heirs. The Clerk will take an account as to whether it is in the interest of the heirs that the land be partitioned or sold. 26 Apr 1876. (P. 134)

J. S. McADOO versus F. S. ANDERSON Et Al. The Clerk is to give an account as to what amount of money is due Matthew Bogle from the estate of Joseph H. Bogle. 26 Apr 1876. (P. 135)

A. B. WITHERSPOON, Administrator, versus J. T. MITCHELL and others. The bill is taken for confessed by the defendants. 26 Apr 1876. (Pp. 135-136)

WARREN CUMMINS versus SARAH HUDSPETH. An account is necessary in this cause in order to adjust the equities between the parties. 26 Apr 1876. (Pp. 136-138)

C. P. BROWN versus H. M. JONES, JAMES A. JONES, Et Al. The bill is taken for confessed. Complainant is entitled to the relief sought. Sale of a tract of land is ordered. 26 Apr 1876. (Pp. 138-139)

W. R. AKERS versus M. R. DUNCAN. There is no equity in complainant's bill. The bill is dismissed but without prejudice. 26 Apr 1876. (P. 140)

J. T. CARTER versus HENRY McBROOM. Consolidated causes. 26 Apr 1876. (Pp. 141-142)

ALF DOWNING Et Al versus McBROOM & COMPANY. 26 Apr 1876. (Pp. 142-143)

SHELTON heirs versus JACOB THOMAS. Process has been served. The bill is taken for confessed. The following defendants have not answered viz. Jacob Thomas and the following heirs of Jesse Alexander, to wit, Mary and husband Thomas B. Carnes, Nancy Black and husband James F., Martha Alexander and husband James M. McKnight, Samuel B. and Gideon Alexander, all of Rutherford County, and against John D. Alexander who is assignee of P. G. Leech who has taken the benefit of the bankruptcy law. 26 Apr 1876. (Pp. 143-144)

J. W. YORK Et Al versus DANIEL S. FORD, Administrator of

Tempy York deceased. Master's Report. The last settlement made by D. S. Ford, Administrator, with the County Court Clerk was 1 Jun 1872. There are eight distributees. 26 Apr 1876. (Pp. 145-147)

E. L. C. WHITLEY and E. J. SUMMERS versus B. F. ROSS and wife SARAH R., R. P. NEAL and husband JAMES, D. J. PRICE, R. B. PRICE, ROBERT PRICE, and N. C. EDWARDS. Partition cannot be made for the advantage of all the parties to have the same. 26 Apr 1876. (Pp. 148-150)

Z. THOMASON Et Al versus R. A. HANCOCK Et Al. Zachariah Thomason and wife Matilda, Benjamin Adamson, Charles J. Hancock, William Adams and wife Elizabeth, Bluford W. Adamson, Olivia Adamson, Ulm L. Adamson, Mary Adamson, the last named three being minors sue by their guardian Bluford Adamson, Bluford J. Hancock, Louis R. Hancock, Ulm L. Hancock, and J. R. Hancock, a minor who sues by his guardian Ulm L. Hancock, R. A. Hancock, J. L. Fare, Administrator of Louis Hancock, Matilda Adamson and husband whose name is unknown who have been served with process. Partition cannot be made advantageously for all the parties. The land contains only 153 acres. There are eight shares. The land is ordered sold. 26 Apr 1876. (Pp. 150-152)

JAMES JAMISON versus MARGARET JAMISON. Claims against the estate of James Jamison deceased are given. 26 Apr 1876. (Pp. 152-155)

THOMAS CUMMINS and wife versus RICHARD SPIDELL. Master's Report. 26 Apr 1876. (Pp. 155-156)

ADAM WEAVER versus L. W. WOODSIDES Et Al. 26 Apr 1876. (Pp. 157-159)

J. A. GOODING, Administrator, versus JAMES L. CAW   ). J. A. Gooding, Administration of Leigh deceased, became the purchaser of a tract of land. 26 Apr 1876. (Pp. 159-160)

S. B. SPURLOCK versus JOHN WOODS Et Al. Complainant is entitled to the relief prayed for. 26 Apr 1876. (P. 161)

LEECH and others versus EZEKIEL ALEXANDER and others. 26 Apr 1876. (Pp. 162-164)

ALFRED ROBERSON and wife Et Al versus W. C. LEECH Et Al. It is decreed by the court that the funds arising from the sale of the Bethel lands be paid to the Thomas heirs in discharge of their claims against Leech and Summers. 26 Apr 1876. (Pp. 165-167)

LUCINDA OWEN Et Al versus ALAMILLA OWEN and WILLIAM POWELL. This cause is dismissed. 26 Apr 1876. (P. 167)

G. W. SMITH versus A. G. PETTY. John Rains was the purchasers of 100 acres. 24 Jan 1876. (Pp. 168-169)

MARY JANE LANCE Et Al versus T. F. WEST and others. Parties have entered into a compromise. 26 Apr 1876. (P. 169)

ZACHARIAH THOMASON Et Al versus R. A. HANCOCK Et Al. 26 Apr 1876. (Pp. 169-171)

(Page 172 is blank)

Chancery Court met at the Courthouse in the town of Woodbury, Cannon County, on the fourth Monday in Oct 1876, it being the 23rd day of said month. Albert S. Marks, presiding. (P. 173)

A number of causes are continued. (Pp. 173-175)

C. P. BROWN versus H. M. JONES Et Al. Clerk's report of sale of a town lot. Bounded east by C. C. Brown's brick store lot supposed to be about one fourth of an acre upon which is situated a brick store house and a grocery. It was purchased by C. P. Brown, the complainant. 20 Sep 1876. (Pp. 175-176)

E. L. C. WITTY and E. J. SUMMERS versus B. F. ROSS and wife Et Al. 23 Oct 1876. (Pp. 176-178)

ROBERT NEELY Et Al versus D. BARKER Et Al. The Clerk will take proof and report the amount due Mrs. Rankhorn in lieu of dower according to the scales of mortality. 23 Oct 1876. (P. 178)

JOHN HAMMONS versus R. F. BELL Et Al. Report of sale. 23 Oct 1876. (Pp. 178-179)

G. W. SMITH versus A. G. PETTY. Master's report. The proceeds of the land sold in this cause will be allowed to settle the lien. 23 Oct 1876. (P. 180)

A. L. DOWNING Et Al versus McBROOM & COMPANY. Report of the Master. 23 Oct 1876. (Pp. 181-182)

S. T. POWELL Et Al versus JOHN A. WOOD Et Al. Master's report. 23 Oct 1876. (Pp. 183-185)

W. B. MILLIGAN versus J. P. MILLIGAN. Master's report. 23 Oct 1876. (P. 186)

THOMAS D. CUMMINS versus RICHARD SPIDELL Et Al. Five dollars is a reasonable fee for the attornies. 23 Oct 1876. (Pp. 186-187)

(Page 188 is blank)

THOMAS D. CUMMINS Et Al versus RICHARD SPIDELL Et Al. Richard Spidell was the purchaser of a tract of land sold at the Courthouse. 23 Oct 1876. (Pp. 189-190)

KENNEDY heirs versus WEST heirs. 23 Oct 1876. (Pp. 190-191)

BILLY YOUNG Et Al versus W. C. TODD and SARAH TODD, Executors of A. F. Todd Et Al. A. F. Todd, Guardian of the minor heirs of J. F. Parton made his last settlement with the County Court Clerk on 5 Jan 1876. Funds were paid to four of his wards. It appears that A. F. Todd was liable as guardian of W. B. Lewis and Mary Parton in the amount of $267.50. 24 Oct 1876. (Pp. 192-194)

E. J. BYNUM and others versus JOHN A. SUMMERS. Final Decree. (Pp. 194-196)

JANE SUMMERS versus J. W. PAGE Et Al. The Supreme Court is of opinion that there is no error except so far as the decree gives the benefit of recovery absolutely to James Summers. The said James Summers is only entitled to the interest arising from the fund. It is ordered that the cause be remanded back to the Chancery Court at Woodbury to secure said fund and to protect the rights of the children of Jane and Ivory Summers. 24 Oct 1876. (Pp. 197-199)

JOHN W. SUMMERS versus LAURA SUMMERS. The Court is pleased to allow the cross bill to be filed. 24 Oct 1876. (Pp. 199-200)

DAVID GRIZZLE Et Al versus JOHN B. WOOD Et Al. W. W. Wood is the purchaser of the land sold in this cause. 24 Oct 1876. (Pp. 201-202)

PETER C. TALLEY versus A. N. FISHER and T. J. JELTON. It appears that complainant Peter C. Talley has paid off and fully satisfied the amount of a decree executed against him by the Supreme Court at Nashville. Said decree was against him as one of the parties in the bond of James S. Odom deceased as guardian of the minor heirs of A. G. Odom deceased. Said recovery is the amount of the proceeds of the sale of a slave by the name of Louisa who was sold under a former decree of this court. 24 Oct 1876. (Pp. 203-204)

WARREN CUMMINS versus S. B. HUDSPETH. Master's report. 25 Oct 1876. (Pp. 205-208)

PETER C. TALLEY versus H. A. WILEY, M. R. RUSHING, J. W. ORAN Et Al. The Court is of the opinion that the deed of J. W. Oran to the defendants H. A. Wiley and M. R. Rushing, dated 23 May 1871, was intended by the parties thereto as a mortgage. 25 Oct 1876. (Pp. 209-210)

WILLIAM PHILLIPS versus M. C. NEELY. The Master will report to the next term of court. 25 Oct 1876. (P. 211)

A. F. McFERRIN versus J. B. DAVENPORT. This cause is continued until next term of court. 25 Oct 1876. (P. 212)

A number of causes are continued. (Pp. 212-217)

MARY ODOM Et Al versus M. M. ODOM Et Al. 25 Oct 1876. (P. 217)

J. B. HAWKINS, Administrator of F. Holt versus FIELDING HOLT Et Al. Sale of a tract of land. 25 Oct 1876. (P. 218)

A number of causes are continued. (Pp. 218-220)

TURNER VAUGHAN versus JAMES H. WOOD Et Al. 25 Oct 1876. (Pp. 220-221)

E. A. LEECH Et Al versus EZEKIEL ALEXANDER Et Al. Master's report. 25 Oct 1876. (Pp. 221-224)

J. W. McADOO versus S. F. ANDERSON. The distributive share of M. S. Bogle in his father's (Joseph H. Bogle) amounted to $258.58. 25 Oct 1876. (Pp. 224-226)

Z. THOMASON Et Al versus R. A. HANCOCK. Master's report. 25 Oct 1876. (Pp. 226-238)

ALFRED ROBINSON and wife and others versus W. C. LEECH Et Al. Consolidated causes. 25 Oct 1876. (P. 239)

WITHERSPOON, Administrator of J. L. Jarratt, versus J. F. MITCHELL. Master's report. The Master reports that the personal assets in the hands of the administrator are insufficient to pay the debts of his intestate's estate. In fact, there are no personal assets in his hands. It will be necessary to sell the land to pay the debts. 25 Oct 1876. (Pp. 240-244)

E. L. C. WITTY versus SARAH R. ROSS Et Al. 25 Oct 1876. (Pp. 245-247)

A number of causes are continued. (Pp. 247-248)

Z. THOMASON versus LARKIN KEATON. 25 Oct 1876. (Pp. 249-252)

J. N. YORK and others versus DANIEL S. FORD, Administrator. 23 Apr 1877. (Pp. 252-253)

A. B. WITHERSPOON, Administrator of J. L. Jarratt, versus J. T. MITCHELL and wife CLEMENTINE, formerly Jarratt, and others. 23 Apr 1877. (Pp. 253-256)

N. G. MADDOX and others versus A. A. WARE and others. Master's report. The Master reports that the land was purchased by the said Maddox. He executed two promissory notes. 23 Apr 1877. (Pp. 257-259)

A number of causes are continued. (Pp. 259-261)

J. B. HAWKINS, Administrator of Fielding Holt, versus FIELDING HOLT and others. 23 Apr 1877. (Pp. 261-263)

J. B. JUSTICE Et Al versus R. STEPHENS Et Al. It appears to the court that defendants are indebted to the complainants. 23 Apr 1877. (Pp. 263-264)

JOSEPH PEDON versus J. M. PEDON. The complainant comes and dismisses his suit. 23 Apr 1877. (P. 265)

(Page 266 is blank)

A number of causes are continued. (Pp. 267-268)

THOMAS D. CUMMINS versus RICHARD SPIDELL Et Al. 23 Apr 1877. (Pp. 268-270)

B. F. McFERRIN versus A. D. FUGITT. Final Decree. 23 Apr 1877. (P. 271)

ALFRED ROBINSON and wife versus W. C. LEECH Et Al. Consolidated causes. 23 Apr 1877. (Pp. 272-274)

G. W. DAVENPORT and wife versus J. W. PAGE, F. F. PAGE, BETTIE PAGE, and WILLIE PAGE. It appears to the court that complainant by reason of his age and intemperate habits was in a measure easily imposed upon. It appears to the court that the defendant, J. W. Page, availed himself of the weakness of complainant and obtained the deed and ought to be impeached by this suit and the Court is therefore of the opinion that neither can stand. It is therefore decreed that said deed and decree be declared void. 24 Apr 1877. (Pp. 274-275)

MARY E. JONES versus HENRY EASON. Master's report. The said Mary E. Jones was the purchaser of the house and lot mentioned in the pleadings. Title is divested out of the said Henry Eason and vested in Mary E. Jones. 24 Apr 1877. (Pp. 275-276)

PIGUE, MANIER, & HALL versus B. L. and W. H. McFERRIN and others. Consolidated causes. 24 Apr 1877. (P. 276)

J. A. GOODING, Guardian of N. A. E. Jamison, a minor, versus WILLIAM SANDERS, Administrator of the estate of M. H. Sanders, and others. Defendant William Sanders' intestate, M. H. Sanders, was appointed guardian of N. A. E. Jamison, a minor. Defendants A. J. Thomas and James Todd were sureties on his guardian bonds. He took charge of and rented out the land of his ward. He received the rents for the year 1861 and from that time on until 1874 during which last year he, said guardian, died without receiving that year's rent. After the death of said guardian, Joseph A. Gooding was appointed as guardian by the County Court. 24 Apr 1877. (Pp. 277-279)

J. H. WOOD versus J. W. McADOO. The motion to dismiss is disallowed. 25 Apr 1877. (P. 280)

MARY G. ODOM versus M. M. ODOM and others. 25 Apr 1877. (Pp. 281-282)

GEORGE PATTERSON Et Al versus T. B. BREVARD Et Al. Decree. 25 Apr 1877. (Pp. 282-285)

J. S. WOOD Et Al versus H. O. WOOD Et Al. Defendants are all non residents. The bill is taken for confessed. 25 Apr 1877. (P. 286)

W. C. NETTLES and wife versus W. C. LOCK and others. Process has been served. The bill is taken for confessed. A hearing is set. 25 Apr 1877. (Pp. 286-287)

B. T. McBROOM Et Al versus MARTHA NELSON Et Al. It was suggested that defendant Martha Nelson has intermarried since the filing of original bill with one George Anderson. The said George Anderson is made a party to this suit. 25 Apr 1877. (P. 287)

JANE McFERRIN versus W. H. McFERRIN. The bill is taken for confessed. It appears to the court that complainant and defendant were intermarried in Cannon County in the year 1866. Since said marriage, defendant has become a habitual drunkard and has failed and neglected to provide for complainant. The bonds of matrimony are dissolved. Complainant is to have the custody of the children, to wit, Emogene, J. B., and Mattie McFerrin. Complainant is to have as alimony all of the property. 25 Apr 1877. (P. 288)

S. B. SPURLOCK and others versus B. A. HANCOCK and others. 25 Apr 1877. (Pp. 289-290)

JOHN McBROOM versus RICHARD FLOYD Et Al. Judgment is entered against defendants Richard Floyd, M. M. Odom and wife Sallie, and Cecilia Floyd. It is agreed that the complainant's bill be dismissed as to all the land embraced in the mortgage except fifty acres. 25 Apr 1877. (P. 290)

R. W. NEELY versus JOHN HAMMONS. The bill is taken for confessed. A hearing is set. 25 Apr 1877. (P. 291)

JOHN R. RIGSBY versus ALMAN RIGSBY. 25 Apr 1877. (Pp. 292-293)

J. T. BELL, Guardian, versus A. C. GOFF Et Al. Master's Report. The report gives the amount received by A. F. Todd for the benefit of his wards. 25 Apr 1877. (Pp. 293-297)

W. L. SULLIVAN versus FRANCES WALKER Et Al. Application of defendants Frances Walker and William Barton to withdraw the answer heretofore filed by them. 25 Apr 1877. (P. 297)

DANIEL GRIZZLE Et Al versus J. B. WOOD Et Al. 25 Apr 1877. (Pp. 298-299)

THOMAS M. BOGLE versus R. R. BOGLE, W. H. TRIBBLE, and others. Master's report. The Master reports on the settlement of R. R. Bogle as guardian of Thomas M. Bogle. (See Wilson County Court record, pages 1 and 2, dated 11 Mar 1868.) R. R. Bogle, guardian of complainant, in connection with the other guardian of Joseph Bogle's children, sold some personal property turned over to them by J. S. Womack for the benefit of their wards. 25 Apr 1877. (Pp. 299-305)

T. M. BOGLE versus R. R. BOGLE, Guardian. The Master reports that the item of Confederate money charged to defendant on page 10 of report is in part erroneous and the report should be modified to that extent. 25 Apr 1877. (Pp. 305-308)

LAURA A. SUMMERS versus JOHN W. SUMMERS. Bill for divorce. Time is given said Laura A. Summers to give security for costs. 25 Apr 1877. (P. 308)

J. T. BELL Et Al versus W. J. BAILEY Et Al. Motion of complainants to take the bill for confessed as to W. J. Bailey, Guardian of William B. Louis, Mary Parton, R. Stephens, Isaac Finley, J. W. McAdoo, and A. Finley. It appears to the court that all of the defendants have been served with process. Judgment is entered against them. 25 Apr 1877. (P. 309)

J. T. BELL Et Al versus W. J. BAILEY Et Al. W. J. Bailey, as guardian of the Parton heirs obtained a decree for two hundred and sixty seven dollars against W. C. and Sarah Todd, Executors of A. F. Todd deceased who was former guardian of the Parton heirs. It appears that said A. F. Todd during his guardianship, to wit, in 1866 and 1867 received into his hands funds belonging to his said wards and invested two hundred and twenty dollars of the same in the lands mentioned in the cross bill. The estate of A. F. Todd is insolvent. Defendant Bailey's wards, to wit, the Parton heirs, have a trust in the land or the funds arising from its sale. It is decreed by the

Court that the Clerk of the County Court apply toward the satisfaction of the decree the said sum of two hundred and twenty dollars. 25 Apr 1877. (Pp. 209-310)

This day, the Court appointed J. C. New as Clerk & Master
of the Chancery Court at Woodbury for the term of six years.
25 Apr 1877. (Pp. 311-314)

W. J. Wood submits his resignation as Special Commissioners
in those causes in which he has been involved during his tenure
as Clerk & Master. John C. New is appointed in his stead. 25
Apr 1877. (Pp. 314-315)

Chancery Court met in the town of Woodbury, Cannon County,
at the Courthouse on the fourth Monday of Oct 1877. Albert S.
Marks, presiding. 22 Oct 1877. (P. 316)

ALFRED ROBERSON and wife versus W. C. LEECH Et Al. Consolidated causes. 22 Oct 1877. (Pp. 316-318)

R. STEPHENS versus B. F. VINSON Et Al. The lands of A. F.
McFerrin, the security of R. Stephens on the land notes for the
purchase money, have been sold under an execution of this court.
22 Oct 1877. (Pp. 318-319)

GEORGE PATTERSON Et Al versus T. B. BREVARD Et Al. 22 Oct
1877. (Pp. 319-321)

ALFRED ROBERSON Et Al versus W. C. LEECH Et Al. Report
showing the amount of indebtedness of W. S. Rhodes to the Thomas
heirs. It is impossible to determine the exact amount due each
of the several heirs. 22 Oct 1877. (Pp. 321-323)

ROBERT W. NEELY Et Al versus D. BARKER Et Al. Consolidated
causes. 22 Oct 1877. The land purchased by B. F. Vinson and
R. Stephens originally belonged to R. W. Neely, A. L. Neely,
J. B. Neely, and Polly J. Neely, now Polly J. Barker. James B.
Neely died intestate without wife or issue. His share of said
land descended to his brothers and sisters or their children,
to wit, R. W. Neely, Polly J. Neely Barker, Sarah A. Neely, now
Vinson, Nancy E. Neely, now Helton, and the heirs of A. L. Neely,
who now represent their father's share. His widow, Harriet D.
Neely, has since married Rankhorn. His other heirs are Elijah
Neely, W. R. Neely, B. F. Neely, and Amanda A. Neely. 22 Oct
1877. (Pp. 323-330)

N. G. MADDOX versus A. A. WARE Et Al. This cause is continued. 22 Oct 1877. (P. 330)

JOHN S. ODOM Et Al versus F. S. ANDERSON Et Al. Master's
report. There was money in the hands of the former Clerk & Master due to the Bogle heirs. 22 Oct 1877. The heirs are Josephine Bogle, Hannah Bogle, George A. Bogle, Thomas Bogle, John
S. Bogle, M. M. Odom, R. L. Odom, and J. H. Odom. (Pp. 332-
334)

S. P. POWELL Et Al versus JOHN A. WOOD Et Al. There was
no bidder to buy the land. It is decreed that the Master take
additional proof and report back. 22 Oct 1877. (P. 334)

ROBERT ROBERSON versus SUE ROBERSON. The complainant comes to dismiss the suit. 22 Oct 1877. (P. 335)

W. C. NETTLES and wife versus W. C. LEECH Et Al and J. L. FARE. The last settlement made by W. C. Leech as guardian was 5 Jan 1861. He had in his hands $287 belonging to his ward. 22 Oct 1877. (P. 336)

R. W. NEELY versus JOHN HAMMONS. Master's report. 22 Oct 1877. (Pp. 337-338)

JOHN McBROOM versus RICHARD FLOYD Et Al. Master's report. Plaintiff recovers of the defendant $600. If the amount is not paid, the Master will sell fifty acres of land. 22 Oct 1877. (Pp. 332-333)

P. D. CUMMINS versus WARREN CUMMINS. The Clerk is to report what additional compensation should be allowed Warren Cummins for his services as Special Commissioner. 22 Oct 1877. (Pp. 340-341)

H. J. ST. JOHN versus MARY WILLIS. An account is taken with Blake Sagely, Guardian of Mary Willis. 22 Oct 1877. (Pp. 342-344)

ALAMINTA OWEN versus MARY TASSEY. Complainant obtained a judgment against the defendant for $464.52 predicated on a promissory note. If the note is not paid, land will be sold to satisfy the judgment. 22 Oct 1877. (P. 344)

JOHN K. RIGSBY versus ALMON RIGSBY. John K. Rigsby was the purchaser of a tract of land. Title is divested out of the said Almon Rigsby and vested in the said John K. Rigsby. 22 Oct 1877. (Pp. 344-346)

THOMAS D. CUMMINS Et Al versus R. S. SPIDELL Et Al. Master's report. The Master is decreed to pay out the funds to the parties entitled as required by law. 22 Oct 1877. (Pp. 346-347)

J. W. WARREN versus J. J. SUMMERS. Defendant is indebted to complainant. 22 Oct 1877. (Pp. 348-350)

S. P. POWELL Et Al versus JOHN A. WOOD Et Al. 22 Oct 1877. (Pp. 350-353)

A. F. and B. L. McFERRIN versus JAMES P. HOLT Et Al. Complainants obtained a judgment against Defendant Holt for $44. Judgment is due. 22 Oct 1877. (Pp. 354-355)

McFARLAND Et Al versus THOMAS G. WOOD, Receiver, Et Al. Defendant has fully performed his duty as Receiver and has faithfully accounted for all sums that have come to his hands. 22 Oct 1877. (P. 356)

S. B. SPURLOCK versus B. L. and W. H. McFERRIN Et Al. The parties enter into an agreement. 22 Oct 1877. (P. 357)

T. J. JELTON versus R. R. BOGLE. 22 Oct 1877. (P. 358)

PIGUE, MANIER, & HALL versus B. L. and W. H. McFERRIN. 22 Oct 1877. (Pp. 359-360)

J. H. WOOD versus J. W. McADOO. The bill is taken for confessed. 23 Oct 1877. (P. 361)

A number of causes are continued. (Pp. 362-363)

NANCY McADOO versus SAM McADOO. It being suggested that the parties are living together, the bill is dismissed. 23 Oct 1877. (P. 363)

R. P. WOMACK versus S. E. BURGER and GEORGE WOOD. A judgment was rendered against the defendant. 23 Oct 1877. (P. 364)

C. M. BARRETT versus WILLIAM ANDY SMITH. The bill is taken for confessed. 23 Oct 1877. (P. 364)

Z. THOMASON versus R. A. HANCOCK Et Al. 23 Oct 1877. (Pp. 365-366)

A number of causes are continued. (Pp. 366-367)

CAL SULLIVAN versus B. L. McFERRIN Et Al. Defendant and purchaser R. A. Hancock bid off the land sold in this cause at 178½ acres. The land has failed to hold out by 12½ acres. The Clerk is directed to credit the note of R. A. Hancock, the purchaser. 23 Oct 1877. (Pp. 367-368)

CALLIE NEW versus C. B. NEW. The Court was pleased to decree the complainant a divorce from bed and board and seventy-five dollars alimony. 23 Oct 1877. (P. 369)

JOHN W. SUMMERS versus LAURA A. SUMMERS. The defendant has been guilty of adultery with one Eli Barrett in Cannon County. The bonds of matrimony are dissolved. 23 Oct 1877. (Pp. 370-371)

LAURA A. SUMMERS versus JOHN W. SUMMERS. The cause was dismissed for lack of security. 23 Oct 1877. (P. 371)

R. W. NEELY versus D. BARKER Et Al. Sarah Vinson, wife of B. F. Vinson; and Polly Barker, wife of D. Barker, were examined by the Chancellor separate and apart from their husbands touching their willingness to allow their husbands credit on their liabilities for the land purchased by them in these causes. 23 Oct 1877. (Pp. 372-373)

W. P. BALTIMORE Et Al versus EMANUEL BURKS Et Al. The bill is taken for confessed except for the heirs of Emanuel Burks deceased. Complainant recovers of all the defendants their shares in two tracts of land as the heirs of James Burks deceased. Complainants and defendants hold the land as tenants in common. 23 Oct 1877. (P. 374)

(Page 375 is blank)

Chancery Court met at the Courthouse in the town of Woodbury on the fourth Monday of Apr 1878, it being the 22nd day of said month. Albert S. Marks, presiding. (P. 376)

J. W. WARREN versus J. J. SUMMERS. J. W. Warren was the purchaser of a tract of land. Title is divested out of the defendant and vested in the complainant. 22 Apr 1878. (Pp. 376-377)

JOHN McBROOM versus RICHARD FLYOD Et Al. John McBroom became the purchaser of a tract of land. Title is divested out of the defendant and vested in the plaintiff. 22 Apr 1878. (Pp. 377-378)

ALAMINTA OWEN versus MARY TASSEY. Complainant became the purchaser of a tract of land containing 130 or 135 acres and known as part of the Fountain Owen tract of land. 23 Feb 1878. (379)

DANIEL GRIZZLE Et Al versus J. B. WOOD Et Al. Consolidated causes. 22 Apr 1878. (Pp. 379-380)

H. C. McBROOM Et Al versus AMEY GANDY Et Al. Master's report. The Master was ordered to rent the saw and grist mill in litigation. S. C. Odom was the renter. 22 Apr 1878. (Pp. 381-383)

A. B. WITHERSPOON, Administrator, versus J. T. MITCHELL Et Al. 22 Apr 1878. (Pp. 383-384)

DANIEL BRYSON Et Al versus C. C. ALEXANDER Et Al. Master's report. 22 Apr 1878. (P, 385)

THOMAS D. CUMMINS Et Al versus R. S. SPIDELL Et Al. 22 Apr 1878. (Pp. 385-386)

DANIEL GRIZZLE Et Al versus J. B. WOOD Et Al. Consolidated causes. 22 Apr 1878. (Pp. 387-388)

ROBERT BRYSON Et Al versus H. J. WOMACK Et Al. Clerk recovers of Joseph Bogle and his surety. 22 Apr 1878. (P. 389)

G. W. SMITH versus A. G. PETTY. Judgment against John Rains, purchaser of a tract of land. 22 Apr 1878. (P. 390)

ROBERT BRYSON, Administrator, Et Al versus MARTHA J. WOMACK Et Al. The Supreme Court is of the opinion that there is no error in the proceedings. 22 Apr 1878. (Pp. 391-392)

JAMES SUMMERS versus B. H. SUMMERS. Leave is granted to complainant to supply the papers. 22 Apr 1878. (P. 393)

R. W. NEELY and others versus D. BARKER and others. The Master reports that there is a suit pending in this court by one of the purchasers, R. Stephens, to rescind the sale of the tract purchased by him until this suit is determined the amount due the married women. It is decreed that the Master cancel the two promissory notes executed in this cause by D. Barker and the account as to B. F. Vinson will await the termination of the suit of Stephens versus B. F. Vinson and others. 22 Apr 1878. (Pp. 294-295)

ISRAEL LONG versus ISABELLA LONG. The defendant is allowed thirty days to file answer. 22 Apr 1878. (P. 396)

A number of causes are continued. (P. 397)

D. B. VANCE Et Al versus Z. L. BREVARD and others. Defendants Mary S. Persley, Anna E. Persley, Alice M. Persley, B. B. Persley, Hattie J. Gollithan, Anna A. Phillips, Edward V. Phillips, and Mary H. Phillips are all minors without guardian. It is ordered that Edward R. Vance, their grandfather, be appointed as guardian. F. L. Turner, W. C. Turner, Annie Turner, Isaac Turner, Jr., Daniel Turner, John Turner, Edna Turner, and Zora Turner are all minors without guardian and are non residents of the State. D. B. Vance is appointed as their guardian. Defendants James W. Brevard, Charlie Brevard, Z. L. Brevard, Jr., and Earnest Brevard are minors without guardian. William F. Brevard, their brother, is appointed as their guardian. 22 Apr 1878. (P. 398)

Adjourned until tomorrow morning at eight o'clock. 22 Apr 1878. (P. 399)

P. C. ISBELL versus F. B. DICKENS and others. Defendants F. B. Dickens and Henry Mankin are non residents of the State of Tennessee. Process has been served. 23 Apr 1878. (P. 400)

MARY TASSEY Et Al versus W. H. MOSES Et Al. Defendants Josephine and Clementine McKnight; W. G., Mary J., Martha R., and N. A. Cook; and James Teague are minors without guardian. James A. Jones is appointed as their guardian. 23 Apr 1878. (P. 401)

P. C. ISBELL versus F. B. DICKENS Et Al. Defendants A. F. Jones and Ruben Adams are allowed thirty days to file their answer. 23 Apr 1878. (P. 402)

ROBERT BRYSON, Administrator, Et Al versus M. J. WOMACK Et Al. It is decreed that D. R. Vance, Executor of T. B. Brevard pay all the costs incident to the cross bill of T. B. Brevard, deceased. 23 Apr 1878. (Pp. 402-403)

S. E. CARNES, Administrator, versus J. M. McMAHAN. The Clerk is ordered to sell a tract of land. 23 Apr 1878. (Pp. 403-404)

MARY J. PRESTON versus WILLIAM C. PRESTON. The cause is continued until next term. The defendant is permitted to go to see his child at reasonable intervals provided he conducts himself in a peaceable, respectful like manner while there. 23 Apr 1878. (P. 404)

P. C. ISBELL versus F. B. DICKENS and others. This cause is compromised and settled as to the defendants A. F. Jones, Bartlett Jones, and Rubin Adams. Defendants relinquish their claim and title to all the lands claimed by complainant for Defendant Dickens outside the lines of an 800 acre tract granted to two of the sons of A. F. Jones. 23 Apr 1878. (P. 405)

B. T. McBROOM versus HENRY McBROOM Et Al. The decree of the Supreme Court states that the decree of the Chancellor is correct and in all things confirmed. 23 Apr 1878. (Pp. 406-407)

J. B. HAWKINS, Administrator, versus J. P. HOLT and others. Mary J. Stone is a minor without guardian. R. B. Capshaw is appointed her guardian. 23 Apr 1878. (P. 408)

S. H. McKNIGHT, Administrator, versus JAMES A. McKNIGHT and others. It is decreed that the administrator report his action to the next term of court. 16 Apr 1878. (Pp. 408-409)

ALFRED ROBINSON and others versus W. C. LEECH and others. Consolidated causes. 23 Apr 1878. (Pp. 410-411)

HANNAH LANCE versus R. T. TATUM and others. The complainant is permitted to have the use and occupation of the land in controversy. 23 Apr 1878. (P. 412)

THOMAS W. WEST versus THOMAS E. WEST. The Court decrees that the settlement made between complainant and defendant about 1 Jan 1872 will not be disturbed and will be taken as conclusion between the parties. Each partner is entitled to a credit. 23 Apr 1878. (P. 413)

Court adjourned until tomorrow morning at eight. 23 Apr 1878. (P. 414)

MARY TASSEY Et Al versus W. H. MOSES Et Al. The bill is taken for confessed as to the unknown heirs of W. H. Moses deceased. They reside in the State of Texas. 24 Apr 1878. (P. 415)

A number of causes are continued. (Pp. 415-416)

P. C. TALLEY versus H. A. WILEY and others. It is suggested that J. C. New is incompetent by reason of relationship to J. W. Orand. The Court appoints a special commissioner to take an account and report at the next term of court. 24 Apr 1878. (P. 417)

H. J. ST. JOHN versus MARY WILLIS. Blake Sagely shall perform all the duties as guardian of Mary Willis, a person of unsound mind. 24 Apr 1878. (P. 418)

SARAH E. WEEDON versus CALVIN SULLIVAN. Parties enter into an agreement. 24 Apr 1878. (P. 419)

MARY TASSEY and others versus W. H. MOSES heirs and others. It appears to the court that the bill is taken for confessed as to Mary Tassey, E. O. P. McKnight, Mary J. Duggin, M. J. Freeman, William T. Wood, John S. Wood, E. J. Wood, M. L. Bivins, Ally Tegue, William Tegue, Gholston Tegue, Alexander Tegue, Sarah Covington, Margaret J. Fite, and the defendants Josephine McKnight, Clementine McKnight, W. G. Cook, Mary J. Cook, Martin R. Cook, N. A. Cook, James Tegue, and the unknown heirs of W. H. Moses and wife Ally, formerly Ally Sutton, as the heirs of Mary Sutton. 24 Apr 1878. (Pp. 420-421)

JANE WALLS versus BENJAMIN FUGITT Et Al. The Clerk is to report if the lands of Edmond Walls can be partitioned or should be sold. 24 Apr 1878. (P. 421)

ROBERT FULLER versus DELILIA FULLER. The bill is taken for confessed. A hearing is set. 24 Apr 1878. (Pp. 421-422)

J. A. WILLIAMS and others versus H. W. DAVENPORT and others. Process has been served on all the defendants, to wit, H. W. Davenport, R. J. Davenport, W. T. Mingles, and Mary Mingles.

The bill is taken for confessed. 24 Apr 1878. (P. 423)

ELIZABETH GRIZZLE by next friend William Grizzle. Ex Parte. It appears to the Court that William Grizzle is the son of Elizabeth Grizzle. He has the sum of about sixty or sixty-five dollars due him in the hands of the County Court Clerk. His mother is in destitute conditions. He is a minor of tender years. She is to be allowed twenty dollars out of the sum. 24 Apr 1878. (P. 423)

SARAH E. MELTON versus JAMES H. MELTON. The bill is taken for confessed. The complainant is entitled to the relief prayed for. The bonds of matrimony are dissolved. Complainant is to have the care of the children. 24 Apr 1878. (Pp. 424-425)

MARY TASSEY Et Al versus G. H. MOSES Et Al. Disinterested parties state that the tract of land is small, rough, and rocky, and has but little tillable land, but little water, if any. There are over twenty heirs and the land is so situated that it cannot be divided without a sale. It is in the interest of the parties that the land be sold. 24 Apr 1878. (Pp. 425-426)

J. A. WILLIAMS Et Al versus H. W. DAVENPORT Et Al. The bill is taken for confessed. Complainant is entitled to the relief sought. Defendant Mary Mingles has no right or title in the land mentioned in the bill. The land is ordered sold. 24 Apr 1878. (P. 427)

A number of causes are continued. (Pp. 428-429)

JOHN S. ODOM and others versus F. S. ANDERSON and others. 24 Apr 1878. (Pp. 430-435)

SARAH E. WEEDON Et Al versus CALVIN SULLIVAN. 24 Apr 1878. (Pp. 436-437)

Chancery Court met at the Courthouse in the town of Woodbury on the fourth Monday of Oct 1878, it being the 28th day of said month. There being no Chancellor present, court was adjourned until the next morning. (P. 438)

Court met pursuant to adjournment. F. A. Burress, presiding as Special Chancellor. 29 Oct 1878. (Pp. 438-439)

JAMES PURSER and wife versus JOHN F. PRESTON Et Al. Defendant moves to have the bill dismissed. 29 Oct 1878. (Pp. 439-440)

THOMAS D. CUMMINS Et Al versus R. S. SPIDELL Et Al. 29 Oct 1878. (Pp. 441-442)

J. A. WILLIAMS Et Al versus H. W. DAVENPORT Et Al. Title to a tract of land is divested out of the defendants and vested in the complainants. 29 Oct 1878. (Pp. 443-444)

MARY J. PRESTON versus WILLIAM PRESTON. Complainant is not entitled to the relief sought. Witnesses state that the defendant's character for peace and chastity is good. He is an industrious, sober, moral man, and provided well for his family. 29 Oct 1878. (Pp. 445-446)

A. B. WITHERSPOON, Administrator of J. L. Jarratt, versus
J. T. MITCHELL Et Al. Master's report. 29 Oct 1878. (Pp. 446-
447)

G. W. SMITH versus A. G. PETTY. Master's report. 29 Oct
1878. (Pp. 447-448)

MINERVA STONE by her guardian. Ex Parte. The Master is
to report as to whether the land mentioned in the proceedings
is worth the amount the parties have agreed to give for it and
whether or not it is a judicious purchase. 29 Oct 1878. (Pp.
449-450)

J. B. HAWKINS, Guardian of Charles M. Jones. Ex Parte.
The Clerk is to take proof as to what would be a reasonable allowance per annum to educate and maintain the minor Charles M.
Jones taking into consideration his standing and rank in society.
29 Oct 1878. (P. 450)

W. B. PARTON by guardian. Ex Parte. The Clerk is to report as to whether the land mentioned in the proceedings is worth
the amount the parties have agreed to. 29 Oct 1878. (P. 450)

E. L. C. WITTY versus SARAH ROSS. 29 Oct 1878. (P. 451)

D. B. VANCE, Executor of T. B. Brevard, versus Z. T. BRE-
VARD, T. J. VANCE, WILLIAM F. BREVARD, JAMES BREVARD, CHARLES
BREVARD, Z. T. BREVARD, JR., EARNEST BREVARD, ELIZA A. BREVARD,
G. A. PURSLEY, MARY S. PURSLEY, ANNA E. PURSLEY, ALICE H. PURS-
LEY, B. B. PURSLEY, JOSEPH VANCE, ED R. VANCE, HATTIE J. GOLLI-
THAN, J. B. GOLLITHAN, JOHN J. BREVARD, SARAH S. TURNER, ISAAC
TURNER, F. L. TURNER, W. C. TURNER, ANNA TURNER, ISAAC TURNER,
JR., DANIEL TURNER, JOHN TURNER, EDNA TURNER, ZORA TURNER,
Z. B. VANCE, SARAH PHILLIPS, THOMAS PHILLIPS, ANNA S. PHILLIPS,
EDWARD PHILLIPS, MARY H. PHILLIPS, J. E. RUCKER, A. C. TATUM,
and J. C. HAYS. The Court decrees that it was the obvious
purpose of the testator that the real estate be converted into
money for all the purposes of said will. The money was bequeathed to his nephews and nieces. The Court decrees that perhaps D. B. Vance is an improper person to act as guardian for
the minors for whom he was appointed. 29 Oct 1878. (Pp. 451-
452)

Court adjoined until Thursday, 31 Oct 1878. (P. 453)

J. A. DEMENT Et Al versus S. T. KELTON Et Al. The bill is
dismissed. 31 Oct 1878. (P. 454)

JOHN S. ODOM Et Al versus F. S. ANDERSON Et Al. Master's
report. 31 Oct 1878. (Pp. 455-457)

R. STEPHENS Et Al versus TIMOTHY MURPHY Et Al. The Court
is of the opinion that this is a proper cause for an account. 31
Oct 1878. (Pp. 457-458)

S. E. CARNES, Administrator, versus J. H. McMAHON. The
land was not sold for want of a bidder. 1 Nov 1878. (Pp. 459-
460)

ROBERT FULLER versus DELILIAH FULLER. Complainant has dismissed his suit on account of the death of the defendant. 1 Nov 1878. (P. 460)

H. C. McBROOM Et Al versus AMY GANDY Et Al. 1 Nov 1878. (Pp. 460-461)

D. B. VANCE, Executor of T. B. Brevard, versus Z. T. BREVARD Et Al. The Clerk is to report whether it is to the interest of all the parties to sell the land instead of waiting until the youngest child of Z. T. Brevard comes of age. 1 Nov 1878. (Pp. 461-462)

A. F. McFERRIN versus E. D. OWENSBY Et Al. This cause is to be heard before a jury. 1 Nov 1878. (Pp. 462-463)

NANCY PARKER versus WILLIAM BARTON Et Al. The Court is of the opinion that there are allegations in the bill upon the question as to the distributive share of complainant due her from her father's estate upon which the bill should be retained in court. 2 Nov 1878. (P. 464)

IVORY SUMMERS versus JANE SUMMERS. 2 Nov 1878. (P. 465)

A. M. DONNELL and others versus J. N. SUMMERS and others. Hearing is set for next term. 2 Nov 1878. (P. 466)

C. M. BARRELL versus WILLIAM ANDY SMITH. Sale of a tract of land. 25 Nov 1878. (Pp. 467-468)

L. ADCOCK and wife versus SARAH B. WOOD Et Al. The Clerk is to determine what would be a reasonable allowance for the services of John K. Rigsby as guardian of Sarah B. Wood. 25 Nov 1878. (P. 469)

J. B. HAWKINS, Administrator, versus J. P. HOLT Et Al. The Clerk is to determine what would be a reasonable fee for St. John and Finley out of the funds brought into the estate of Fielding Holt. 25 Nov 1878. (P. 470)

JAMES PURSER and wife versus JOHN F. PRESTON Et Al. The bill of Purser and wife is dismissed. They pray an appeal to the Supreme Court in Nashville. 25 Nov 1878. (P. 471)

T. W. WEST versus T. E. WEST. The Clerk will make a report to the next term. 25 Nov 1878. (P. 471)

A number of causes are continued. (P. 472)

JOHN S. WOOD versus H. O. WOOD Et Al. The complainant is entitled to the relief sought. 25 Nov 1878. (P. 473)

ALFRED OWEN Et Al versus H. A. OVERALL Et Al. Consolidated causes. 25 Nov 1878. (Pp. 473-474)

LEONARD ADCOCK Et Al versus SARAH B. WOOD Et Al. Consolidated causes. 26 Nov 1878. (Pp. 475-489)

WILLIAM DAVENPORT versus DANIEL TRAVIS. The defendant is allowed time to file his answer. 26 Nov 1878. (P. 489)

C. W. MOORE Et Al versus A. F. McFERRIN Et Al. The demurrer is not well take. 26 Nov 1878. (P. 490)

A number of causes are continued. (P. 490)

WILLIAM W. McKNIGHT versus E. O. P. McKNIGHT. Process has been served on defendants E. O. P. McKnight, W. P. Duggin and wife M. J., L. A., P. C., and M. A. McKnight, and D. B. Vance, Clerk. The bill is taken for confessed as to all the defendants except B. E. J. McKnight, the lunatic. The complainant as husband of Elizabeth McKnight is entitled to a life estate. The defendants are enjoined from proceeding to sell the life estate of complainant. By consent of complainant, the court consents to act for the lunatic, B. E. J. McKnight's one fourth interest in complainant's estate. It is decreed to E. O. P. McKnight to take care of, support, and maintain the lunatic and in return will receive the share for taking care of her. The said E. O. P. McKnight is a brother of the lunatic. 26 Nov 1878. (Pp. 491-492)

RACHEL A. CAWTHON versus PLEASANT A. CAWTHON. The Court decrees a temporary divorce from bed and board until the next term of court. Complainant is restored to all the property attached. 26 Nov 1878. (P. 493)

MELVINA STONE by her guardian. Ex Parte. The tract of land mentioned in the pleading is well worth $400, the amount the parties have agreed to. There is a pretty fair dwelling on the premises, very good barn and stable, a garden, a good smokehouse, wheat house, etc. There are 64¼ acres. It is in the interest of the minor to have her means invested in the tract. 26 Nov 1878. (Pp. 494-495)

WILEY HENDRIXSON versus J. Y. HIPP. The defendant appeals the ruling to the Supreme Court. 26 Nov 1878. (P. 496)

D. B. VANCE, Executor of T. B. Brevard, versus Z. T. BREVARD Et Al. Master's report. 26 Nov 1878. (Pp. 496-499)

S. P. POWELL Et Al versus JOHN A. WOOD Et Al. Petition of Lucile B. Dunington and E. R. Dunington, Executrix of F. C. Dunington, to become parties in this suit. They are permitted to file a cross bill. 26 Nov 1878. (P. 500)

JANE WALLS Et Al versus BENJAMIN FUGITT Et Al. Judgment rendered against the defendant. 26 Nov 1878. (P. 500)

J. A. DEMENT Et Al versus S. T. KELTON Et Al. Complainant's bill is dismissed. 26 Nov 1878. (P. 501)

J. B. HAWKINS, Administrator, versus J. P. HOLT Et Al. The Court is to determine whether the land assigned as a homestead of R. Holt by the Sheriff is subject to sale for the payment of the judgment rendered. The Court is of the opinion that the homestead is liable and subject to sale under the proceedings. 26 Nov 1878. (P. 502)

WILLIAM JUSTICE Et Al versus HENRY McBROOM. The death of William Justice was suggested. The cause was revived in the name of Henry Justice. 26 Nov 1878. (P. 503)

S. E. BRAGG versus NANNIE B. BRAGG. The cross bill is dismissed. 26 Nov 1878. (Pp. 503-504)

J. B. HAWKINS, Administrator, Et Al versus J. P. HOLT Et
Al. It appears to the Court that the complainants and defendants who are set out as heirs of Fielding Holt are purchasers
from the heirs are the owners of the land mentioned in the proceedings. 26 Nov 1878. (Pp. 504-505)

H. C. McBROOM Et Al versus AMEY GANDY Et Al. Consolidated
causes. 26 Nov 1878. (P. 506)

J. B. HAWKINS, Administrator, Et Al versus J. P. HOLT Et
Al. (Pp. 507-510)

S. P. POWELL Et Al versus JOHN A. WOOD Et Al. Master's
report. 26 Nov 1878. (Pp. 510-511)

All the business of the Court having been dispatched, the
Court adjourned until the next term. (P. 511)

Chancery Court met at the Courthouse in the town of Woodbury, Cannon County, on the fourth Monday of Apr 1879, it being
the 23rd day of said month. James W. Burton, presiding. (P.
512)

J. B. HAWKINS, Administrator, versus J. P. HOLT Et Al. 23
Apr 1879. (Pp. 512-514)

D. B. VANCE Et Al versus Z. L. BREVARD Et Al. Report of
sale. 23 Apr 1879. (Pp. 514-523)

LEONARD ADCOCK and wife versus SARAH B. WOOD Et Al. Consolidated causes. 23 Apr 1879. (Pp. 523-526)

N. C. HILL, Administrator, versus SAMUEL M. HILL Et Al.
Master's report. 23 Apr 1879. (Pp. 526-527)

A number of causes are continued. (Pp. 527-528)

T. D. CUMMINS versus R. S. SPIDELL Et Al. Master's report.
23 Apr 1879. (Pp. 528-529)

S. E. CARNES, Administrator, versus J. H. McMAHON. Master's
report. 23 Apr 1879. (Pp. 529-530)

C. M. BARRELL versus WILLIAM ANDY SMITH. Master's report.
Sale of a tract of land. 23 Apr 1879. (Pp. 531-532)

S. K. McKNIGHT, Administrator, versus J. M. McKNIGHT Et Al.
Master's report. It appears to the court that all the funds in
the hands of the administrator have been paid out under the order of the court. This cause is strickened from the docket. 23
Apr 1879. (P. 532)

P. C. TALLEY versus H. A. WILEY Et Al. Master's report. 23
Apr 1879. (Pp. 533-534)

(Page 535 is blank)

Court met pursuant to adjournment. F. R. Burrus was com-
missioned by the governor to hold the Chancery Court where the
said James W. Burton is incompetent. Said Burrus presented his
commission. 29 Apr 1879. (Pp. 436-437)

A number of causes are continued. (Pp. 537-538)

H. A. WILEY versus W. L. COVINGTON and wife. The land was sold on 30 Sep 1868. Trustees paid to William Barton, Trustee for Mrs. Covington fifty dollars and the balance due on note. It is ordered by the Court that the Clerk & Master and Commissioner pay to the said William Barton the funds that are in his hands. 30 Apr 1879. (Pp. 539-540)

J. A. FARMER versus J. L. LAWRENCE. The sum is due on the sale of a tract of land. If not paid, the land is to be sold. 30 Apr 1879. (P. 541)

J. B. HAWKINS, Administrator, versus J. P. HOLT Et Al. 30 Apr 1879. (P. 542)

S. B. CROUK versus IRENE CROUK. The bill is taken for confessed. 30 Apr 1879. (P. 542)

SARAH L. WHITLOCK versus WILLIAM BARTON. Complainant to pay the cost. 30 Apr 1879. (P. 543)

S. B. CROUK versus IRENE CROUK. The allegations in the bill are sustained. Parties were married on 24 Nov 1876. Defendant has wilfully absented herself and without just cause for more than two years before the filing of this bill. The bonds of matrimony are dissolved. 1 May 1879. (P. 543)

J. B. HAWKINS, Administrator, versus J. P. HOLT Et Al. 1 May 1879. (Pp. 544-545)

IVORY SUMMERS versus JANE B. SUMMERS. Master's report. 1 May 1879. (Pp. 546-548)

ANNA STROUD versus MITCHEL DANIEL Et Al. This cause was heard by jury. They find that W. D. Stroud was last with his family in the early part of 1867. W. D. Stroud and his wife executed a deed for the land in controversy to James Cook on 1 Dec 1852. The said Cook executed a deed to the land to Pelham and Daniel. The bill is dismissed. 1 May 1879. (Pp. 548-549)

JANE B. SUMMERS versus JOHN W. PAGE Et Al. 1 May 1879. (P. 549)

NANNIE BRAGG versus S. E. BRAGG. The bill is taken for confessed. The cause will proceed ex parte. 1 May 1879. (P. 550)

ANN E. TODD versus JOHN TODD. The bill is taken for confessed. The bonds of matrimony are dissolved. Complainant will have custody of the two children. 1 May 1879. (P. 550)

A number of causes are continued. (P. 551)

NANCY E. BUSH versus HARVEY ARNOLD. The Court is pleased to enjoin defendant and wife from further proceeding with their suit in the County Court. 1 May 1879. (P. 552)

Report of John C. New, Clerk & Master, of the funds on hand at the Apr Term 1879. (P. 552)

A. B. WITHERSPOON, Administrator, versus J. T. MITCHELL Et Al. 1 May 1879. (Pp. 552-555)

146

P. C. ISBELL versus F. B. DICKENS. The bill is taken for confessed. A hearing is set. 2 May 1879. (P. 556)

T. Y. DAVIS versus WILLIAM PHILLIPS. In order to avoid the trouble of litigation, William Phillips agrees to the Chancery Court entering a decree. A tract of land is to be sold. 2 May 1879. (Pp. 556-557)

J. C. NEW, Clerk & Master, makes his bond. 2 May 1879. (Pp. 558-559)

A. D. LEWIS versus ALICE LEWIS. The bill is taken for confessed. The bonds of matrimony are dissolved. Complainant will be restored to the custody of the child. 2 May 1879. (P. 560)

J. N. YORK Et Al versus D. S. FORD Et Al. Master's report. 2 May 1879. (Pp. 560-561)

B. T. McBROOM versus HENRY McBROOM Et Al. Master's report. 2 May 1879. (Pp. 561-564)

J. W. McADOO versus J. H. MITCHELL Et Al. 2 May 1879. (P. 565)

NANNIE BRAGG versus SAMUEL BRAGG. Parties were married on 3 Dec 1877. The defendant made false and unjust accusations against the chastity and virtue of the complainant. He had wilfully neglected and refused to provide for her. He drove her away from home without just cause. The bonds of matrimony are dissolved. Complainant is restored to her maiden name of Nannie E. Stephenson. Complainant is to have custody of her child. 2 May 1879. (Pp. 565-566)

JAMES JAMISON versus MARGARET JAMISON. Master's report. 2 May 1879. (Pp. 566-571)

CALLIE NEW, Administratrix, versus NANCY NEW Et Al. Defendants are allowed time to answer. 2 May 1879. (P. 571)

JOHN FARLEY versus W. F. MASON Et Al. Defendants are allowed time to answer. 2 May 1879. (P. 572)

ACHILLES ALEXANDER versus T. G. SULLIVAN. Defendant is allowed time to answer. 2 May 1879. (P. 572)

HIRAM TENNISON versus JAMES TODD and wife ELIZABETH. The death of defendant Elizabeth Todd was suggested. No further steps were taken. 2 May 1879. (P. 573)

WILLIAM DAVENPORT VERSUS DANIEL TRAVIS. Defendant is given time to make an answer. 2 May 1879. (P. 574)

RACHAEL A. CAWTHON versus PLEASANT CAWTHON. The charges in the bill are not sustained by the proof. The complainant's bill is dismissed. 2 May 1879. (P. 574)

A. OWEN versus H. A. OVERALL Et Al. Consolidated causes. 2 May 1879. (P. 575)

NANNIE E. BRAGG versus S. E. BRAGG. Five hundred dollars would be reasonable alimony for the complainant. 2 May 1879. (P. 576)

OLLY and FRANK NEELY versus JOHN E. MASON Et Al. John E. Mason makes application for a receiver for the land in controversy. 2 May 1879. (P. 577)

RACHEL M. SULLIVAN and husband versus JOSEPH HOLLIS Et Al. It appears to the court that all the equities in the bill are met and denied in the answer. The proof fails to establish the allegations in the bill. Complainants' bill is dismissed. 2 May 1879. (P. 577)

Z. L. BREVARD, JR. and others by their next friend Z. L. Brevard, Sr. Ex Parte. 2 May 1879. (Pp. 578-580)

The Court having disposed of all business ready for hearing adjourns until court in course. (P. 580)

(Page 581 is blank)

Chancery Court met at the Courthouse in the town of Woodbury, Cannon County, on the fourth Monday in Oct 1879, it being the 27th day of said month. John W. Burton, presiding. (P. 582)

L. A. FARMER versus J. T. LAWRENCE. Master's report. Sale of 25 acres in the 5th District. Title is divested out of the defendant and vested in the complainant. 27 Oct 1879. (Pp. 582-583)

?. Y. DAVIS versus WILLIAM PHILLIPS. Master's report. Sale of a tract of land. 27 Oct 1879. (Pp. 584-585)

MARY TASSEY Et Al versus W. H. MOSES Et Al. 27 Oct 1879. (Pp. 585-586)

JAMES JAMISON versus MARGARET JAMISON. 27 Oct 1879. (Pp. 586-587)

D. B. VANCE, Executor of T. B. Brevard, versus Z. L. BREVARD Et Al. Master's report. 27 Oct 1879. (Pp. 588-590)

L. ADCOCK and wife versus SARAH B. WOOD. Consolidated causes. 27 Oct 1879. (Pp. 590-591)

R. STEPHENS Et Al versus TIMOTHY MURPHY Et Al. It appears to the court that M. E. Murphy and Martha C. Murphy are minors without guardian. James H. Cummings is appointed as guardian. 27 Oct 1879. (P. 592)

ACHILLES ALEXANDER versus Z. G. SULLIVAN. The Court is pleased to decree that the complainant is entitled to recover of the defendant the money paid by complainant for the land embraced in the deed from defendant. 27 Oct 1879. (P. 593)

J. P. ELKINS versus A. YOUNGBLOOD. Complainant dismisses his suit. 27 Oct 1879. (P. 594)

A number of causes are continued. (Pp. 595-596)

WILLIAM BLACKBURN versus JOSEPH CLARK. Sale of a tract of land and town lots. 27 Oct 1879. (Pp. 597-598)

FRANK NEELY and wife versus J. E. MASON Et Al. 28 Oct 1879. (Pp. 599-602)

MARY G. ODOM versus M. H. ODOM. This cause is continued. 28 Oct 1879. (P. 603)

The Chancellor having failed to attend, the Court is dismissed. 23 Nov 1879. (P. 604)

Court met in pursuance to adjournment. N. W. McConnell, presiding. 25 Nov 1879. (P. 604)

L. ADCOCK and wife versus SARAH B. WOOD Et Al. Consolidated causes. 25 Nov 1879. (Pp. 605-606)

J. N. YORK Et Al versus D. S. FORD Et Al. Master's report. 25 Nov 1879. (Pp. 606-607)

JAMES JAMISON versus MARGARET JAMISON. 25 Nov 1879. (Pp. 607-608)

FRANK and OLLY NEELY versus JOHN E. MASON Et Al. Master's report. Sale of a tract of land in the 6th District to John E. Mason. 25 Nov 1879. (Pp. 509-510)

A. L. HANCOCK versus WILLIAM BARTON Et Al. 25 Nov 1879. (Pp. 611-612)

R. STEPHENS versus B. F. VINSON Et Al. 25 Nov 1879. (P. 612)

FRANK NEELY and wife versus JOHN E. MASON Et Al. 28 Nov 1879. (P. 613)

(Page 614 is blank)

MARY G. ODOM versus M. H. ODOM Et Al. Judgment against defendants M. M. Odom and H. C. Odom. The have four months to pay the money into court. 28 Nov 1879. (P. 615)

JOHN A. MILLIGAN versus JAMES H. MITCHELL Et Al. Complainant is entitled to the relief prayed for. 28 Nov 1879. (P. 616)

The Court having disposed of all the business ready for trial is adjourned to meet the third Monday in Jan 1880 at which time a special term of this court is appointed to meet. (P. 616)

Court met pursuant to adjournment. John W. Burton, presiding. There being no business, the Court adjourned until Thursday, Feb 12, 1880 at which time a special term of the court is appointed. 19 Jan 1880. (P. 616)

Special term of Chancery Court met pursuant to adjournment at the Courthouse in the town of Woodbury, Cannon County, on 12 Feb 1880. John W. Burton, presiding. (P. 617)

ANNA SULLIVAN versus T. G. SULLIVAN, Administrator, Et Al. Process has been served on some of the defendants, but not all of them. Complainant is allowed to amend her bill so as to make one Isaac Sullivan, a citizen of Illinois, a party defendant. 12 Feb 1880. (P. 618)

MARY TASSEY Et Al versus W. H. MOSES' heirs Et Al. 12 Feb 1880. (Pp. 618-619)

FRANK NEELY versus JOHN E. MASON Et Al. 14 Feb 1880. (P. 620)

(Page 621 is blank)

Chancery Court met at the Courthouse in the town of Woodbury, Cannon County, on the fourth Monday of Apr 1880, it being the 26th day of said month. John W. Burton, presiding. (P. 622)

J. C. HENEGAR and wife Et Al versus ISAAC FOSTER Et Al. It is ordered by the Court that the Clerk take and state an account between the heirs of William York deceased and E. T. Dillon and report what amount went into the hands of said E. T. Dillon as commissioner for the sale of the land mentioned in the pleadings. 26 Apr 1880. (P. 622)

JAMES JAMISON versus MARGARET JAMISON. Master's report. The Master reports that he paid T. G. Jamison, attorney in fact for Sarah A. Cates, formerly Sarah A. Jamison, and husband Thomas Cates the sum of $58.58. 26 Apr 1880. (P. 623)

MARY G. ODOM Et Al versus M. M. ODOM Et Al. Master's report. 26 Apr 1880. (Pp. 624-625)

FRANK NEELY and OLLY NEELY versus JOHN E. MASON Et Al. 26 Apr 1880. (Pp. 625-626)

JAMES BRAGG, Guardian, versus ELIZABETH E. J. McKNIGHT. M. W. McKnight is appointed guardian of the defendant who is a lunatic. 27 Apr 1880. (Pp. 627-628)

A. C. GUNN versus W. C. PRATER Et Al. Complainant filed a written order to dismiss his bill. 27 Apr 1880. (P. 629)

ALIMINTA OWEN versus MARY TASSEY. Master's report. 27 Apr 1880. (Pp. 630-631)

J. H. YORK Et Al versus D. S. FORD Et Al. The Master reports that he has paid N. P. Stiles and husband, daughter of W. F. York the sum of $10. 27 Apr 1880. (Pp. 631-632)

C. M. BARRELL versus WILLIAM ANDY SMITH. Master's report. P. C. Isbell, attorney for C. M. Barrell, became the purchaser of fifty acres of land sold at the Courthouse. Bounded on the east by the Barrell lands. 27 Apr 1880. (Pp. 633-634)

IRA HOLLINSWORTH, Guardian of Laura A. Murphy. Ex Parte. It appears to the Court that the petitioner is antagonistic to the interest of the minor. It is ordered to W. C. Houston be appointed as guardian. 27 Apr 1880. (P. 634)

MARY TASSEY versus W. H. MOSES' heirs Et Al. Master's report. John McAlexander and wife Hanna M. became the purchasers of a tract of land. Title is divested out of Mary Tassey and others and is vested in the said McAlexanders. 27 Apr 1880. (Pp. 635-637)

W. L. BATES Et Al versus A. BURGER Et Al. The Master was ordered to report the amount of cost that was incurred by the complainants and defendants in a survey and portion and divisions among the heirs of William Bates. 27 Apr 1880. (Pp. 637-638)

TOLBERT FUSTON and wife versus T. J. McMAHAN Et Al. Motion to dismiss as to John T. McMahan because he had neither given bond or take the oath prescribed for poor persons. 27 Apr 1880. (P. 638)

W. G. CRAWLEY versus DANIEL SMITH, Administrator, Et Al. Consolidated causes. 27 Apr 1880. (P. 639)

JANE B. SUMMERS versus JOHN W. PAGE Et Al. Master's report. 27 Apr 1880. (Pp. 639-640)

IRA HOLLINSWORTH, Guardian of Laura A. Murphy. Ex Parte. The Master is to report what means of support, if any, said minor has other than that mentioned in the pleadings. 27 Apr 1880. (P. 641)

WILLIAM CARSON Et Al versus MARTHA PEAY Et Al. J. A. Jones, an attorney of this Bar, is appointed as guardian for Laura Peay, Eliza Peay, John Peay, and R. D. Peay, the minor defendants. 27 Apr 1880. (P. 641)

E. L. C. WITTY versus SARAH B. ROSS Et Al. 28 Apr 1880. (Pp. 642-644)

JAMES JOHNSON versus ASA NICHOLS. The demurrer is overruled. 28 Apr 1880. (P. 644)

ANNA SULLIVAN VERSUS T. G. SULLIVAN Et Al. J. H. Cummings is appointed guardian for the minors John Stone, M. Stone, Sallie Stone, and Isaac Sullivan. 28 Apr 1880. (P. 645)

J. N. YORK Et Al versus D. S. FORD Et Al. It is agreed between the parties that each of the heirs of William F. York receive of the funds in the hands of the Clerk & Master. 28 Apr 1880. (P. 646)

153

Bates, William L. 21,26,
  50,54,56,70,76,79,81,
  83
Batton, L. G. 88
Bawley, Susan J. 127
Bawley, Zachariah 127
Beard, Frances A. 35
Beard, John A. 35
Beaty, Allen 5,6,7
Beaty, Elizabeth 5,6
Bell, B. F. 99
Bell, Elizabeth S. 46
Bell, J. B. 95
Bell, J. T. 134
Bell, Mary W. 46
Bell, R. F. 72,76,103,
  126,130
Bell, R. L. 90
Bell, Rebecca 49
Bell, Robert 99,108,
  109,110
Bell, Robert F. 96
Bell, W. W. 49
Bell, Wiley W. 38,46
Bennett, Joannah 47
Berry, Richard 2,3,5,
  7,8
Bethel, Chester F. 78
Bethel, Susan C. 120
Bigsby, John 61
Bivins, M. L. 140
Black, James F. 128
Black, Nancy 128
Blackburn, William 148
Blair, Ann E. 105
Blair, Caroline 46
Blair, J. T. 105
Blair, James 46
Blair, T. J. 107
Blanks, William 118
Bogle, A. L. 86
Bogle, Douglas 62
Bogle, Eliza J. 77
Bogle, Elizabeth H. 37
Bogle, Enxina C. 41
Bogle, Exena E. 37,38,39
Bogle, G. 97
Bogle, George 10,11,62,
  63,77,89,102
Bogle, George A. 37,135
Bogle, George, Sr. 8
Bogle, Hannah 135
Bogle, James 72
Bogle, James H. 41
Bogle, James J. 70
Bogle, Jane 70,86,92

Bogle, Jane J. 120,123
Bogle, Joel 40
Bogle, Johite 86
Bogle, John 42,118
Bogle, John S. 135
Bogle, Joseph 57,80,98,108,134,
  138
Bogle, Joseph H. 38,41,54,100,
  125,128,131
Bogle, Josephine 37,92,108,135
Bogle, M. S. 40,41,43,45,55,62,
  131
Bogle, Margaret 89
Bogle, Mathew L. 37,38,49
Bogle, Mathew S. 39,41,54
Bogle, Matthew 100,128
Bogle, Nancy 62
Bogle, Nancy C. 92
Bogle, R. P. 94
Bogle, R. R. 89,113,134,136
Bogle, Sarah 86,118
Bogle, T. M. 134
Bogle, Thomas 89,135
Bogle, Thomas B., Jr. 89
Bogle, Thomas M. 92,134
Bogle, Thomas N. 37
Bogle, Thomas W. 92
Bogle, Unis 92
Bogle, W. R. 80,87
Bogle, William R. 58
Boling, Levi 8
Boman, Lucy 25
Boman, William J. 25
Borum, Delphia 29
Borum, Joseph 29
Bowen, Absolom 65
Bowen, Elizabeth 65
Bowen, Ellen 65
Bowen, James R. 65
Bowen, John W. 9
Bowen, Josephine 65
Bowen, Martha E. 65
Bowen, Sally 65 .
Bowen, Sarah 65
Bowen, Sarah J. 9
Bowen, William M. 65
Bower, Ellen 70
Boweraman, Richard 41
Boweraman, Sarah 41
Bowerman, Michael 54,56
Bowerman, Mikiel 54
Bowerman, Samuel 54
Bowerman, Sarah 54,56,57
Bowers, Enoch 48
Bowers, Frances 48
Boyd, Lucinda 55

Boyd, R. L. 55
Boyett, John 87,94
Boyle, Mary A. 40
Boyle, Sarah A. 40
Boyle, William 40
Bradford, James 65
Bradford, Polly 65
Bragg, D. F. 111,112,
   113,116
Bragg, D. L. 108
Bragg, Edward 13,15,17
Bragg, Elizabeth 40
Bragg, James 150
Bragg, Joseph 40
Bragg, Nannie 146,147
Bragg, Nannie B. 144
Bragg, Nannie E. 147
Bragg, S. E. 144,146,
   147
Bragg, Samuel 147
Bragg, William 108,116
Brandon, J. J. 84
Brandon, R. B. 126
Brandon, Robert 118
Brevard, Charles 142
Brevard, Charlie 139
Brevard, Earnest 139,
   142
Brevard, Eliza A. 142
Brevard, James 142
Brevard, James W. 139
Brevard, John J. 142
Brevard, T. B. 20,109,
   112,115,116,117,133,
   135,139,142,143,144,
   148
Brevard, William F. 139,
   142
Brevard, Z. L. 29,84,
   138,139,145,148
Brevard, Z. L., Jr. 148
Brevard, Z. L., Sr. 148
Brevard, Z. T. 100,142,
   143,144
Brevard, Z. T., Jr. 142
Brevard, Zachariah L. 23
Brevard, Zebulon L. 20
Brewer, B. 23
Brewer, Benjamin 20,23,
   24,26,30
Brewer, David 53
Brewer, E. G. 116
Brewer, Elizabeth 23
Brewer, Elizabeth L. 24
Brewer, Erasmus 23
Brewer, Erasmus G. 20

Brewer, J. L. 116
Brewer, Jesse 20,23,24,26
Brewer, John 20
Brewer, John L. 23,24
Brewer, John S. 30
Brewer, L. L. 116
Brewer, Martha 20,23
Brewer, Robert 20,116
Brewer, Robert H. 23,24
Brewer, Russell 100
Brewer, Susan 20
Brewer, T. W. 115,116,117,124,
   126
Brewer, Thomas 53
Brewer, Thomas W. 20,23,115
Brewer, William 20,116
Brewer, William M. 24,24
Bridges, Allen 7,8
Bridges, Allen H. 10
Bridges, Esther 7,8,10
Brien, John L. 36
Brien, J. S. 46
Brien, John S. 30,51
Brien, Manson M. 3,4
Bright, James 81
Bright, Sarah 81
Brison, A. J. 40
Brison, Cinderilla 40
Brison, J. J. 40
Brison, Susan 40
Brison, T. B. 108
Britton, Washington 44
Brogan, John A. 9
Brogan, Lucy 9
Brooks, George 101
Brown, Anna 1
Brown, C. C. 109,112,113,130
Brown, C. P. 83,91,128,130
Brown, E. P. 85
Brown, James 1
Brown, James M. 1,3,4,35
Brown, James M., Jr. 41
Brown, James M., Sr. 41
Brown, John 1,2
Brown, John S. 18
Brown, L. S. 108,111
Brown, Nancy 1,2,8
Brown, Polly 1
Brown, Sarah P. 1,3
Bryan, E. L. 108
Bryan, Elmira F. 93
Bryan, Nelson 120
Bryan, Thomas L. 93,108
Bryant, J. W. 105
Bryson, A. A. 110
Bryson, A. J. 52,86,90,93,98,

Bryson, A. J. 103,105,
  107,117,118,120,121
Bryson, Daniel 106,
  110,111,113,127,138
Bryson, E. P. 127
Bryson, Emily 106
Bryson, Emily C. 110
Bryson, F. T. 110
Bryson, Francis 18,20,
  23,28,54
Bryson, H. T. 110
Bryson, J. J. 118
Bryson, M. J. 127
Bryson, Nancy 127
Bryson, R. 106
Bryson, Robert 62,63,
  89,95,97,102,109,
  113,118,139
Bryson, Susan 98,103,
  118
Bryson, William 18,47,
  54
Bucy, Sarah 84,89,91,
  97
Burge, James 1
Burger, A. 7,44,46,47,
  52,54,76,79,91,107,
  110,112,116,150
Burger, Abraham 3,11,
  50,118
Burger, Jacob 1,2
Burger, James 4
Burger, Lockey J. 67,
  102,105
Burger, S. E. 91,106,
  137
Burger, S. N. 81,83,94
Burger, S. W. 81
Burger, Samuel 76
Burger, Samuel C. 68
Burger, Samuel E. 1,2,
  63
Burger, W. M. 32,67,
  118
Burger, W. W. 114
Burges, Abraham 39
Burke, Clementine 50
Burkett, Andrew 55,60,
  68
Burkett, Jermiar 60
Burkett, John 53,60
Burkett, John J. 55
Burks, Caroline 92
Burks, Elizabeth 92
Burks, Elza 92
Burks, Emanuel 92,102,

137
Burks, George 92,102
Burks, James 137
Burks, John 92
Burks, R. F. 92
Burks, Rebecca 92
Burks, Richard 124
Burks, Verice 92
Burress, F. A. 141
Burrus, F. R. 145
Burton, H. M. 30
Burton, James W. 145
Burton, John W. 148,150
Burton, Lavina 30
Burton, Luvina 28
Bush, Amanda M. 31
Bush, Berry 79
Bush, H. L. 56
Bush, Jeremiah 65,68,69,71
Bush, Lucinda 45,48,55,79
Bush, Melchisidac 45
Bush, Nancy E. 146
Bush, Willis W. 31
Bush, Zachariah 7,48,55
Butcher, Richard 4,5
Byford, Aaron 7
Byford, John H. 21
Byford, Susannah 21
Bynon, John 108
Bynon, W. B. 108
Bynum, Caroline 65
Bynum, E. J. 128,130
Bynum, George W. 31
Bynum, Jane 65,69,71
Bynum, John 65,119,127
Bynum, Lucy A. 31
Bynum, Martha 65
Bynum, Mary 65,127
Bynum, Redmond 65
Bynum, Sam 65
Bynum, W. B. 119,127
Caffey, Medford 15
Campbell, A. G. 8,15
Campbell, Albert G. 8,12,13
Campbell, Alice 118
Campbell, E. H. 32,33,34,38,42
Campbell, Francis 28
Campbell, John 73
Campbell, John D. 34,37
Campbell, Josa E. 73
Campbell, Thomas 55,74
Campbell, W. B. 114
Campbell, W. R. 120,121,123
Campbell, William 39
Campbell, William B. 23
Cannon, A. F. 25

Curlee, P. B. 75
Curlee, Stephen 64
Curlee, Theodocia 64
Curlee, Widow 75
Daniel, Mitchel 146
Darby, Elizabeth 125
Darby, J. N. 125
Daugherty, Harvy 91
Daugherty, Henry 59,63,
  68,75,81,85,96,100
Davenport, Carrol 42
Davenport, Elisha 72
Davenport, G. W. 132
Davenport, George W. 118,
  125
Davenport, H. W. 140,141
Davenport, Henry 100,104
Davenport, J. B. 131
Davenport, John 42
Davenport, R. J. 140
Davenport, Wiley 60,66,
  87,98,106,111
Davenport, William 143,
  147
David, Elizabeth J. 81
Davidson, Hugh 7
Davis, Caleb B. 7
Davis, Elizabeth J. 81
Davis, John S. 41
Davis, Rebecca C. 45
Davis, T. Y. 147,148
Dawson, William J. 17
DeLong, Narcissa 117
DeLong, W. J. 117
Dement, J. A. 142,144
Denby, Margaret J. 108
Dennis, Henry 65,68,75,
  84,95
Dennis, Martha 95
Dennis, Mathew 60,65,68,
  75,84,91
Derickson, Samuel B. 28
Dewitt, Daniel G. 37
Dewitt, Mary S. 37
Dickens, B. B. 7,17
Dickens, Baxter B. 20,26
Dickens, Catherine L. 104
Dickens, F. B. 139,147
Dickens, Fielding 116
Dickens, J. F. 104
Dickens, J. H. 102
Dickens, J. T. 96
Dickings, James H. 89
Dickings, W. F. 89
Dill, Joseph 87
Dillin, Martha E. 108

Dillon, E. T. 114,150
Dillon, Sallie 114
Dodd, David 46,47,100
Dodd, John S. 90
Dodd, Nancy 90,101
Donnell, A. M. 143
Donnell, W. C. 100
Douglas, J. J. 61
Douglas, Rosaline 61
Downing, A. L. 130
Downing, Alf 128
Driver, Kezie 125
Driver, William 125
Duggin, Charles 86
Duggin, M. J. 144
Duggin, M. S. 118
Duggin, Mary J. 140
Duggin, Nancy 86
Duggin, P. L. 118
Duggin, Polly 86
Duggin, Richard 86
Duggin, Sarah 86
Duggin, Thomas 86
Duggin, W. P. 144
Duggin, William H. 86
Dunaway, D. W. 53,56
Dunaway, Paralee 53,56
Duncan, Cicero B. 11,14,19
Duncan, I. W. 111
Duncan, John 96
Duncan, John W. 112
Duncan, M. R. 125,128
Duncan, T. W. 11
Dunington, E. R. 144
Dunington, F. C. 144
Dunington, Lucile B. 144
Dunn, J. M. 115,126
Dye, Lee 94
Dye, Polly A. 94
Earle, Nathan 92
Earles, D. J. 102
Earles, Joseph R. 102
Earles, William G. 102
Earthman, Isaac 33
Earthman, Margaret 32,40
Earthman, William 33
Easley, Eliza 23
Eason, Henry 121,133
Edwards, David 9
Edwards, J. W. 56
Edwards, M. J. 56
Edwards, Mathew 3,5
Edwards, N. C. 129
Edwards, Paery 3
Edwards, Patra 5
Edwards, Polly 5

Francis, J. D. 75,99,
103
Francis, James 33,87,89
Francis, James J. 34,46
Francis, John D. 53
Francis, M. 33,34,46,95,
106
Francis, Margaret 87,89
Francis, Margaret D. 33,
34
Francis, Mary P. 52
Francis, Melchisdic 34
Francis, Nancy 52,53,63
Francis, Sarah 52,89
Francis, Sarah A. 33,34,
46,87
Freeman, M. J. 140
Frierson, Samuel D. 29
Fuget, A. D. 23,24
Fugett, A. D. 30,34
Fugett, Alfred D. 20
Fugett, Benjamin 23,24
Fugitt, A. D. 110,132
Fugitt, B., Sr. 123
Fugitt, Benjamin 114,
144
Fugitt, Townsend 123
Fuller, Delilia 140,142
Fuller, I. N. 128
Fuller, Isaac N. 30,31
Fuller, Robert 140,142
Furguson, Harriet 108
Furguson, John O. 108,
109
Furguson, R. B. 108
Fuson, J. R. 113,115,
122,124,127
Fuson, James R. 102
Fuson, Joseph 110
Fuson, S. R. 110
Fuson, Sarah 102,110,
113,115,122
Fuston, Josiah 14,19
Fuston, Sarah 124,127
Fuston, Tolbert 151
Gaither, Isaac 108,111,
112,113,116
Gaither, Sarah A. 61
Gaither, W. P. 61
Gandy, Amey 138,143,145
Gandy, Anny 117,121
Gandy, Sophia 117
Gann, M. M. 90
Gann, Nathan 90
Gannon, A. J. 114,120,
121,123

Gannon, J. K. 60
Gannon, James N. 60
Gannon, John P. 61,68,72
Gannon, M. A. 60
Gannon, S. 60,66
Gannon, S. M. 60
Gannon, S. P. 66,70
Gannon, Sarah E. 60
Gannon, Susannah 75
Garmany, William 11
Garrett, J. A. 98
Garrison, Jeremiah 70
Gasaway, Benjamin 17
George, John A. 11,42
George, Miles 83
George, Nancy A. 42
George, William F. 27,28
Gibson, Richard 15
Gibson, William 15
Gideon, Elizabeth J. 61
Gilbert, S. E. 39
Gillam, J. H. 110
Gilley, Dorcas J. 45
Gilley, Jesse 69
Gillman, J. H. 113
Gilly, John W. 28
Givan, William 30,32
Givens, Margaret 40
Givens, William 33,40
Glascock, Maxey 89
Glascock, Millie 89
Glasscock, Moses H. 15
Glenn, William 17
Goacher, Fannie 89
Goacher, Labner 89
Goad, Polly 50
Goad, W. H. 116,121
Goad, William 89,93,100
Goff, A. C. 134
Goff, Amanda 109
Goff, Ann C. 113
Goff, L. P. 109,113
Goforth, Mariah 72
Gollithan, Hattie J. 138,142
Gollithan, J. B. 142
Goad, J. 23
Goad, Sarah J. 25,28,29
Goodall, Nancy 10
Gooding, J. A. 122,123,129,133
Gooding, Joseph A. 133
Gooding, Paralee 103
Gooding, William 103
Goodloe, Henry 47,49,54
Goodloe, Henry, Jr. 47
Goodloe, James 47
Goodner, James 28

Gordon, Luma 22
Gordon, Robert 22
Graham, Louisa A. 72
Graham, Mary E. 72
Gray, Matilda 119
Gray, S. H. 119
Green, Lucinda 39
Green, Polly A. 39
Gribble, James 116
Gribble, James S. 97,
  119,124
Grigg, Daniel 89
Grimes, Britter 81
Grimes, Britton 71,81
Grimes, Fanny 81
Grimes, Grief 81
Grimes, Jane 81
Grimes, Jemima 71,81
Grimes, John 81
Grimes, Mary 81
Grimes, Nancy A. 81
Grimes, Rachael 81
Grimes, Susan 81
Grimes, Tempe 81
Grimes, William 71,81
Grimes, William F. 81
Grimes, William H. 81
Grimmett, William H. 26
Grizzle, Dan 104
Grizzle, Daniel 97,108,
  114,121,134,138
Grizzle, David 77,131
Grizzle, Elizabeth 141
Grizzle, George 114
Grizzle, John R. 114
Grizzle, Lucinda 61
Grizzle, Margaret J. 77,
  114
Grizzle, Mary 46
Grizzle, William 43,44,
  46,55,57,61,63,68,114,
  141
Groom, W. A. 92
Gross, E. C. 31,33,34
Gross, Ephraim C. 12,
  13,16,17
Gunn, A. C. 150
Gunter, Analiza 117,118
Gunter, Ann E. 125
Gunter, Isaac 42,57
Gunter, Levina 53,57,60
Gunter, Malinda 56
Gunter, Mary 57
Gunter, Nancy 59
Gunter, P. A. 60
Gunter, P. D. 56
Gunter, Pleasant D. 59

Gunter, Rebecca 57
Gunter, S. M. 57
Gunter, Samuel 2
Gunter, William 5,39,59
Guthrie, W. P. 61
Guy, James 96
Guy, Narcissa 96
Hagewood, Zachariah 13
Hailey, James A. 65
Hailey, Mary A. 65,68
Hailey, William B. 65
Hale, John P. 101
Hale, John W. 5
Hale, Mary 122
Haley, Caroline 89
Haley, Elizabeth 89
Haley, Green M. 89
Haley, Isaac T. 36
Haley, Mary A. 36
Hall, J. S. 93
Hall, Richard 120
Halpain, Frances 126
Hambleton, S. C. 62
Hamilton, Martha 106
Hamilton, Micajah 106
Hamilton, S. C. 62,72,74
Hammer, A. R. 32,35,37,40,43,46,
  47,52,53,63,72,82,84
Hammer, C. A. 98
Hammons, C. A. 108
Hammons, C. H. 80
Hammons, Elijah R. 80
Hammons, John 126,130,134,136
Hammons, Larkin W. 80
Hanagar, George W. 12
Hancock, A. L. 33,36,38,42,51,
  124,149
Hancock, Alaminta 37,38
Hancock, B. A. 127,133
Hancock, Bluford J. 129
Hancock, C. C. 12,33,36,37,38,
  40,42,51,69,124
Hancock, Charles J. 17
Hancock, Christopher C. 13
Hancock, Frances 17,18,19,22,23,
  25
Hancock, Lewis 18,19,23,25
Hancock, Louis 17,129
Hancock, Louis R. 129
Hancock, R. A. 129,132,137
Hancock, R. H. 104
Hancock, Richard 12,13,16,17,31,
  33,34,40,51,124
Hancock, Robert 33,37
Hancock, Samuel 7
Hancock, Ulm L. 129
Hardaway, Daniel 7

Harding, G. S. 93
Harding, Giles 109
Harding, Giles S. 65,79,
   102
Harding, Thomas M. 79
Hare, James 95,99,100,
   115,123
Hare, Millie D. 115
Hare, Millie E. 99
Hare, Minnie 95
Harmon, Samuel 51
Harper, James 2
Harris, Francis 72
Harris, J. C. 128
Harris, John W. 72,110
Harris, Sarah E. 72
Harris, Thomas N. 72
Harris, William P. 6,7
Harrison, Sarah J. 93
Hart, Henry 2,3,4
Hart, Laura 86
Hart, W. T. 86
Hawkins, J. 105
Hawkins, J. B. 83,105,
   107,122,123,131,132,
   139,142,143,144,145,
   146
Hawkins, Jacob B. 95
Hawkins, James 94
Hawkins, John 122
Hayes, John 42
Hayes, John C. 124
Hayes, Lydia J. 73
Hayes, Mary J. 42
Hayes, Minerva E. 73
Hayes, Nathaniel 26
Hays, Henry 81
Hays, J. C. 142
Hays, Susan 81
Helton, James 85,97,
   100
Helton, Nancy E. 135
Henderson, Agnes 15,19
Henderson, Baldy 15
Henderson, James T. 19,
   25,27
Henderson, Robert C. 15
Hendrickson, Jonathan 29
Hendrixson, Wiley 144
Heneger, J. C. 105,107,
   150
Heneger, John 105
Hennessee, Martha A. 119
Hennessee, William 119
Heriel, Elizabeth 61
Heriel, Thompson 61

Herrod, Frances 109
Herrod, John B. 109
Hibbitt, James R. 27
Hicks, Abraham 31
Hicks, Archebald 63,68,76,81,91
Hicks, Elizabeth M. 31
Higgin, Alexander 8
Higgin, Elijah 8
Higgin, James 8
Higgin, John 8,11
Higgin, Mary 8
Higgin, Wesley 8
Higgin, William 8,10
Higgins, J. P. 86,91
Higgins, James 70,78,94
Higgins, John 94
Higgins, John P. 70,73,78,94,95
Higgins, Susan 70,73,78,86,91,94,
   95
Hill, Cady F. 107
Hill, J. H. 107
Hill, J. W. 93
Hill, John H. 111,115
Hill, Kady 111
Hill, Kedy F. 108,111
Hill, Lettice J. 107
Hill, Letty 111
Hill, Lottie J. 108
Hill, N. C. 114,126,145
Hill, Nancy C. 107,108,111
Hill, Samuel 108
Hill, Samuel M. 107,108,111,114,
   126,145
Hill, W. C. 111
Hill, W. R. 43
Hipp, G. B. 110
Hipp, J. Y. 144
Hodges, R. K. 66
Hollan, Martha 110
Hollinsworth, Dillard 74,87,92
Hollinsworth, Elizabeth 74,87
Hollinsworth, Ira 71,74,84,87,
   92,94,101,116,120,121,123,150,
   151
Hollinsworth, James 74
Hollinsworth, James G. 92
Hollinsworth, John 92
Hollinsworth, Josiah 82
Hollinsworth, Sarah 82,121
Hollinsworth, Susan 74,87,92
Hollinsworth, William 74,92
Hollis, David 11,13
Hollis, John 3,4
Hollis, Joseph 11,13,148
Hollis, Samson 11
Hollis, Simeon 13

Laughlin, Elizabeth 2
Lawrence, E. J. 86,95,
  100
Lawrence, J. L. 146
Lawrence, J. T. 148
Leach, E. A. 74,104
Leach, P. G. 86
Leech, Amanda 45
Leech, Amanda C. 82
Leech, Amanda E. 106
Leech, E. A. 82,89,96,
  99,100,104,131
Leech, L. G. 34
Leech, L. H. 82
Leech, P. G. 33,39,40,
  41,42,45,48,49,51,
  54,62,63,90,93,100,
  102,105,107,112,117,
  119,120,121,125,128
Leech, P. J. 27
Leech, W. C. 67,82,104,
  106,113,119,129,132,
  135,136,140
Leech, William C. 20,
  22,42,45,59,66,72
Lefevre, Barbara 4
Lefevre, Barbary 3
Lefevre, John 3,4
Leigh, Deliliah A. 133
Leigh, Louela 123
Leigh, Mary A. 123
Leigh, William 123
Leigh, William J. 123
Leman, Daniel 19
Lemons, Asa 102
Lemons, Isaac 102
Lemons, James 102
Lewis, A. D. 147
Lewis, Alice 147
Lewis, Eliza 51,52,53,
  55,58,100
Lewis, Miles 100
Lewis, W. B. 130
Lillard, Thomas 53
Lillard, W. B. 127
Lillard, William B. 59
Lock, W. C. 133
Long, Elizabeth 62,67,
  77,84,94
Long, George 89
Long, Isabella 138
Long, Israel 62,67,77,
  94,138
Long, Matilda 89
Louis, William B. 134
Lowe, Charles F. 3,5

Luck, William C. 19
Lyon, Elijah 51,54,127
McAdoo, Azaline 19,27
McAdoo, Berthina A. 27
McAdoo, Eliza 14
McAdoo, J. S. 128
McAdoo, J. W. 75,115,131,133,
  134,137,147
McAdoo, James W. 41
McAdoo, Jane R. 29
McAdoo, Margaret J. 19,27
McAdoo, Nancy 27,137
McAdoo, Nancy C. 28
McAdoo, Parthenia 19
McAdoo, Sam 137
McAdoo, Thomas B. 19,27
McAdoo, W. S. 34
McAdoo, William 14
McAdoo, William S. 28
McAdow, James W. 1,3,7,11,15,20,
  22
McAdow, Nancy C. 19,22,32,34
McAdow, Parthenia A. 32
McAdow, William 19,22,29,32
McAdow, William L. 19
McAdow, William S. 26
McAlexander, Hannah M. 150
McAlexander, John 150
McBroom, Abel 32
McBroom, Abel, Jr. 27,30
McBroom, Abel, Sr. 27
McBroom, Amy 79
McBroom, B. T. 91,93,105,107,113,
  118,133,139,147
McBroom, Benjamin 119
McBroom, Benjamin T. 22,23,27
McBroom, Elizabeth H. 65
McBroom, Giles 93
McBroom, Giles H. 65,79
McBroom, H. C. 117,121,124,128,
  138,143,145
McBroom, Henry 28,105,119,128,
  139,144,147
McBroom, Henry D. 22,23,26,27,30
McBroom, Isaac 60
McBroom, J. D. 93,105,118
McBroom, John 134,136,138
McBroom, John D. 27,30,79,91,113
McBroom, John P. 107
McBroom, John W. 65,79,93
McBroom, Mary A. 65,79,93
McBroom, Ruth 117
McBroom, Sarah 27,28,29,30
McBroom, Sarah A. 79
McBroom, W. T. 91,93,100,102,109
McBroom, William H. 65,79

Maddox, N. G. 114,124,
132,135
Mankin, Henry 139
Marcum, J. T. 96
Markham, A. 67
Markham, Archibald 67
Markham, John 67
Markham, Nancy 67
Marks, Albert S. 91,
95,99,104,107,110,
112,115,120,121,123,
126,130,135,137
Marks, Isaac 3
Markum, J. S. 89
Marshall, D. C. 20
Marshall, David C. 24,
26,30
Marshall, F. L. 20,24
Marshall, Finis L. 26,
30
Marshall, Hugh E. 26
Marshall, H. L. 20
Marshall, Hugh L. 24
Marshall, Hugh R. 30
Marshall, John J. 20,
24,26,30
Marshall, R. F. 20
Marshall, Robert F. 24
Martin, Barclay 74
Martin, Frances 61
Martin, J. C. 17
Martin, James 28
Martin, John 4,5,7
Martin, John C. 2,3,8,
61,65,65,66,75
Martin, John, Jr. 5,6,
8,10
Martin, John, Sr. 6,8,
10
Martin, Joseph G. 61,
109
Martin, L. 108
Martin, Richard 34,37
Martin, Sophia B. 61,
64,65,66,75,108,109,
112,115,116
Martin, Taswell 61
Mason, J. E. 148
Mason, John E. 30,31,
148,149,150
Mason, R. H. 21,36,45
Mason, Raymon H. 17
Mason, Robert 98
Mason, T. P. 116
Mason, W. F. 147
Massey, W. S. 44

Mathis, J. B. 110,113,116
Matthews, Nancy 105
Mattox, N. G. 122
Maxey, Peter 77,84,90
Mears, Elijah 21,22,23,26
Mears, Emily S. 127
Mears, John 69
Mears, Lydia 11
Mears, Mary C. 66,69
Mears, William 11,66,69
Medford, Henry 11
Medford, Mary 11
Meekes, Isaac 5
Melton, Ansel 46,57
Melton, Elizabeth 46
Melton, George 126
Melton, Green 46
Melton, James 46
Melton, James H. 141
Melton, Jarratt 97
Melton, Jo D., Jr. 46
Melton, Jo D., Sr. 46
Melton, John W. 46
Melton, Lucinda 43,44,46,55,63,
68
Melton, Malinda 56,59
Melton, Martha 46
Melton, Mary 46,57
Melton, Rutha A. 58,59
Melton, Sarah B. 107
Melton, Sarah E. 141
Melton, Sarah F. 94
Melton, William 43,46,55
Melton, William J. 46
Miles, Catharine 10,11
Miles, L. W. 78
Miles, Mahaley 10
Miller, Elizabeth J. 44,46
Miller, Elnora 44,46
Miller, George D. 44,46
Miller, Jenny W. 46
Miller, Martha 24,43
Miller, Martha E. 44,46,51,52,54
Miller, Sarah L. 44,46
Miller, Terry W. 44
Miller, Thomas T. 44,46
Miller, William 27
Miller, William C. 24,26,43,44,
46,47,51,52,54
Miller, William H. 44,46
Milligan, A. 94,101
Milligan, A. C. 65
Milligan, A. P. 91
Milligan, Alcena E. 86
Milligan, Alexander 70,72,74,78,
79,81,86,87,91,92,95,101,116,

168

Milligan, Alexander 120, 123
Milligan, Elizabeth 92
Milligan, Henry 86
Milligan, J. P. 94,130
Milligan, James 74,79,92
Milligan, John 74,79,81
Milligan, John A. 91,92, 101
Milligan, W. B. 130
Milliken, A. C. 43,56
Milliken, A. G. 12,47, 56,68,71,85,97,100, 110,111,119
Milliken, Albert G. 13, 15,18,20,46
Milliken, Elizabeth 8
Milliken, Inde 12
Milliken, J. P. 127
Milliken, James 8,56
Milliken, Jesse 13,15, 18,20,41,43,44,46,47, 54,56,57
Milliken, Jesse A. 44, 46,47
Milliken, Jesse M. 56
Milliken, Jesse N. 43
Milliken, John W. 43,44
Milliken, M. B. 127
Milliken, N. G. 54
Mills, Martha 23
Mills, William C. 23
Mingles, Mary 140,141
Mingles, W. T. 140
Mitchell, Clementine 132
Mitchell, Daniel W. 30
Mitchell, Elizabeth 51
Mitchell, J. F. 132
Mitchell, J. H. 147
Mitchell, J. N. 115
Mitchell, J. T. 128,132, 138,142,146
Mitchell, James H. 47,51, 149
Mitchell, John N. 115, 117,118,120
Mitchell, Mary 118
Mitchell, Stephen A. 15, 17,19,20,22,30
Moore, Alex 75
Moore, C. W. 143
Moore, Jacob 4
Moore, John A. 87,95
Moore, Ruth 47
Moore, Samuel 47
Morah, Joseph 8

Morah, Sarah 8
Morford, Jane 16
Morford, Josiah F. 16
Morgan, Alex 15
Morgan, Alexander 14,16
Morgan, Allen 73,74,100
Morgan, Catharine 14,16
Morgan, James A. 73
Morgan, Jemima 81
Morgan, Joseph D. 41
Morgan, Matilda J. 73
Morgan, Rebecca C. 73
Morgan, Robert A. 73
Morgan, Serina 73
Morris, Ann 58
Morris, Cole A. 58
Morris, Elisha 58
Morris, Hiram 11
Moses, Alcy 22
Moses, Aley 20,119
Moses, Ally 140
Moses, G. H. 141
Moses, W. H. 139,140,148,149,150
Moses, William H. 20,22,25,27,28, 29,119
Mullinax, A. P. 74
Mullinax, Eliza 74,92
Mullins, John 2,3,4,6
Muncy, Eli 45,46
Muncy, John 45,46
Murfy, Laura 70
Murphy, Laura A. 74,150,151
Murphy, Lucy A. 92
Murphy, M. E. 148
Murphy, Martha C. 148
Murphy, Timothy 142,148
Murray, John 45
Myers, William 106
Napier, E. L. 52
Napier, Eliza 52
Neal, James 129
Neal, R. P. 129
Neeley, Amanda A. 61,66,67
Neeley, B. F. 66,67
Neeley, Elijah 61,65,66,67
Neeley, Francis 61
Neeley, H. D. 65
Neeley, Harriet 67,72
Neeley, J. R. 62,67,73,74,86,93, 99
Neeley, James B. 67
Neeley, Nathan L. 67
Neeley, Polly J. 67
Neeley, R. W. 66,67
Neeley, Robert 67
Neeley, W. R. 66

Neeley, William R. 61,
  67
Neely, A. L. 135
Neely, Amanda A. 135
Neely, Anna 101
Neely, B. F. 101,135
Neely, Elijah 31,37,
  101,113,115,116,121,
  135
Neely, Elijah, Jr. 113
Neely, Frank 105,148,
  149,150
Neely, Harriet D. 135
Neely, Isaiah 113
Neely, J. B. 135
Neely, J. R. 46,64,93,
  96,115,124,126
Neely, James B. 135
Neely, Jeremiah 124
Neely, M. C. 118,119,
  124,126,131
Neely, N. L. 125
Neely, Nancy E. 135
Neely, Olly 148,149,
  150
Neely, Polly J. 135
Neely, R. W. 115,116,
  121,123,125,134,135,
  136,137,138
Neely, Robert 130
Neely, Robert W. 101,
  113,135
Neely, Sarah A. 135
Neely, Sarah E. 113
Neely, Thomas L. 113
Neely, W. R. 135
Neely, William R. 101
Nelson, Martha 133
Nesbitt, Ephraim 18,21
Nettles, W. C. 133,136
New, C. B. 137
New, C. L. 23
New, C. T. 24,30
New, Callie 137,147
New, Charles T. 20
New, J. C. 135,140,147
New, John C. 146
New, Nancy 147
New, T. C. 23,34
Newby, Harriet C. 72
Newby, Thompson 4
Nichols, Abagail 4
Nichols, Asa 151
Nichols, Joseph W. 4
Nichols, Joshua 4
Nichols, Louisa E. 4

Nichols, Mary E. 4
Nichols, Phebe 4
Nichols, William 5
Nokes, Martha 18
Nokes, Mary 18
Nokes, Sarah 18
Nokes, Susan 15,18,20
Nokes, Thomas 15,18
Nokes, W. B. 63
Nokes, W. R. 119
Nokes, William 15,18
Nunley, Lydia 73
Nunley, Lydia A. 39,54
Oatried, Catherine 109
Oatried, T. J. 109
Odenheimer, John M. 27,28
Odineal, Catherine 61
Odineal, T. J. 61
Odom, A. G. 78,82,90,131
Odom, A. Z. 45
Odom, Armstead G. 85
Odom, C. B. 36,37,39,42,47,58
Odom, C. C. 36,86,87
Odom, F. 84
Odom, H. C. 149
Odom, Hannah E. 92
Odom, Henry C. 92,104,106
Odom, J. H. 78,116,135
Odom, J. J. 62,84,85,87
Odom, J. L. 74
Odom, J. M. 59
Odom, J. S. 106
Odom, James 81
Odom, James H. 41,45,82,92,109
Odom, James S. 41,45,62,68,71,82,
  84,85,87,95,97,131
Odom, John J. 68,71,76,95,97
Odom, John L. 85
Odom, John S. 41,45,78,82,86,92,
  100,106,107,109,117,118,135,
  141,142
Odom, Josephine B. 107
Odom, M. H. 149
Odom, M. M. 131,133,134,135,136
Odom, Martha M. 45
Odom, Mary 59,131
Odom, Mary G. 133,149,150
Odom, Mathew M. 41,92
Odom, Matthew 82
Odom, R. L. 41,45,76,82,92,95,97,
  105,107,116,120,135
Odom, Richard L. 82
Odom, S. C. 117
Odom, S. J. 59,74,99,100
Odom, Sallie 134
Odom, Sam C. 108

Odom, W. L. 74
Odom, William C. 36, 37,39,42,47
Odom, William F. 55, 74
Odum, Armstead G. 26
Odum, H. C. 89
Odum, Hannah 89
Odum, James H. 89,108
Odum, James S. 55
Odum, John S. 55,89
Odum, Mathew 55,89
Odum, R. L. 89
Odum, Rufus 55,89
Odum, Samuel C. 6
Odum, William C. 2,6
Oran, J. W. 121
Orand, J. W. 140
Orand, John W. 71,81
Orran, John 15
Orrand, N. L. 29
Osborn, H. 69
Osborn, Henry 72
Osborn, Naomi 68,72
Overall, H. A. 84,91, 121,143,147
Overall, Horace 67,71, 73,76
Overall, Mary C. 67
Owen, A. 67,71,76,84, 86,91,95,99,104,107, 147
Owen, Alamilla 129
Owen, Alaminta 33,39, 40,125
Owen, Alford 75,101
Owen, Alfred 67,73,111, 143
Owen, Allimenta 67,136, 138,150
Owen, Anthony 55,70,76, 78,94
Owen, Araminta 63
Owen, Cancie 101
Owen, Christopher 18, 86,105
Owen, Eliza 67
Owen, F. 51,64,86
Owen, Fountain 33,36, 37,38,39,40,42,47,62, 64,67,76,94
Owen, H. A. 64
Owen, J. C. 101
Owen, John C. 105,120,
Owen, Josiah 101
Owen, Lafayette 101

Owen, Lucinda 124,129
Owen, Mary 67,84
Owen, Permelia 18
Owen, R. L. 55,59,62,63,64,68,71, 81,84,85,87,124
Owen, Richard L. 67
Owen, W. J. 124
Owensby, E. D. 143
Page, Bettie 125,132
Page, F. F. 118,132
Page, J. W. 111,112,118,119,131, 132
Page, John W. 110,118,146,151
Page, Nellie 125
Page, T. F. 125
Page, Willie 132
Pain, Robert 128
Parker, Adam 39
Parker, John W. 13,15,17
Parker, Joseph 24
Parker, Levi 17
Parker, Nancy 24,143
Parker, Sarah 17
Parkes, Francis 6
Parris, John B. 31
Parton, Calinda 97,104,105,107, 110
Parton, Celinda 122,123,125
Parton, J. F. 130
Parton, Louis 124
Parton, Mary 124,130,134
Parton, W. B. 142
Parton, William B. 124
Patterson, George 117,133,135
Patterson, John 83
Patterson, Lewis 7
Patterson, Robert 83,89
Pattie, James D. 3
Pattie, John D. 4
Patton, David 17,20,26
Patton, P. C. 128
Pearson, John 28
Peay, Eliza 151
Peay, John 151
Peay, Laura 151
Peay, Martha 151
Peay, R. D. 151
Pedon, J. M. 132
Pedon, Joseph 132
Peebles, Martin 82
Pelham, Caroline 73,74
Pelham, Levi 73,74
Pelham, William 73,74
Pendleton, Andrew 41
Pendleton, Ann E. 16
Pendleton, Benjamin 1,2,7,13,14,

Pendleton, Benjamin 16, 41
Pendleton, Catherine 41
Pendleton, Dillard 41
Pendleton, Edmond 41
Pendleton, Eliza 13,14, 16
Pendleton, John 42
Pendleton, Mary 41
Pendleton, Stay A. 41
Pendleton, Thomas 41
Perrer, Jesse 21
Persley, Alice M. 138
Persley, Anna E. 138
Persley, B. B. 138
Persley, Mary S. 138
Petty, A. G. 124,129, 130,138,142
Petty, Alex 99
Petty, Ambrose 50
Petty, Ann 50
Petty, Charles 99
Petty, David 50
Petty, Dorcas J. 45
Petty, Frances 102
Petty, Frances C. 95
Petty, G. A. 102
Petty, G. W. 98
Petty, George 113
Petty, George W. 50
Petty, J. A. 84
Petty, James 50,87,96
Petty, James A. 99
Petty, John 50
Petty, John C. 50
Petty, Mary 50
Petty, Nancy A. 50
Petty, Nancy C. 99
Petty, Nathan A. 99
Petty, Newton 95,99
Peyton, William H. 22
Phillips, Anna A. 138
Phillips, Anna S. 142
Phillips, Benjamin F. 52
Phillips, B. H. 33,36,37, 50
Phillips, Benjamin H. 34, 35,47
Phillips, Benjamin L. 7
Phillips, Edward 142
Phillips, Edward V. 138
Phillips, Elizabeth 7
Phillips, H. F. 33
Phillips, Mary H. 139,142
Phillips, Nancy A. 75
Phillips, Peter H. 36,37

Phillips, R. H. 33,36
Phillips, Robert H. 33,34,35
Phillips, Samuel 82,90
Phillips, Sarah 142
Phillips, Thomas 142
Phillips, William 75,86,93,96,98, 102,110,113,131,147,148
Pierce, Jesse 19,27,28,29
Pinkerton, Joseph 20,34,116
Pinkerton, Nancy 20,116
Pinkston, Joseph 23
Pinkston, Nancy 23
Pitman, James M. 83
Pitman, Nancy 83
Pogue, James 1
Pogue, James E. 2
Pogue, Nancy 2
Pogue, William 1
Porterfield, Charles 1,2
Porterfield, Mariah E. 2
Powell, Paralee 121
Powell, S. P. 121,124,135,136,144 145
Powell, S. T. 130
Powell, William 129
Praitor, James M. 96
Praitor, John H. 96
Praitor, Martha 96
Praitor, T. E. 96
Praitor, Thomas P. 96
Prater, James J. 80,90
Prater, W. C. 150
Prator, F. E. 104
Prator, J. J. 104
Prator, M. J. 104
Preston, John F. 28,29,32,141,143
Preston, Mary J. 139,141
Preston, Thomas J. 34
Preston, William 141
Preston, William C. 139
Price, D. J. 129
Price, Elisha 53
Price, Elizabeth 53
Price, Jackson 53
Price, James 9
Price, R. B. 129
Price, Robert 129
Price, Sarah 53
Purser, James 141,143
Pursley, Alice H. 142
Pursley, Anna E. 142
Pursley, B. B. 142
Pursley, G. A. 142
Pursley, Mary S. 142
Quarles, James C. 42
Quarles, James T. 42

172

Robinson, Richard 86
Robinson, Silas A. 16
Robinson, Silus 92
Robinson, Stephen 78,87,
  90
Robinson, William 86,99
Robinson, William J. 17
Robison, W. M. 118
Rodgers, Elizabeth 14,15,
  16
Rodgers, Elizabeth, Sr. 17
Rodgers, Henry 14,16
Rodgers, James 14,16,17
Rodgers, Jane 14,16
Rodgers, John 14,16
Rodgers, Polly A. 39,57
Rodgers, William 14,16
Rogers, Polly 53
Rogers, Polly A. 53,54
Rogers, Tinsey 53
Rose, Eliza 63
Rose, Elvira B. 63
Rose, Jane A. 63
Rose, Leroy 63
Rose, Tennessee 63
Ross, B. F. 129,130
Ross, Sarah 142
Ross, Sarah B. 151
Ross, Sarah R. 126,128,
  129,132
Ross, Zeno C. 9,11
Rucker, Anderson 45,62,
  118
Rucker, Bennett 47,49,54
Rucker, J. E. 142
Rucker, Josia 61
Rucker, Mary J. 61
Rucker, Permelia 45
Rucker, Thomas 61
Rucker, William 61
Rucks, Elizabeth 25,27
Runnells, Nancy 50
Rushing, A. 49
Rushing, Abel 45,56,71,
  76,78,82
Rushing, Amanda F. 66
Rushing, John 45,49,62
Rushing, M. R. 44,45,46,
  48,66,131
Rushing, Parmelia 49
Rushing, Sarah 45
Rushing, W. A. 66
Rushing, William A. 66
Ruyle, Jasper 20,69
Safford, Milas 65
Safford, Teletha 65

Sagely, Aaron 7
Sagely, B. 101,104
Sagely, Blake 83,86,93,106,136
Sanders, M. H. 133
Sanders, William 133
Sandridge, Caroline 23,25
Sandridge, Dabney 23,25
Sandridge, Eliza 89,91
Sands, Mary B. 62
Sanford, Betty 70
Sanford, Betty V. 59,72,95,97,
  104,111
Sanford, Elizabeth N. 44
Sanford, Elizabeth V. 48
Sauls, William 60,66,87,98,106,
  111
Savage, A. M. 23
Scissim, Albert 37,41
Scissim, William 37
Scissom, M. A. 74
Scissom, Mary A. 64,68
Scissom, Thomas 64,68
Scissom, William 38
Seawell, Abigail 26
Seawell, Francis M. 26
See, Andrew 77
See, Nancy 77
Seitz, A. L. 53
Sewel, Abigal 50
Sewel, Abyel 21
Sewel, Frances M. 21,50
Sewell, Abigal 107
Sexton, John W. 32
Shacklett, John 74
Shacklett, Lucy A. 94,107
Shanks, William 5
Shelton, Elbert 110,114
Shelton, F. M. 114
Shelton, James 110,114
Shelton, Martha 110,114
Shelton, Mary L. 110,114
Shelton, William 89,96,101,103,
  110,114
Sherley, John W. 58,59
Sherley, Margaret E. 59
Shirley, John W. 71
Shirley, Margaret E. 71
Shockley 56
Shockley, John 79
Silvertooth, G. W. 21
Silvertooth, George W. 22,25
Simpson, Joseph 21
Sisson, Albert 42
Sisson, C. W. 60
Sisson, I. G. 60
Sisson, Mary A. 60,62

Stacy, William 18,21
Stanley, Jane 77
Stanley, Thomas 77
Star, L. D. 80
Starr, John 93,97,104,
  105,107,110,122,123,
  125
Starr, Joseph 93,112
Starr, L. D. 93
Starr, Lewis 105
Starr, Mary 112
Steel, E. G. 34
Steel, Edward G. 33
Steel, John P. 58
Steele, John P. 63,67,
  71
Stephens, Joanna C. 95
Stephens, Joshua 99
Stephens, Mary J. 58,
  61
Stephens, R. 132,134,
  135,138,142,148,149
Stephens, Robert B. 61
Stephens, Robert H. 2,
  5
Stephens, Robert K. 58
Stephens, Thomas 99
Stephens, Thomas D. 95
Stephens, W. P. 89,90,
  103,116,120
Stephens, William P. 84
Stephenson, Nannie 147
Stiles, N. P. 150
Stokes, William B. 84
Stone, Archibald 12,
  13,25,35,37,39,45,56,
  85
Stone, Henry D. 65,66
Stone, John 151
Stone, John W. 8,12,13
Stone, Julia 56
Stone, Julian 59
Stone, M. 151
Stone, Margaret 101
Stone, Mary J. 139
Stone, Melvina 144
Stone, Minerva 66,142
Stone, Minerva A. 65
Stone, Sallie 151
Stone, Sarah 8
Stone, William 59,71
Stone, William L. 98
Stroud, Anna 146
Stroud, John H. 25
Stroud, John W. 21,23,
  28,29,30

Stroud, Mary A. 23,29
Stroud, W. D. 146
Stroud, Walter 23,25,28,29
Stroud, William 56
Stroud, William D. 56
Sublett, Elizabeth 32,35
Sublett, George A. 32,35
Sullivan, Andrew 67
Sullivan, Ann 112,127
Sullivan, Ann D. 29
Sullivan, Anna 149,151
Sullivan, Cal 137
Sullivan, Calvin 11,67,85,90,98,
  105,108,115,127,140,141
Sullivan, Hampton 42
Sullivan, Isaac 151
Sullivan, James 46,51,52,53,55,
  58,67,83,85
Sullivan, Jane 59
Sullivan, John E. 83,85,93,97
Sullivan, John R. 17,29,91,112
Sullivan, Rachel M. 148
Sullivan, T. G. 147,149,151
Sullivan, W. L. 124,126,134
Sullivan, William 11,59
Sullivan, Z. G. 148
Summar, John R. 28
Summar, John W. 26
Summer, Aleena C. 40
Summer, Anthony 74
Summer, C. B. 60,67
Summer, D. D. 52
Summer, David 40,42,81
Summer, David D. 48,52
Summer, E. J. 57
Summer, Elijah 60
Summer, Elizabeth 40
Summer, H. C. 40
Summer, Ivory 61
Summer, J. M. 40
Summer, J. N. 40
Summer, James B. 40,48,61
Summer, James C. 40
Summer, James M. 40
Summer, Jefferson 60
Summer, John B. 31
Summer, John R. 30
Summer, John W. 26,32,60
Summer, Lehanna 40
Summer, Mira L. 40
Summer, M. P., Jr. 40
Summer, N. W. 52,53,57,63
Summer, Robert 40
Summer, Sarah A. 40
Summer, T. R. 40
Summer, Thomas 26

Williams, Thomas A. 52
Williams, Thomas H. 55
Williams, Thomas L. 3
Williams, William 52
Williams, Williamson 52
Williams, Zachariah 52
Williamson, William 55
Willis, Mary 83,86,101,
  106,136,140
Willis, Miles 114
Willis, William 83
Wilsher, Thomas A. 54
Wilson, A. J. 112,113
Wilson, Betty A. 109,
  112,113
Wilson, Martha L. 52
Wilson, Robert 7,8
Witherspoon, A. B. 128,
  132,138,142,146
Witherspoon, Ebenezar 8
Witherspoon, Elihu 7
Witherspoon, Eliza 7,8
Witherspoon, Elizabeth 7
Witty, E. L. 45,46,47,96,
  112,114,125,126,128,130,
  132,142,151
Womack, A. B. 77
Womack, Cicero 109
Womack, Elizabeth G. 77
Womack, H. J. 138
Womack, J. B. 109
Womack, J. S. 100,112,119,
  120,125,134
Womack, M. J. 139
Womack, Margaret 109
Womack, Martha J. 87,109,
  138
Womack, R. P. 137
Womack, S. M. 106
Womack, Sarah J. 109
Womack, T. A. 80,109
Wood, A. J. 3
Wood, A. R. 87,94
Wood, B. F. 23
Wood, Benjamin F. 19,25
Wood, E. J. 140
Wood, Eliza 87
Wood, G. G. 121
Wood, George 137
Wood, H. O. 121,133,143
Wood, J. B. 108,134,138
Wood, J. H. 133,137
Wood, J. S. 109,133
Wood, James 2,23,25,124
Wood, James A. 121
Wood, James G. 87

Wood, James H. 36,44,77,80,85,
  109,120,122,131
Wood, John 86,121,124
Wood, John A. 66,94,104,121,130,
  135,136,144,145
Wood, John B. 77,121,131
Wood, John H. 2,3,19,22,25,35,
  37,85,89
Wood, John S. 94,140,143
Wood, John W. 39
Wood, Roxana 22
Wood, S. H. 68,71
Wood, Sarah B. 72,74,77,85,87,92,
  95,98,100,101,143,145,148,149
Wood, T. G. 85
Wood, T. W. 60,65,121
Wood, Thomas C. 50,58
Wood, Thomas G. 7,12,18,21,23,25,
  29,30,39,40,42,43,67,81,82,87,
  89,90,98,111,114,125,126
Wood, Thomas J. 77
Wood, Thomas W. 55
Wood, W. J. 94,121,135
Wood, W. W. 89,97,104,131
Wood, William 55,77,85,87
Wood, William T. 140
Wood, William W. 77,121
Woodall, Mary D. 34
Woodall, William C. 34
Woodruff, J. T. 43,93
Woodruff, Robert 15
Woodruff, T. J. 114
Woods, Eliza 83
Woods, George 106
Woods, James 1,83
Woods, James H. 98
Woods, John 102,115,117,129
Woods, John F. 83
Woods, S. H. 51
Woods, William 98
Woods, William H. 96
Woodside, L. M. 127
Woodsides, L. W. 129
Word, Thomas C. 3,12,13,15
Word, T. W. 61
Wrather, Elizabeth 28
Wrather, F. D. 18
Wright, E. 2
Wright, Ebenezar 3,4
Wright, Jacob 1
Wright, Susan J. 61,109
Wright, William 61
Wright, William B. 109
Yoakum, Henderson 1
York, I. N. 91
York, J. H. 105,124,150

York, J. N. 73,74,105,
132,147,149,151
York, J. W. 128
York, James 105
York, Jeremiah 105
York, Paralee 105
York, Tempy 129
York, William 74,105,
150
York, W. F. 150
York, William F. 151
Young, Adaline 59
Young, Billy 124,130
Young, Delphia 29
Young, F. 77
Young, F. A. 56
Young, Henry 28
Young, Isaac 35
Young, Isaac B. 35,37
Young, J. B. 110
Young, Jane 121,122,
123
Young, John 22,25,97,
122
Young, Joseph 121,122,
123
Young, M. L. 98,109
Young, Mark L. 19,26,
27,28
Young, Mary 35,37
Young, Sarah F. 121,
122
Young, Tersey 77
Young, William 5,29
Youngblood, A. 148
Youree, Eliza I. 70
Youree, Joseph 67,70
Youree, Julia A. 70
Youree, Sara 67,70
Youree, Thomas N. 4

MISCELLANEOUS INDEX